The Twelve Dels of Christmas

ALSO BY DAVID JASON

My Life
Only Fools and Stories
A Del of a Life

The Twelve Dels of Christmas

DAVID JASON

CENTURY

1 3 5 7 9 10 8 6 4 2

Century
20 Vauxhall Bridge Road
London SW1V 2SA

Century is part of the Penguin Random House group of companies
whose addresses can be found at global.penguinrandomhouse.com.

Penguin
Random House
UK

Copyright © Peglington Productions Ltd 2022

David Jason has asserted his right to be identified as the author of this
Work in accordance with the Copyright, Designs and Patents Act 1988.

First published by Century in 2022

www.penguin.co.uk

A CIP catalogue record for this book is available from the British Library.

'. . . and a partridge up your pear tree' from 'Christmas Crackers',
Only Fools and Horses, John Sullivan

ISBN 9781529136142 (hardback)
ISBN 9781529904451 (trade paperback)

Typeset in 13.25/17.5 pt Goudy Old Style by Jouve (UK), Milton Keynes

Printed and bound in Great Britain by Clays Ltd, Elcograf S.p.A.

The authorised representative in the EEA is Penguin Random House Ireland,
Morrison Chambers, 32 Nassau Street, Dublin D02 YH68

www.greenpenguin.co.uk

CONTENTS

INTRODUCTION

'It is at Christmas time that want is most keenly felt, and abundance rejoices.'

Charles Dickens, *A Christmas Carol*, 1843

Not that long ago, over lunch at a rather fancy restaurant in London, an executive from ITV looked me in the eyes and said, 'David, you know what? You would make the most perfect Scrooge.'

Which, I have to say, caused me to pause briefly from chewing on my chicken escalope and take a moment.

Well, how would *you* feel if someone came straight out and said, 'I saw you and thought of Scrooge'?

Because, yes, of course, we all know that Ebenezer Scrooge turns out to be a good guy *in the end.* After the three ghosts of Christmas have pitched up and finished frightening him half to death, the old scrimper's human spirit is unlocked, he realises the true cost of his meanness, and finally grows a heart and puts it to some use. That's the Scrooge story, or what we would now call, on the back of the reality television shows, his 'journey'. (I'm officially old enough to remember when a journey meant actually going somewhere, but let's not get into that now.)

However, our image of Scrooge tends to be, as it were, front-loaded, does it not? By which I mean, if you describe someone as Scrooge-like, you're not generally implying they're the type to knock on your door on Christmas morning with a big grin on their face, a huge turkey under their arm and a bottle of champagne all ready to pop.

On the contrary, you're thinking of the sour-faced tightwad from the beginning of the tale, the bloke who barks, 'Bah! Humbug!' – the character who is, in Dickens's words, 'a squeezing, wrenching, grasping, scraping, clutching, covetous, old sinner'.

And just to remove any remaining traces of doubt about it, Dickens went on: 'The cold within him froze his old features, nipped his pointed nose, shrivelled his cheek, stiffened his gait; made his eyes red, his thin lips blue; and spoke out shrewdly in his grating voice.'

Hence, dear reader, my moment of personal reflection back there in the restaurant with a mouthful of pricy chicken.

Scrooge? Who, *moi*?

But such, of course, are the daily knocks and setbacks, the low blows and blindside rabbit-punches, for the humble thespian and small-screen entertainer as he goes about his business of attempting to enthral and delight the watching nation. It's called 'casting', obviously, and anyone who goes into acting expecting a life of unbroken flattery in this department is going to be sorely disappointed somewhere along the line.

Saw me and thought of Scrooge? I'd heard worse, frankly. Indeed, I got one of my most important breaks in television when, essentially, Ronnie Barker saw me and thought of a hundred-year-old gardener called Dithers. I was about thirty at the time, with a spring in my eye and a twinkle in my step, but no matter.

And actually, now we're on the subject, 'I saw you and thought of a deluded cockney chancer flogging hooky gear off a market stall' wasn't a completely complimentary thing to hear, either. But that didn't work out too badly.

No, as time and experience have taught me, the only thing to do at these moments is to bite your lip, jut out your chin and think of the work. The fact was, the man from ITV was offering me a part in a new production of *A Christmas Carol* – a starring role in a big and no doubt handsomely budgeted festive number, and, well, you don't go sneezing at those, with a 'nipped' and 'pointed' nose, or otherwise. So, plenty to consider there and much to discuss before they came round with the dessert trolley.

Yet, as I resumed chewing thoughtfully and began to weigh the pros and cons of this potentially nice little earner, another question started rotating somewhat naggingly in my mind.

What *is* it about me and Christmas?

When I survey the wondrous tapestry, if you will, of my acting career, it's extraordinary how frequently Christmas comes into the picture. And not just in the sense of once a year, which you might reasonably expect. No, somehow Christmas bulks much larger than that. So many key moments in my professional life seem to be associated with that time. And it's been that way from the start.

My first ever appearance on television? Christmas Day, 1965. Soon after 4.50 p.m., to be precise, in the BBC pantomime, which was an annual fixture in those days – what we would now call 'appointment television', even. In my family, certainly, we cleared the Christmas lunch away and ritually plonked ourselves in front of the set for it, in various states of turkey-and-pudding-stuffed disrepair, and 1965 was no exception. The only difference that year was that the entertainment for which we all plonked ourselves down (me on the sofa, next to my mum and my aunt, my dad in his armchair) featured . . . me.

Or kind of. More on this monumental occasion and its life-changing consequences for the occupants of the sitting room at 26 Lodge Lane anon. At this point, let the record merely show that the pantomime laid that evening before my proud parents and the rest of the country was *Mother Goose*. And let the record further state that if you strained your eyes at one point, I could be briefly glimpsed playing a swinging policeman.

No, not *that* kind of swinging. *Literally* swinging – by a wire from the ceiling.

So, yes – not one of the greater roles in the theatrical canon, I grant you. And not an especially dignified one, either, because, let me tell you, those theatrical harnesses, when they get yanked up around your softer regions mid-flight, chafe like nothing on earth.

Was it ever like this for the nation's greatest thespians on their various routes to glory? I wonder. For the likes of Giel-gud, Olivier, McKellen? Instinctively I feel that it almost certainly was not.

Yet this was where I found myself, as the rocket containing my small-screen career trundled tentatively onto the launch-pad. Never mind Scrooge or a hundred-year-old gardener: someone at the BBC saw me – twenty-five years young, lithe and willowy, his innocent head aflutter with dreams of major parts as a romantic lead – and thought of . . . a flying policeman.

There were other bits and pieces of Christmas panto in those early years, too – even less distinguished, if you can imagine it – and one of them so grim around the edges that I almost gave up acting and went back to being an electri-cian. But Christmas was already doing its bit to shape my course.

And then there was *Only Fools and Horses*. Now, none of us who were involved in that show had any inkling at the outset about exactly what it would turn into. But I think it's fair to say that it ended up meaning a great deal to an awful lot of people. And it seemed to mean a great deal to people in particular at Christmas.

There were eighteen *Only Fools* Christmas specials in total, beginning with one at the end of the first series in 1981 – the 'Christmas Crackers' episode from which the words of Del quoted at the beginning of this introduction are taken. From then on, our ugly mugs started looming in the corner of the nation's sitting rooms at Christmas pretty much annually. Indeed, from 1991 onwards, after the end of the seventh series, *Only Fools* existed *solely* at Christmas, the team reuniting only to film extended stories for the holiday period – 'our Christmas present to the nation', as the BBC liked to call them.

Would the nation have preferred money or perhaps a gift token? Quite possibly. But instead the nation got given us, doing increasingly daft things in increasingly far-flung places.

Accordingly, it was at Christmas that the world saw Rodney, Del and Uncle Albert set sail in a battered old tub for Holland, pausing to seek directions from an oil rig. It was at Christmas that the entire cast was spotted decamping by coach to sunny Margate, only to watch the coach go up in flames. And it was Christmas that sent Del and Rodney to Miami to encounter both the Mafia and a member of the Bee Gees. (Nice bloke, Barry Gibb. And nice and warm, Miami. No complaints from me and Nick Lyndhurst about that particular location shoot.)

It was also at Christmas that Raquel moved in with Del, that Peckham Spring Mineral Water was first marketed, and that the world's least likely Batman and Robin duo emerged on a foggy street. Those episodes might have been shown at Christmas but they very quickly stopped being *about* Christmas. John Sullivan, the late, great creator of *Only Fools*, seized on those specials as an opportunity to widen the show's scope – to be daring, tell bigger stories over longer time frames, deepen the characters and our attachment to them. John was a pioneer, and it's my opinion that, in those eighteen festive numbers, he pretty much single-handedly rewrote the rules around Christmas shows – about what a Christmas edition of a comedy programme was and what it could be allowed to do.

But more about that later. For now, let me simply try and dizzy you with some numbers that still, genuinely, dizzy me. On the list of the twenty most-watched programmes ever broadcast on Christmas Day, there are seven episodes of *Only Fools*. Well, seven out of twenty sounds like the kind of mark I used to get at school on a good day. But in the context of the entire history of Christmas broadcasting . . . well, I guess seven out of twenty is pretty impressive.

What's more, the 'Time on our Hands' episode, which was the concluding part of the 1996 Christmas trilogy, attracted an audience of 24.35 million. Now, my dear mother taught me not to blow my own trumpet – and also to be careful about blowing other people's trumpets. But at the same time, unashamedly contradicting herself, my mum also told me not to hide my light under a bushel, advice I would have gladly heeded if bushels hadn't been so vanishingly few and far between in the Finchley area in the forties and fifties – even fewer and farther between than trumpets, actually.

Facts are facts, though, and, setting all bushels and trumpets aside, 24.35 million is the kind of audience which tended only to gather in front of television sets for space missions and royal weddings. Yet that number of people eagerly assembled that Christmas to find out what was going on with a bunch of fictional wallies in a Peckham tower block.

Just to put this in some kind of perspective, 1996 was the year England played Germany at Wembley for a place in the final of football's European Championships – a game of some interest to the nation, you could say, given what we know about England and football, and also what we know about the rivalry between England and Germany. Yet, amazingly, some six million fewer people tuned in to watch that match than tuned in to see how much Del and Rodney could get for the pocket watch that they had just unearthed among the Showaddywaddy LPs and iffy Eastern European electronics in their garage lock-up.

Then again, unlike England v. Germany, I suppose at least our show had a happy ending. Germany, you may not need reminding, went through on penalties that time, whereas Del and Rodney . . . well, thanks to that Sotheby's auction, after years of dreaming about it, they were finally millionaires, weren't they? And this time next year, no doubt – Del was sure of it – they'd be *billionaires*.

Anyway, the point is, that Christmas, 'Time on our Hands' became the UK's most-watched comedy show of all time, and I think we can be fairly confident now that we're looking at a record there that won't ever be broken. If only the same could be said for those Showaddywaddy LPs.

I can still only shake my head in wonder about it, really. I think back to the beginning of the voyage, the first time the cast gathered together for this completely new sitcom in a shabby room at the BBC's Television Rehearsal Centre in Acton, all carrying the scripts we'd been sent and looking around the place in various states of anticipation, with that first-day-at-school atmosphere in the air, as it always is on such occasions.

Now, imagine if the director had clapped his hands at the start of that session and said, 'Right, listen up, everyone. Come Christmas a few years from now, the world and his dog will be tuning into this show, to the point that, when they all put the kettle on at the same time for a cup of tea afterwards, it'll produce a 1600 megawatt power surge and practically crash the National Grid. So look sharp.'

We'd have assumed he'd banged his head on the way in.

Yet it came to pass. And, incidentally, my formal apologies, belatedly, to everyone working overtime at power stations that Christmas for the inconvenience caused. I speak in solidarity with you as a former electrician who has touched enough live wires in his time to know a thing or two about power surges. However, I can't say I'm not lastingly proud to have been part of something which had that effect. Proud and astonished.

The Christmas connections don't end with *Only Fools*, by the way. In the 1990s, *The Darling Buds of May*, in which I played Pa Larkin, spawned two Christmas specials. Indeed, the second of them went out on ITV on Boxing Day, twenty-four hours after 'Mother Nature's Son', which was that year's *Only Fools* special, had gone out on the BBC. Thus did I straddle two channels for Christmas 1992 – which I suppose was less painful than it sounds, but which should still probably only be attempted under properly qualified supervision and with medical support to hand.

Even *A Touch of Frost*, which, as a detective show revolving around the solution of frequently grisly murder cases, might not automatically have been your first stop for festive frolics, ended up getting a Yuletide spin at one point. In 1999, Detective Inspector Jack Frost took up ninety minutes of the nation's Christmas Day, sandwiched between two bursts of the *Who Wants to Be a Millionaire?* Christmas special.

Or what about the year I was borne aloft in a flying sled alongside a hooded figure – only for the studio to flood and the power to go out, leaving the pair of us hanging in mid-air while everyone else evacuated the building? Again, precise details to follow. But these inconveniences occurred during the filming of Sky TV's adaptation of *Hogfather*, Terry Pratchett's tale of Christmas on Discworld, which eventually, when the power came back on, got completed and went out over the holidays in 2006, with me in the role of Death's manservant, Albert. The producers of that show had the ambition to create something that would be reshown at Christmas every year – and it has.

All things considered, it was no real surprise to me that, when the BBC brought back *Open All Hours* as *Still Open All Hours* in 2013, they chose to make a Christmas thing out of it and launch it on Boxing Day. It was the same when ITV unveiled *Micawber*. That was an idea that John Sullivan had after *Only Fools* – a comedy drama using characters from Dickens's *David Copperfield*. Great hopes attended the Christmas debut of that show – ITV's, John's, and mine, too, because I was playing Mr Micawber. We thought we were really onto something – a potential winner that could run and run. Alas, it didn't work out that way. But the ones that fell on stony ground are part of my Christmas story as well.

All in all, I somehow became someone who seemed to have his own reserved parking space in the Christmas double issue of the *Radio Times*. Indeed, one year the front of that magazine was a picture of me, warmly wrapped in a coat and a red scarf, lightly sprinkled with artificial snow, and smiling suavely. The headline read 'MISTER CHRISTMAS'.

Michael Bublé, eat your heart out! It was as if I had come to define the season: a tree with lights on, a bowl of Brazil nuts that nobody was going to touch, and something with David Jason in it on the telly. Fair play to the *Radio Times* editors, though, for that one. There were spells in my career when I was on television on Christmas Day so regularly that I began to think I knew how the Queen must feel.

And here's the thing: I don't even *like* Christmas that much. Can I confess that here? It's just between the two of us, obviously, and I'm trusting you to take it no further. But I'm someone with a long-held aversion to shopping and a mild anxiety about large gatherings of people, and . . . well, Christmas often seems to be offering both of those things in a sandwich. A turkey sandwich, obviously. Which I'm also not that keen on.

And don't get me started on the cheesy department store ads that nowadays seem to begin in August, the same jingly tunes wherever you go, the heart-sinking corporate Christmas cards ('with best wishes for the season from all of the team at Pepto Financial Planning Services'), the mind-boggling consumption, the enforced jollity, the sense of being held hostage in the house for two days by your relatives, the neighbours dropping in, the obligatory participation in board games and (worse) charades, the faked enthusiasm for unwanted gifts ('A tie-hanger! You really shouldn't have!'), the feelings of intense disorientation and unease which can only occur after forcing a seventh consecutive mince pie into an already bloated stomach . . .

Oh yes, and the tree lights which, despite the fact that you carefully coiled and packed them away last January with an attention to detail which would have impressed the captain of a sailing ship, have just emerged from their box in a knotted clump that is about to cost you seven and a half hours of unpicking before you finally give it up as a lost cause and go out to buy some more.

I could go on. But let me just say (and I suspect my wife, Gill, will meaningfully confirm this), when the season once again looms into view and conversation turns to those apparently urgent 'Christmas plans', the expression 'Bah! Humbug!' has been known to escape my lips quite naturally, and entirely unprompted by executives from ITV.*

So how is it, then, that I, of all people, became a decoration on the nation's Christmas tree at this special time of the year? – the *most wonderful* time of the year, as Andy Williams, among others, will sometimes try to persuade you, although of course Andy Williams never spent it dressed in a policeman's uniform and hanging by a wire from the rafters. Or not to the best of my knowledge he didn't, and he might have had something different to sing about it if he had. And he'd probably be singing it falsetto.

Or to put it another way, by what strange workings of fate did someone like me end up on the cover of the *Radio Times*, dusted with fake snow and labelled 'Mister Christmas'?

That, dear reader, is the subject of this book.

* * *

* Footnote from my wife, Gill: 'I meaningfully confirm this.'

This is my fourth volume of memoirs and musings – the fourth time that I have adjourned to the musky privacy of the library at Jason Towers, pulled up a chair at the antique oak desk, and dipped my freshly sharpened quill in the bronze ink flask. (I really must get round to replacing the cartridge in that printer.) If you've joined me in print before, then welcome back. And if you haven't, then welcome, too, and worry not, because I am assured by my superiors at Penguin Random House that sales staff will be passing among you during the interval with the three preceding volumes on trays, attractively packaged for your further reading pleasure.

Coincidentally, as I began this book – in November 2021 – and commenced the work of gently lifting time's gauzy veil to look back across my illustrious and frequently tinsel-strewn career, another festive season was almost upon us. And yet another one will be drawing near by the time the work is finished and published, this being very much the nature of Christmas, as I have observed it: it tends to come round, whether you like it or not, and very quickly. Increasingly quickly, actually, because in my experience life speeds up the longer you live. Time hurries on its restless way and before you know it, the holiday season is upon us, the lights are going up again (assuming I can unknot them), the geese are getting fat and the amaryllis bulbs are once more planted in the gazunda.

Amaryllis in the gazunda? It sounds like a cryptic crossword clue, or perhaps the kind of thing a spy would say

to another spy on a remote park bench in order to iden-
tify himself. 'The amaryllis is in the gazunda.' But in fact
it's a Christmas tradition for Gill and me. Each year in the
late autumn/early winter, we plant three bulbs, with their
spaghetti-like roots, in a pot of earth and try to time it so that
at least one of them flowers on Christmas Day. This turns out
to be harder than it sounds. We've had some near misses on
either side, but we've yet to hit it spot on and come down
on Christmas morning to be greeted by a freshly blooming
amaryllis. Hope springs eternal, though, and, as someone
once said, 'This time next year . . .'*

Actually, to be strictly accurate, we've only been using the
gazunda since 2021. Various other receptacles for the bulbs
have been deployed in the past, but that year, after extensive
consultations and a return to the drawing board, we made
the decision to up our game. Needless to say, this was not a
decision we took lightly. But sometimes in a long-term cam-
paign like this, when you've experienced repeated setbacks,
you've simply got no choice but to bring out the biggest
weapon in your armoury. So we dusted off the gazunda.

Not that it worked, of course. Far from greeting us
brightly that Christmas morn, those bulbs eventually did

---

* Amaryllis: a flowering bulb species native to the Cape Provinces of South
Africa, and commonly white-petalled, but occasionally purple or pink.
Not to be confused with Amarillo, a city in Texas which Tony Christie
was always asking directions to. I guess, in the age of satnav, nobody really
needs to ask the way to Amarillo any more. It's pop music's loss.

us the honour of flowering in mid-January. Still, it looked impressive.

'But what's a gazunda?' you may well be asking. It's a bedpan or potty – a 'pisspot', I suppose we might have said in coarser times, but called a 'gazunda' in politer circles because it 'goes under' the bed. My decision to find a home for the amaryllis bulbs in this unusual container met with some initial reservations from Gill, who wondered whether we might regret the overtones implicit in making such an item our Christmas centrepiece, not to mention parking a potty in the vicinity of the place where we regularly eat. But I managed to persuade her that it wasn't just any potty – it was a Victorian potty and, moreover, an artefact of great historic merit which ought to be put to good use.

The artefact in question, by the way, is in china, with a delicate flower motif around the outside, and, seeing as you asked, I bought it back in the eighties while on a trawl of antique shops with Ronnie Barker. It was Ronnie – who was eleven years older than me and in his early fifties at this point – who introduced me to the pleasures of antique hunting, something he loved and was very good at, having a practised eye for it. He was so good at it, in fact, that he eventually opened an antiques business of his own.

When we were in South Yorkshire, filming *Open All Hours*, Sunday would often be our day off, and the pair of us would venture into the surrounding countryside in Ronnie's chauffeur-driven car – something which I found rather grand at the time, though it was a perfectly common perk for the star of the show. It was on one of these trips around the local dealerships that I happened on an old 3D advert for Player's cigarettes, which I snapped up in a hurry and which hung in my house for quite a while. And it was on another of those voyages that I came upon this charming gazunda – a piece of redundant technology, of course, since the invention of the flushing lavatory.

I'm not sure why, really, but this item caught my eye and, with Ronnie's encouragement, I gladly parted with a couple of quid for it. All these years later, it remains in extremely good condition, with the exception of a small crack that has appeared in the handle. But I guess that's not by any means the first crack this particular item has seen. Anyway, it's now been promoted to the role of Christmas planter. And I'm still backing it to repay my confidence in it and come good with the blooms eventually.

While we're all waiting for that to happen, though, here's a view of my life, as seen through a Christmas lens. And, drawing on the example set by Dickens, I'll be compiling it with the help of my own personal Spirit of Christmas Past, whom I've ordered online, at what seemed to me to be a very reasonable hourly rate, or certainly on the basis of the figures I was seeing on the Spirit of Christmas Past price comparison websites. With, I hope, some handy assistance from this hired Spirit, I'll be examining my various interactions with the festive season across the decades, loosening history's ribbons, parting the wrapping paper of obscurity, and peering at what emerges in order to work out what went right, and what went wrong, and, if possible, why it even happened at all. And as I do so, I'll do my best to reach any important conclusions about life, work and the meaning of it all that I can usefully pass on to you – baubles of wisdom if you like. Or certainly a lot of old baubles.

Think of this volume, then, as a Christmas special in book form, from someone who, deliberately or otherwise, has found himself in the middle of a few such – but a Christmas special very much in the John Sullivan style, I hope, being about much more than just Christmas. Or, as Derek Trotter would probably try to flog it, a Christmas special for all seasons.

And who knows? Maybe as a consequence of meeting the ghosts of my Christmases past, not to mention the ghosts of my Christmases present, and, no doubt, the ghosts of my Christmases future, too, I'll end up changing some of my *own* fixed views about the season, as mentioned above. I mean, if it could happen to Scrooge . . .

And mixed in, as usual, will be my latest reports from the frontline of the life I find myself leading as a direct consequence of putting in some of those Christmas shifts – a life which, honestly, remains a source of abiding amazement to me and something I can never quite get my head around, let alone take for granted. For, as I constantly have cause to reflect, none of what has come to pass these past fifty years or so was ever a foregone conclusion on my own 'journey', from north London fishmonger's son and budding electrician with his own van and business card, to multiple-BAFTA-winning television actor, knight of the realm and international man of mystery.

So, will I be recounting herein my recent hours spent in the skies with an astronaut? I will indeed. Will I be attempting to explain my essential and perhaps even history-making duties on the Mall during the celebrations for the Queen's Platinum Jubilee in the summer of 2022? Yes I will. (Those parades don't get watched on their own, you know.) Will I be recalling composing and filming the good luck message I was asked to send the England football team ahead of the final of the 2021 European Championships when they stood so tantalisingly on the verge of trophy-winning glory for the first time since 1966, and just needed that little bit of help from a qualified actor to tip them over the edge? Try and stop me. Ditto my recollections of when *Strictly Come Dancing* came a-calling.

And will I be writing up in detail my recent encounter with fellow dashing screen icon (and fellow helicopter pilot) Tom Cruise? Reader, I may be able to contain myself for, ooh, whole pages before I get round to that one.

So that's where we're heading. And hopefully we'll find something to laugh about along the way, because heaven knows we could do with some laughs in these days when pandemic and warfare seem to be working on a rota basis to mess us all up. Indeed, laughs may be the best means we have of fighting back. For, to quote Charles Dickens in *A Christmas Carol* once more: 'While there is infection in disease and sorrow, there is nothing in the world so irresistibly contagious as laughter and good-humour.'

To which I can only say: good point, Dicko, me old son, and well made.

And that role as ITV's all-new Scrooge, offered to me over lunch that day and for which, as you now know, I was so temperamentally suited?

Well, let me tell you what actually happened there. But before I do that, I just need to get up and let the Spirit of Christmas Past in at the window. He's turned up a bit early, which I suppose is a good sign – showing willing, and all that – but he's been clanking his chains and making a right old racket out there for about twenty minutes now and he'll be annoying the neighbours. So let's get him in here and ask him if he wouldn't mind being an awfully good fellow and spinning us back a few years . . .

ON THE FIRST DEL OF CHRISTMAS . . .

Tinsel and puddings

'The Spirit put out its strong hand as it spoke, and clasped
him gently by the arm. "Rise! and walk with me!"'

A Christmas Carol

Right, Spirit: now that you've finished hanging your coat
up and plugging in your laptop, your first vision, if you
please . . .

Ah, now this I recognise. It's a make-up room at BBC
Television Centre. It is 1981, late December, the holiday
season fast upon us, and I am sitting in a chair, wrapped in a
protective sheet and having a large make-up brush flapped
in my face by one of the BBC's crack squad of powder-puff
artists. Ahead of me lies an evening of recording in front
of a studio audience, an exciting but always nerve-jangling
prospect, and no less so on the occasion of the first ever *Only
Fools and Horses* Christmas special.

Suddenly there appears, reflected in the illuminated mirror

in front of me, a woman in a bright blue silky outfit and a pair of white high-heeled boots. On her head is a jewelled cap from beneath which falls a long cascade of platinum-blonde hair. She has drifted in from the corridor and it is clear that she is lost.

'Can you help me?' she says.

It is a sight, dear reader, which causes my jaw to drop to the floor – thereby briefly admitting the make-up brush and its dusty contents to my mouth, which is never entirely advisable. Nevertheless, despite the fact that I am essentially trapped under a sheet and have a tongue which is now lightly coated with face powder, I somehow retain the wherewithal to make my feelings clear.

'I think I'm in love,' I say.

The beatific reflection in the mirror acknowledges this open-hearted declaration with an indulgent smile. But before I can rise from the chair, shake off the sheet that binds me, spit out the face powder (but in a decorous and ultimately attractive way, hopefully) and pledge my troth more fully, the make-up artist standing behind me intervenes.

'Where are you meant to be?' she asks.

While I merely sit under my sheet and look on helplessly, like a dental patient mid-treatment, the lost woman mentions a studio number, the make-up artist points her in the right direction, and the lost woman in turn says her thanks. And then I watch as the reflection of this dream in bright blue turns in the doorway and steps back into the corridor.

And with that, Agnetha from ABBA walked out of my life, never to return.

Ah, ships that pass. And what a potentially pivotal moment that could have been for the history of popular culture. In only mildly different circumstances, I could have ended up joining ABBA. Or Agnetha could have ended up joining the cast of *Only Fools and Horses*. Or we could both have decided to throw it all in, there and then, turn our backs on the world and depart forthwith for a life of isolated bliss on a remote Scandinavian island, there to spend the long dark winters happily weaving jumpers for each other. But either way, how very much altered the world as we now know it would be.

As I was discovering, though, now that I was working there regularly, the BBC's various rehearsal and studio spaces were quite the place for worlds briefly colliding. Quite apart from members of ABBA wandering into your make-up session, you might find yourself down in the canteen at lunchtime, tray in hand, queuing for sausage and chips, or whichever other gastronomic speciality the BBC was fuelling its workforce with that day, looking across at someone tucking into a steamed pudding with custard and thinking, 'That bloke looks exactly like Bruce Forsyth,' only to realise that there was a very good reason for that – namely, because the person tucking into steamed pudding with custard actually *was* Bruce Forsyth. And isn't that Angela Rippon over there by the window? And, blimey – isn't that the whole of Pan's People beside the coffee cups?

I can't deny that I got quite a buzz out of it all – this strong sense, which it would be impossible to duplicate today, of being at the British broadcasting industry's beating heart.

Really that canteen in itself, with all its various comings and goings, would have made a good setting for a sitcom. But we already had one of those to think about – and now it was making its first Christmas special. And making it in something of a hurry, I have to say – filming a session in the studio on 20 December for broadcast just over a week later, on the 28th.

Talk about leaving your shopping until the last minute. And it wouldn't be the last time our team ended up going down to the wire in the wrapping of its Christmas gifts to the nation.

To be honest, there was something rather ad hoc and hurried about all of the arrangements around 'Christmas Crackers', as this episode of *Only Fools* was named. It seemed to have been a last-minute gift idea on the BBC's part, too, who commissioned it late and foisted it on John to write at speed. The episode was entirely studio-bound, there being no time for any external location business and perhaps, knowing the BBC, no budget for any, either. Neither Martin Shardlow nor Ray Butt, the director and producer who had worked on the show regularly to this point, were available at short notice, so in came, on a one-off basis, to fill both those roles, Bernard Thompson, who had worked on *Are You Being Served?* and *Last of the Summer Wine*.

Now, I don't think I'll be going out on a limb if I suggest that the slightly slapdash circumstances in which the episode came together ended up showing in the finished product – right the way through to that title, 'Christmas Crackers'. In naming the special editions from here on in, John would never again hit the target so squarely and flatly on the nose. And nor would their content be quite so straightforwardly mainstream, either.

All sitcoms are fundamentally about people who are trapped by their circumstances and yearning in some way to get out. Classically, then, the Christmas special version of a sitcom, when given the standard treatment, will be about those same people being trapped by those same circumstances, but at Christmas – which is kind of a double trap, compounded by the fact that everywhere is closed and the world has shrunk even further.

This is very much the predicament in which we find Del, Rodney and Grandad in 'Christmas Crackers'. Grandad takes charge of the turkey roasting, but leaves the giblets inside, in their plastic bag, and also underdoes the cooking by a number of hours. Nigella Lawson will back me up here: this is not the best way to release the full flavour and succulence of your chosen bird on the big day.

Grandad's Christmas pudding, on the other hand – well, I think we can agree that that could have done with a little less time on the stove. He's basically produced a serving of coal. Again, Nigella will be turning in her apron.

These culinary horrors aside, plus an equally obligatory sequence featuring an exchange of Christmas presents, nothing much develops, apart from a trip to the miraculously open Monte Carlo nightclub where Del and Rodney attempt – unsuccessfully, of course – to pair themselves off. So, not the show's finest hour, let's gently say, and certainly not broadcast at the BBC's finest hour: the show went out at 9.55 p.m. following directly after *Val Sings Bing*, in which the crooner Val Doonican put his silken tones to the songs of Bing Crosby. In that unpromising and very much non-family-oriented slot, our show picked up 7.5 million viewers, which wasn't too bad for that time of night, although many of them, one suspects, were people who, having survived Val singing Bing, decided they could survive anything, and many of the rest were probably just staying awake for the main news, read by Richard Baker.

Not spectacular, though, however you carve it. A bit like Grandad's turkey.

Fast-forward a year to December 1982, though, and things are already starting to move, both for *Only Fools*'s general place in the Christmas scheme of things and for my own. Indeed, by 1982, the show is deemed worthy of not one but two appearances over that Christmas – albeit one of them is only eight minutes long, so perhaps has to qualify more as a head-popped-round-the-door than a fully-fledged visit to the nation's living rooms.

This was for something called *The Funny Side of Christmas* – a set of short skits featuring the casts of already running series, a compendium of miniature Christmas specials, if you will, offered to the country for its delectation on the Bank Holiday Monday, 27 December. Also featured were shows like *The Fall and Rise of Reginald Perrin*, *The Last of the Summer Wine* and *Butterflies* – all well-established sitcoms with their feet well under the BBC table at this point. So this was quite a vote of confidence for our relatively young show, just eighteen months and two series old at this stage, and with its place in the nation's affections still far from secured.

And who is that dapper gentleman in the pink bow tie whose job it is to link together this eighty-minute televisual patchwork on a Christmas theme? Why, that's the raconteur and comedy-writing polymath Frank Muir, of course, the kind of suave, verbally florid presence that, I think it's fair to say, television is simply less inclined to show us these days, at Christmas or any other time. They appear to have gone the way of the pink bow tie.

Often described as a 'lost episode', and not much seen since the night it went out, John Sullivan's contribution to Frank's patchwork was a sketch called 'Christmas Trees', in which Del is charged with going out on the street to flog 150 dismally droopy-looking fake firs – folding tinsel monstrosities, which Del optimistically describes as microchip-driven but which actually seem to need some fairly heavy manual encouragement just to fold away. Needless to say, despite Del's very best sales patter, these items seem to be going down among shoppers, as Del sighingly concedes, 'about as well as Union Jacks in Buenos Aires'.*

I loved doing all those street-selling scenes, and this one in particular gave me some room to get going:

> . . . Now, if you went up Harrods you'd pay 27 quid for one of these and you'd think you were getting a right result. Well, I'm not going to ask you for 27 quid. I'm not even going to ask you for a score. Who said 15? . . .

Another vocation missed, clearly. But this was one of those acting occasions when I could genuinely say I'd done my research – specifically on Oxford Street in the late 1970s. While walking to work at the theatres from my place in Newman Street, I would often pause to watch the hawkers who had thrown down a blanket on the pavement and laid out their wares: watches, perfumes, underwear, toys, whatever was fresh off the back of that morning's lorry. The set-up fascinated me. I could stand there in the throng for ages, just watching it all develop, seeing these wannabe entrepreneurs do a roaring trade or die a cold and eerie death, depending – seeing them pack up in a hurry and scarper when the scout, posted up the road to keep an eye out, returned hotfoot to tip them off to the imminent arrival of a member of Her

---

* Topical joke by John, there: the Falklands War had ended six months prior to this. Probably still works as a joke even now, though.

Majesty's Metropolitan constabulary. You could see a whole story get told in a matter of minutes.

You soon picked up the tricks – the member of the team who pretends to be a customer, handing over a tenner and heading off up the street with his purchase, thereby getting the ball rolling, only to drift back furtively later with the goods tucked under his jacket, ready for resale. But the thing that most hooked me was the patter – the rhythm and pace of it, the reaching out to engage with someone in the audience and, in the process, bring everyone in on it. It was extraordinary to watch those guys cultivate relationships with strangers out of thin air.

How do you persuade somebody that they need something? First of all by persuading them that they can trust you. The manipulating, the tempting, the subtle cajoling – these were, frankly, theatrical tricks. I've said it before and I'll say it again, and in fact I'll keep saying it until the world decides to call it Jason's Theorem . . . but: flogging hooky gear from a suitcase with one eye out for an approaching copper and the noble profession of acting have an awful lot in common when you get down to it.

The slightly odd thing about that Frank Muir compendium is that Nick Lyndhurst and I appear in it twice, both playing roles that were ours before *Only Fools* came along. The inclusion of Carla Lane's *Butterflies* means that Nick pitches up opposite Wendy Craig and Geoffrey Palmer as Adam, the younger of their teenage sons, in a scene set in the wake – yet again – of a clearly thunderously inedible Christmas lunch. Clearly, whether it's a Peckham flat or the middle-class suburban home of a dentist and his frustrated wife, the law of the Christmas special states that crippling indigestion will dominate the conversation.

'What did she stuff the turkey with?' Adam's brother Russell, played by Andrew Hall, asks him from a semi-paralysed position on the sofa.

'A sort of herbal putty,' is Adam's reply.

And then, because *Open All Hours* also got a slot in the show, I additionally graced the screen as Granville the corner-shop assistant, opposite my great friend and mentor Ronnie Barker's Arkwright. It was the fate of *Open All Hours* to be mostly overlooked at the first time of asking (1976, on BBC2), but then to catch fire when the series was casually repeated on BBC1 to fill a hole in the schedules. Suddenly, after a four-year gap in which we'd all reluctantly reached the conclusion that the show was sunk, we were back in business, and the subsequent three series went out in 1981, 1982 and 1985, overlapping with the birth of *Only Fools* and keeping me rather busy, not least, clearly, over this particular Christmas.

In Roy Clarke's eight-minute *Open All Hours* skit, it was Christmas Day – the only day of the year that stingy old Arkwright would consent to close the shop – and nobody had indigestion because it was the morning and Christmas dinner (over the road at Nurse Gladys Emmanuel's) was yet to come.

In the meantime, though, eagle-eyed viewers – and perhaps not so eagle-eyed ones as well – had a moment to ponder the miracle by which, appearing as Granville, I had a dark and lustrous head of hair, which was somehow less in evidence in my portrayal of Derek Trotter in the very same broadcast.

No miracle, in fact – unless you count a little supplementary help with a clip-on hairpiece around the crown area, courtesy of the aforementioned BBC make-up people. Ah, once again, the indignities of the trade. But one is a professional and one weathers them and soldiers on.

The official *Only Fools* Christmas special that year went out three days later, on 30 December, at 7.55 in the evening – so by no means at the centre of the Christmas schedules, but nevertheless glamorously sandwiched between *Top of the Pops* and an episode of *'Allo 'Allo*. This special was called 'Diamonds are for Heather' and, after the conventional Christmas offering which was 'Christmas Crackers' the previous year, it showed pretty quickly that John Sullivan was already loosening the knots a bit and starting to do his own thing when Christmas came around.

OK, so the story was still pegged in time to the Christmas season – John hadn't yet had the nerve to fly in the face of that extremely robust convention, and he wouldn't do so at the next time of asking, either: indeed, 'Thicker Than Water', the 1983 special, will be set, in full compliance with tradition, on Christmas night in the Trotters' flat. There was no pushing the boundaries here in terms of length, either: 'Diamonds are for Heather' was a standard half-hour episode.

But it's quietly revolutionary in its own way, and even pretty daring. For here is a story intended for Christmas consumption, yet not about badly roasted turkeys and cooped-up families getting tetchy with one another while suffering indigestion, but about thwarted love – which can feel a lot like indigestion after consuming the wrong kind of stuffing, it's true, but which is ultimately a very different thing.

Here is a story in which Del falls head over heels for a single mum called Heather – played by Rosalind Lloyd – investing himself wholly in both her and her little son, only to be rejected by her in the end. Out went the full-on festive jollity you'd probably been expecting, then, and in came a heartstring-tugging romance, with an unhappy ending.

And what was on display as a consequence of that move were aspects of Del's character which had only really been hinted at up to now – that sense of Del as a thwarted father and home-builder. For all his striving, boisterous, best-foot-forward nature and for all his ducking and diving and bobbing and weaving, he's a man with this hinterland of tenderness inside him – someone who has had the responsibility for his brother and grandfather dropped on his plate by the death of his mum and has had to make a lot of sacrifices.* All that

---

* Contrary to some suggestions online, there is no cream you can get for a tender hinterland, or certainly not over the counter, anyway.

was a development for Del's character, and a development for me, playing him.

So, at the end, instead of everyone sitting around a groaning table in a tinsel-festooned room, pulling crackers, you get sadness and melancholy – and a rendition of 'Old Shep'.

Ah, that song – that terrible old song. On 'Spanish Night' in the Nag's Head, just before noticing Heather drinking alone at the bar, a deeply downcast Del orders the pub's specially booked Spanish live music act (more Greenwich in origin than Granada, it turns out) to sing 'Old Shep', a depressing hillbilly tune from the 1930s about a boy and his beloved but now unfortunately dead dog which Elvis Presley famously turned his hips to. So 'Old Shep' effectively brings Del and Heather together – it kicks off the conversation between them – and weeks of successful and happy courtship then ensue, capped off with the application of a 'DEL – HEATHER' sun-strip to the Reliant Regal, than which, clearly, there could be no firmer declaration of a man's best intentions. In the early 1980s, a marriage proposal was virtually a foregone conclusion after a demonstration of loyalty as solid as that.

Lo, over a candlelit curry, Del does indeed propose. But Heather respectfully turns him down, intending to reunite with her previously vanished husband and the father of her child, who has now, it seems, come back on the scene and is happily employed as a department store Father Christmas in Southampton.* Del is back to square one, then, and, in a typically neat Sullivan loop-around, the rejected and thoroughly dejected Del, out on the street, gets some carol singers to sing him . . . 'Old Shep'.

This is a song so dreary, remember, that the 'Spanish' pub singer in the Nag's Head tells Del that there is no way he can sing it and hope to remain employed. Yet John Sullivan manages to get it performed in a sitcom's Christmas special, twice.

Those weren't just any old carol singers, by the way. They were played by the Fred Tomlinson Singers, about whom you possibly know more than you realise because Fred Tomlinson and his people supplied the choral requirements of the Monty Python team. Yes, my old nemeses the Pythons return to haunt these pages yet again. Indeed, Fred wrote the music for 'The Lumberjack Song', which must have earned him a bob or two, and he and his singers performed it with the Pythons for the show, as well as the almost equally notorious 'Spam Song'. Not a lot of people know that, as Michael Caine never actually said.†

---

* Very good terms and conditions with that job, as Del drily points out. 'Free uniform, luncheon vouchers, forty-eight weeks' holiday a year.'

† According to Michael Caine it was something that Peter Sellers said about him during a television interview as a wind-up – that Caine had the habit of repeating facts from the *Guinness Book of Records* and then saying, 'Not a lot of people know that.' The myth stuck – and so fast that Caine then ended up carrying that catchphrase around with him. He did eventually utter those words in the film *Educating Rita*, which came out in

But in between these renditions of that really quite awful song, much that is truly poignant has unfolded, not least in the scenes of Del enthusiastically bonding with Heather's boy, Darren, and embracing the self-appointed role of 'Uncle Del', on a day out round London. And if I managed to make something ring true about Del's predicament in those scenes then maybe that wasn't entirely a surprise, given where I was in my own life at that stage. When we filmed this episode, I was getting into my forties, and surrounded by friends and colleagues who had long since started having families, and naturally wondering if, having wholeheartedly dedicated the last fifteen years to doing all the acting I possibly could and to trying to build a career, I might have missed the boat in that regard.

Of course, with regard to that particular boat, I got exceptionally lucky eventually – as, indeed, would Del in due course. But in the meantime I definitely had the odd bout of anxious reflection in this area about the pros and cons of the choices I had so far made. I tend to resist comparisons between myself and Del, the two of us being – as I am always extremely keen to point out – such different people. But in the case of the kind of melancholy thoughts about his future that Del was having in 'Diamonds are for Heather', and the enthusiasm he brought to those scenes with Heather's child,

---

1983, but by then the association of Caine with the line was so rife that was an in-joke. Not a lot of people know all *that*, either.

I can make a small exception. Like with the street salesman patter, you could say: this was acting for which I'd done a bit of research.

After the studio shoot was completed, Rosalind and I went out to meet some of the audience, which was something the cast frequently did, just to thank them for turning up, being patient with us when we screwed up and generally being a part of it all. And as we mingled, a woman, still looking a little bit emotional, came up to us and said, 'God, I wasn't expecting that: you two made me cry.'

That was quite a moment for me. I mean, it was a nice compliment for Rosalind's and my acting, and actors will always bite your hand off for one of those. But beyond that – getting people to cry at a shoot for a Christmas sitcom? It made me realise what *Only Fools* was turning into and what it could become.*

All in all, I've got quite a soft spot for 'Diamonds are for Heather'. Coming so early in the show's history and long pre-dating the big set-piece Christmas numbers, it can get over-looked. But it was actually a rather lovely and fully formed episode, in my humble opinion, and in terms of seeding the

* Top tip: should you ever find yourself face-to-face with an actor and required to compliment them after a performance that, to be perfectly honest, you weren't entirely sure about, simply look them directly in the eye, beam warmly and say, in a tone of overawed wonder: 'Darling, you've done it again!'

direction for Del's character and the narrative direction of the series as a whole, a formative episode, too.

Even though it went out in what was very much not one of the prime Christmas slots, it still managed to attract 9.3 million viewers, which was nearly two million more people than the previous year's Christmas special had managed to drum up. The slightly disappointing thing was that it was about a million fewer people than had watched the most recent regular series episode of the show, a little less than a month previously – 'A Touch of Glass', which is the one where a chandelier doesn't come off too well from the Trotters' attempts to detach it for cleaning.

One step forward, two steps back, then. But the progress of *Only Fools* often felt a bit that way in those early years. Still, at the time, I wasn't inclined to split hairs. Ten million, nine million . . . these seemed like pretty big numbers to me – a decent chunk of the country.

Little did I know, but we were only just getting started in that respect.

Humble beginnings, then. But that was very much my story, too.

ON THE SECOND DEL OF CHRISTMAS . . .

Ghosts and movies

'The Ghost smiled thoughtfully, and waved its hand: saying as it did so, "Let us see another Christmas!"'

A Christmas Carol

What have you got for me now, my reasonably priced Spirit? Something much older this time?

Ah, yes. It's a cold, clear winter's night, and a small boy and his mother have got their coats on and are heading up Finchley High Road in north London in the direction of the Gaumont cinema.

The small boy in question? Well, draw a little closer, dear reader, because that's me, young David White. I'd be around eleven years old, by the look of it, which would make this 1951 or thereabouts, and I'm a shy and rather cautious little chap at this point in my life, although certainly sharp enough to tell you, if you ask me, how many beans make five. The answer being, 'A bean, a bean, a bean and a half, half a bean and a bean.' (Trust me, this little piece of repartee was considered the height of wit among eleven-year-olds in 1951.)

I'm also slightly on the short side, and a bit self-conscious about it, truth be told. Hard not to be. To my great alarm, a number of my contemporaries at school have begun getting tall before my very eyes – abruptly departing in the direction of the ceiling as if there is something in the light bulbs that they urgently need to get hold of. Some of them seem capable of adding whole feet to their height in the space of a single weekend. I, by contrast, can only watch all this rampant growth from a position closer to the ground and hope that I'm playing a longer game.

Spoiler alert: I am actually in the process of rising by tiny increments towards the giddy height of . . . er, five foot six, actually, where, in three years' time or so, at the age of about fourteen, my body will decide that it's had enough of getting taller, and stop. Here's an encouraging thought, though, gleaned in passing from a documentary I happened to be watching recently: back in the eighteenth century, the height of the average full-grown British male was (small drum roll here, please) . . . five foot five. Something positive to reflect on there, for all of us five-foot-sixers. Only three hundred years – a mere stitch, surely, in the unfathomable trousers of time – has separated us from a place among the giants.

As history shows us, over and again, it's all about perspective.

Anyway, here I am in 1951, fairly tiny, with my mum, who is not so tall herself, now you come to mention it, heading up the street for a night at 'the pictures'. This is not a rare outing for us. On the contrary, this is something we might do twice a week and sometimes even three times – occasionally joined by my father, though he generally, after a long day on his feet at the fishmonger's, prefers to stay at home and read the paper and listen to the radio. Fair enough. But for me and my mum . . . well, why wouldn't we go frequently, when the cinema costs so little – ninepence for a child in the cheap seats, one and six for a grown-up – and when it's basically on our doorstep, or at any rate a simple half-mile walk, up the road and turn right?

And what a cinema, too. The Finchley Gaumont is a majestic, towering, curve-fronted, art deco building whose glass-walled frontage sits behind the splendidly named Tally Ho Corner – not, as it turns out, a part of Aintree racecourse, but a broad road junction, laced overhead by a jumble of wires for the trolley buses.

Don't bother looking for the Gaumont today. It was demolished in the 1980s. And don't bother looking for the trolley buses, either, nor their wires, which, to be honest, were already going out of fashion in 1951, eased aside by the free-roaming diesel vehicles which people seemed to have decided were the future.

And while we're on the topic, don't bother looking for my house half a mile away at 26 Lodge Lane, either, which has long since been knocked down and concreted over, and now takes the form of a municipal car park, round the back of a Starbucks. Alas, then, no blue plaque marks my childhood home. And if it did, it would have to be nailed up somewhere between a Pay & Display machine and a selection of extremely sugary muffins.

Nevertheless, take it from me, on this particular Thursday evening in 1951, both the Gaumont and 26 Lodge Lane are still very much in business, along with these two figures walking out into the night. And if a certain urgency quickens the step of Mrs White and her son along the High Road, it's because they don't want to be late to join the queues which they know will already be forming on the street under the cinema's sweeping glass canopy.

Sure enough, the line when they reach it is already stretching up the pavement, but they take their place in it. And from then on, as the queue shuffles slowly forward, you will notice an eleven-year-old boy repeatedly leaning out from behind the overcoat in front of him and craning his neck to look ahead, in fear of the sight that will spell doom to the whole evening: the uniformed commissionaire emerging from the foyer and plonking down the HOUSE FULL sign.

What a heart-sinker that used to be when it happened – which was quite often, on account of the raging popularity of cinema-going at this moment in history. I should point out that the auditorium at the Gaumont held more than two thousand people and, even then, if you mistimed it, you could find yourself turned away. And there was never a plan B on those cinema nights. Go for a meal or a drink instead, as one might nowadays? Unthinkable behaviour! If the place sold out, my mum and I would simply turn round and walk home the way we had just come.

Tonight, though, after the usual anxious spell on the pavement, we're in luck. We're through the doors. And what a sight it is that greets us, in that immense entrance hall: the red-carpeted steps, the silver pillars soaring upwards into the high ceiling, the hanging globe lights giving off an orangey glow, the walls painted in shades of peach and gold and green. To my young eyes, all of this is unimaginably exotic – and to my mother's older eyes, too, actually, as we reach the window and she pushes the coins under the glass in exchange for our tickets.

And from there it's just a few more paces up another short flight of carpeted steps and we're through the internal doors and into the stalls of that massive auditorium. The enormity of the place never failed to impress my young mind – very different from your modern multiplex. None of that hobbling three miles down a dimly lit corridor to find Screen 14 in what was possibly once a broom cupboard – taking care to leave a trail of popcorn behind you, of course, so that you can find your way back to the entrance later. At the Gaumont, the big screen really did mean the big screen.

And oh, the warmth! I touched on this a bit in my last book, but a large part of the appeal of a night at 'the pictures' in those immediately post-war years had to do with basic creature comforts: things we largely take for granted now, like light and heat. Trust me: if, as was the case for the White family, electricity won't be reaching your terraced street for another couple of years yet, and television not for a couple of years after that; if the main source of warmth in your house is a single coal fire in the back parlour, and most of the other rooms, including the whole of the top floor, simply stay cold; and if the smallest room in your house isn't a room at all but actually takes the form of a tiny and punishingly draughty brick-built lean-to in the backyard, where the cold wind whistles under the door, as well as under several other things . . . well then, somewhere as wonderfully appointed and sumptuously heated as the Gaumont greets you as something which has just landed from the future.

And we haven't even mentioned the gents, with their gleaming porcelain sinks and shining mirrors. What promised land was this?

My point is, they didn't call them 'picture palaces' for nothing, and this, surely, as much as anything, accounted for the powerful magnetism of the cinema in those frequently colourless post-war years, and was what brought us working-class families flocking in such numbers two or three times a week. Never mind the movies – feel the grandeur. Even the commissionaire who minded the queue was loaned the magnificent authority of a peaked cap and a frock coat with gold-braided epaulettes, as if he was the doorman at Buckingham Palace, and for us he might as well have been.

And tonight in these sumptuous surroundings my mum and I will see something called *Scrooge*, a film about which I know very little in advance, but which, it's no exaggeration to say, I will know a lot about for ever more. At this point, though, the limits of my knowledge are that it stars someone named Alastair Sim. I know this because his name is emblazoned right across the top of the poster – 'IN HIS FIRST GREAT DRAMATIC COMEDY ROLE' – a poster which I have already examined carefully under glass outside the cinema, just as I closely scrutinised all the movie posters fixed to that wall, seeking to unlock the promise they contained.

But not too much else is given away in this case, the poster mostly being dominated by a painted image of a smiling elderly man, wrapped up in a red scarf and blue coat and under a top hat, with just a hint of a Victorian London street scene poking itself into view along the bottom edge. The colours on the poster, of course, are something of a liberty because the film we are about to see is in black and white. But it wouldn't occur to any of us to complain about that little detail, nor even really to notice it.

We have barely settled when the room thrillingly darkens and the curtains draw aside and a giant card silently fills the screen: 'RENOWN PICTURES CORPORATION LIMITED'. There is then, suddenly and out of nowhere, a thunderous burst of dark and jagged orchestral music that practically throws me backwards over my seat. The orchestra then gives way to a few voices hesitantly singing 'Hark the Herald Angels Sing', which also sounds threatening and eerie at first but then gradually gets louder, rising in confidence until it sounds strong and ultimately triumphant. Though I don't realise it yet, the whole story of the film is in that overture.

Meanwhile, on the screen, a hand has fetched down a volume from a shelf and solemnly opened it to reveal the film's titles and that name again, 'Alastair Sim', and the narrator has made himself heard for the first time.

'Old Marley was as dead as a doornail. This must be distinctly understood or nothing wonderful can come of the story I am going to relate . . .'

And straight away here comes Ebenezer Scrooge through an ominous-sounding wind, brutally brushing aside the pleading of a debtor outside on a set of icy steps, deriding Christmas in short order as 'a humbug' and crisply dismissing the carol singers outside his house: 'Be gone!'

I'm spellbound already, and I continue to be as I watch this glowering and instinctively mean figure return to his spacious but sparsely furnished and almost entirely comfortless home. With its creepy clock and its long shadows, it's a place set for a haunting if ever there was one and . . . well, what do you know? Before long there is a terrible clanking and creaking out on the stairs while Scrooge sits frozen over the most unappetisingly pale-looking bowl of soup you've ever seen in your life. He continues to stare in open-mouthed terror at the back of the closed door as (brilliant touch, this) his spoon, paused on its way up, tilts and slowly empties its unappealing contents back into the bowl.

By the time that door bursts open and the ghost of Jacob Marley enters, my eleven-year-old self is pinned to his seat, as open-mouthed as Scrooge and, if the lights were up, probably as pale as that awful soup. Because, by the wonders of film trickery, we are now looking at *a see-through man*.

How utterly terrifying is that? I mean, no disrespect to anyone recently hired in this line of work who might currently be sitting on the other side of my study with his feet up, and occasionally looking in a slightly bored way at his watch. But in those days, they knew how to do a Spirit of Christmas Past properly.

Marley's ghost in *Scrooge*, by the way, is played by Michael Hordern. That's the same Michael Hordern whom, some thirty-two years after this, I will stand alongside in a recording studio, creating the voices for the animated film version of *The Wind in the Willows* – him giving the world his Badger while I give the world my Toad. In other words, while Scrooge is encountering his past up there on that screen, I'm staring directly up at my future. But, aged eleven, I'm in no position to know that, and, even if I was, I'm too busy right now gripping the edge of my tip-up seat in horror to really give it much thought.

As it turned out, being in the presence of Michael Hordern was pretty scary, even when he wasn't playing a partly invisible ghost. But perhaps that's a story for further on in these pages. What I'll say now is that, following a preview of the film, the critic from the American trade paper *Variety* felt compelled to warn the world that *Scrooge* was 'a grim thing that will give tender-aged kiddies viewing it the screaming-meemies'.

And what can I tell you? As a tender-aged kiddie, the screaming-meemies – or certainly the nearest British equivalent – were a large part of my reaction, sat there in the stalls with whitened knuckles.

But, of course, that's precisely what I loved about it. Because, let's be honest, there's nothing some tender-aged kiddies like more than being scared witless by a movie now and again, and that was certainly true of *this* tender-aged kiddie. And if it leads directly to some screaming-meemies, then all the better, surely, and money well spent.

'A grim thing'? Well, yes. But that was the point, and what made *Scrooge* so great. This was a story about the consequences of meanness and about meanness overcome – and if you, in the audience, didn't encounter and feel the full force of that meanness in the first place, then there was no redemption in the tale. The director and producer of *Scrooge*, Brian Desmond Hurst, knew that. The film doesn't gloss over the darker aspects of the Dickens story. Even the snow – which falls throughout the film in accordance with the law affecting Christmas-themed movies – has a chilly, hostile bleakness about it.

In the US, the film was released under the more proper title, *A Christmas Carol*. Well, I say more proper, but if we're going to be pedantic about it, the title that Dickens actually gave his story was: *A Christmas Carol, in Prose: Being a Ghost Story of Christmas*. So stick that on your backlit marquee.

Anyway, *Variety* back then didn't care much for the film, whatever it was called. 'Adults will find it long,' the reviewer suggested – which is quite a contention to make about a film that clocks in under an hour and a half. Adult-wise, I can only speak for my mum, who, like me, was agog through-out. Generally there was a quite strong divide in those days between what my mum enjoyed at the cinema (romantic comedies, anything with Rock Hudson and Doris Day) and what I enjoyed (westerns featuring John Wayne and lashings of gunfire). But here, in *Scrooge*, we found an easy meet-ing place. This was storytelling which reached across the divides, generational and otherwise.

And as for the *Variety* critic's allegation that 'Alastair Sim stalks through the footage like a tank-town Hamlet' . . . well, at that point I feel I have no alternative but to reach for the traditional expression at moments of bewilderment while reading film reviews: 'Was this person watching the same movie as me?'

Also, what's a 'tank-town' when it's at home?

OK, I've looked it up: it's American for 'small-town'. But

a small-town Hamlet? Alastair Sim? No, surely not. There was so much that was clever about that performance, and so much that was adeptly done. You laughed at Scrooge, and you recoiled from him, and you understood that there was something monstrous about him. But you also saw his fear and understood it, and eventually came to sympathise with him. It's a rare and deft kind of acting that can command that range of response in an audience.

Anyway, an hour and a half later the credits rolled. Did the young boy in our tale then wander forth from the Gaumont and make his dazed way home, his head a-spin with visions of what acting could do and with the seeds of ambition now sown deep in his heart? Well, if this book was itself a movie, maybe you would play it that way. (And incidentally, film rights to these recollections do remain available at the time of writing: any interested Hollywood producers, please address your approaches to my agent in the usual fashion.)

But in truth, no: there were no dreams of acting for me at this point. There couldn't have been. The place in which there were people called actors, who got together and made entertainments for people like me and my mum, might as well have been another planet entirely. It was so far removed from my own world as to be completely unimaginable – not even, at this point, a fantasy land running parallel to our own that I might dream about finding the portal to. All that was a long way off, in every sense.

So what happened after I watched *Scrooge* was, I went home to bed. I used to love doing that walk back from the cinema – especially in the winter. I loved that burst of cold air as you came out onto the pavement and which caused you to tighten your coat around yourself. And I loved that feeling of tiredness at the end of the day, and knowing that your bed was waiting for you, and not so far away.

But most of all I loved the way that the dark night, as you walked, helped you keep the movie you had just seen running in your head. Summer nights just weren't the same for film-going in that respect. Coming out at around half past nine into the lingering evening light and the warm air somehow made the magic evaporate more quickly. In the depths of winter, when it was properly dark and cold enough to draw you into yourself, you could stay in the world of the film for just that little bit longer.

So I headed home with the story of *Scrooge* rolling around my imagination, and with those ghosts, in particular, accompanying me – and following me up the dark stairs to my bedroom and putting a bit of extra energy in my legs as I scampered under the blankets to get warm. If any seeds were sown, on this and all those other young nights at the cinema, it was in beginning to understand how things can leap off a screen and touch people – how a simple piece of entertainment can reach into people's hearts and minds and lodge there, not just for the whole of the journey home, but for good.

*   *   *

I saw Alastair Sim in the cinema again several times after that. Most notably, he played the headmistress, Miss Millicent Fritton, in *The Belles of St Trinian's*, that now classic comedy set in the legendarily rebellious girls' school, and which I saw in the Gaumont when it came out in 1954. The character of Miss Fritton was a proper 'grande dame' part originally written for Margaret Rutherford, but when she proved unavailable someone had the bonkers yet brilliant idea of giving it to Sim, who was also cast in the film as Clarence Fritton, the headmistress's brother. What I love about Sim's Miss Fritton is that he doesn't play it as cabaret, which a broader and less capable kind of comedian might have been tempted to do. He doesn't aim for the exaggerations where the belly laughs might have been. He goes for something much closer and more careful – a character study. And it's perfect in every detail.

Sim died in 1976, but he will always be high on my list of the greats. And I'm by no means alone in holding him there, of course. In the early seventies, John Cleese apparently pleaded and badgered and downright begged his way into an episode of the BBC comedy series *Misleading Cases*, purely because he wanted to be able to say he had acted with Alastair Sim. I wish I'd thought of that.

I did at least get to see Sim work onstage, though. I drove out of London to the Chichester Festival Theatre one evening in 1969 to see him play Aeneas Posket in the nineteenth-century Pinero farce, *The Magistrate*. I got lucky, because some now rank that as Sim's finest theatrical performance – stuffed full of unscripted sequences, unique bits of business and tours de force. At one point he spent a long time trying, and failing, to get a pair of braces under control; at another, he spent the best part of five minutes simply washing his face and getting into all sorts of difficulties with the soap and the towel. His control, both of what he was doing and of us in the audience, was masterful. Opposite him as Agatha Posket was Patricia Routledge. It was quite a night, all in all.

I go back to Alastair Sim's *Scrooge* every Christmas, marvelling yet again at the depth of its cast. Patrick Macnee, later of *The Avengers*, is in there, and so are Hattie Jacques and Jack Warner from *Dixon of Dock Green*. And so is George Cole, who would have been twenty-six at the time, playing the younger Scrooge and talking in a slightly higher register voice in order to do so. George's path and mine ended up crossing a lot further down the line, too.

But mostly I marvel at Alastair Sim. He made something there for Christmas which doesn't fade. Which is why, when we wind forward across the ages to that restaurant table in London a few years ago, where the man from ITV was offering me the extremely tempting chance to play Scrooge myself, I didn't have to think too hard or for too long.

'No, thank you very much,' I said. 'I don't think that's for me.'

The thing was, I'd seen other productions of A *Christmas Carol* in the meantime, and . . . well, no names, no pack drill, but I'd found myself sitting there and thinking: 'No! No! Why did you even attempt it?' And now that the carrot was being dangled in front of me, it would have felt hypocritical to snatch at it. It would certainly have felt daunting.

I mean, I was as up for a challenge as any other actor, and always had been, from day one. I was also up for a job, as most actors tend to be, too, acting being a famously precarious business in which you never quite know when the next offer might be coming along – and that's true no matter how successful you are. The problem was, I sincerely believed that Alastair Sim had achieved the summit with that interpretation of Scrooge, and if I were to take it on, I would only end up kicking about in the foothills. His version had left such an impression on me that I didn't see how I could do anything other than a pale imitation of it. So I decided to turn this rather generous opportunity down.

Which either makes me a man of unimpeachable integrity or a bit of a wally, depending how you look at it.

There's a useful saying, though: 'Talent hits a target no one else can hit. Genius hits a target no one else can see.'

Who wrote that? Well, I did, just now, of course. But I believe the first person to set down those words in that order was Arthur Schopenhauer, the nineteenth-century German philosopher whose hugely influential works – I'm sure I don't need to tell you – I am forever taking down from the shelves of the library at Jason Towers and pondering anew. In the original German, obviously.

Actually, I think I might have seen it on a wall somewhere – possibly at the dentist's? Or was it at the recycling centre?

Doesn't matter. The point is, it's true. Talent does indeed hit a target no one else can hit. And genius does indeed hit a target no one else can see.

And just occasionally the wisest course is not even to take aim.

I finished my chicken escalope, thanked the man from ITV for his kind offer – and prayed another part would come along soon.

ON THE THIRD DEL OF CHRISTMAS . . .

Pantomimes and turkeys

And what scene is this now that my reasonably priced Spirit of Christmas Past, who's hanging about over there by the fireplace, bids me contemplate with his bony, pointing finger? Ah yes: I know this vision well enough, and these figures within it extremely well, though it is even older, surely, than the last scene he cooked up for us.

This is 1948, did you say? And if this is 1948, that would make me . . . what? Eight, going on nine – and even smaller than I was in the previous chapter, if such a thing is physically possible. And there I am, in the hall at home with my mother, putting on our coats. But this time the pair of us are heading, not for the Finchley Gaumont, but for the Golders Green Hippodrome, a short bus trip away. And this time, it's not the cinema we're going to. We're bound for the pantomime.

To which you are legally obliged to shout, 'Oh no, you're not.'

And to which I, in turn, am legally obliged to reply, 'Oh yes, we are.'

But wait. Before we finish buttoning ourselves up and set off for the evening, the Spirit invites you and me to put our heads into the Lodge Lane kitchen, just briefly, and observe the scene there.

And what a scene it is. There, piled around the sink and on the table, are Christmas turkeys. Also Christmas ducks and large-size Christmas chickens. Mounds of them. Whole piles of uncooked meat, stacked high. And there, somewhere in among those mounds, sits my father, working away with his bare hands and a sharp knife. You would say it looked like a butcher's in here at the moment, and there's a good reason for that, because it is.

At any rate, being a fishmonger, my father knew the local butcher well and, come Christmas, when the butcher was overwhelmed with orders, my dad could make himself a couple of extra quid by taking in a delivery of fowl at home and preparing it for the butcher's counter: plucking it and disembowelling it, as required. Eventually the butcher's van would come back to load up the now shop-ready meat – and I'm sure the deal was sweet enough to ensure that my father got to set aside a decent-sized bird for the family in part payment.

So this was how my dad would spend his evenings in the run-up to the Christmases of my childhood. He would roll up his sleeves, pull up a dining chair and set to work on a batch of freshly slaughtered turkeys. The smell, like the feathers, would fill the kitchen. I used to pitch in and help with the plucking. I drew the line at the disembowelling, though. Health and safety? Well, we washed our hands, didn't we?

And these, in turn, were the sights and sounds that I came to associate with the festive season, as readily as I associated it with paper chains, glued together at the dining table by me and my sister, June, and then looped across the sitting room through the light fitting in the middle. Christmas at 26 Lodge Lane was about the decorations, yes, and about the stockings hung by the chimney which would end up filled with sweets and nuts, and the pillowcase at the foot of the bed that would miraculously come to contain a clump of presents in the short gap between going to sleep on Christmas Eve and waking up bright and breezy the next day. In that sense, it was probably no different from most other people's. But it was also that time of the year when our kitchen became, briefly, a butcher's outhouse.

Is it any wonder that I later developed mixed feelings about the season and an indifference to turkey sandwiches?

But enough of this. Let us turn away from the kitchen now, and its mounds of partly prepared poultry, and leave by the front door. Me and my mum have got a bus to catch and a pantomime to go to. In fact, by the magic of the written word, we're already there. We're taking our seats in the Hippodrome, which turn out to be in the stalls, but a long way back in this cavernous music hall theatre – so far back that the balcony formed by the circle is not far above our heads, making our position below it quite snug. And this, as we wait for the show to commence, is causing me considerable agitation.

It's nothing to do with claustrophobia because, don't worry, the seating isn't *that* tight. And, of course, my less than exceptional height, which I think I may have mentioned already, has at least one lifetime benefit: I'm normally quite well off for headroom. (You've got to look on the bright side.)

No, my anxiety is entirely about what this position in the auditorium means for my view of the upcoming entertainment. Because the show we have come to see is *Jack and the Beanstalk*. And despite this being my first time at the pantomime – my first time at a professional theatrical production of any kind, actually – I haven't come into this experience entirely unbriefed. On the contrary, I am bringing with me the advance knowledge that the tale of Jack and the Beanstalk features . . . a giant. This I know, as well as I know how many beans make five. (See previous chapter if you're still struggling with the maths.)

And although, as a theatre-going novice, I hardly qualify as an expert in this area, I am immediately certain of one thing about these seats under the circle that fate and the woman in the box office have dealt my mother and me – and that's that they can't possibly lend themselves to the clear and unobstructed viewing of giants.

And this is a worry.

Indeed, as we settle into these seats and wait for the lights to go down, I am leaning forward as far as I can go in my place and straining, unsuccessfully, to peer out from under the circle's low ceiling to get a view of the very top of the curtains. Because that's surely what I'm going to need if I'm going to be able to take in the full enormity of this giant when he eventually pitches up, which will be, by most informed estimates, sometime around the beginning of Act Two.

I mean, you wouldn't want to miss it, would you? Imagine going to *Jack and the Beanstalk* and only being able to see the giant up as far as his knees. That's the kind of disappointment that would live with you for a while afterwards.

So I'm getting up and leaning forward, and sitting down and getting up again, and tilting my head to one side until it's practically upside down to see if that makes any difference . . . doing everything, basically, to work out what's possible, from a sightlines point of view. Meanwhile my mum is trying to reassure me that when the lights go down and the curtains open, all will be well, just you wait and see. (And please, for heaven's sake, would you just stop *fidgeting*.)

And my mum, of course, is right. For it turns out that my childish imagination has rather got ahead of me on this occasion, as childish imaginations are prone to do. In due course, as the entertainment unfolds, it will emerge that the part of the giant is being played, not by an actual giant, flown in from the Land of Giants and appearing by special arrangement with the Land of the Giants Tourist Board, but by a man of slightly above average height in a pair of stacked heels.

I should immediately say that this is by no means a bare-bones production, here in Golders Green. On the contrary, the Hippodrome is a pukka theatre and a landmark home for significant performances from quality performers, and we're not talking Trotter Entertainments by any means. Corners have not been cut. Why, the part of Muggles is being played by Max Wall, no less. This, of course, flies over my eight-year-old head entirely, and perhaps, dear reader, it flies over yours now, too. But in Max Wall I am watching a comedy great at work, a man who will know national fame for his character, Professor Wallofski, and his silly-walk routine – which, as John Cleese readily admits, was the prime inspiration for Monty Python's Ministry of Silly Walks. (I'm sure Wall would thank me for mentioning that he was a great serious actor, too, by the way – strong enough, along with Buster Keaton, to attract the patronage of Samuel Beckett, who was famously picky when it came to actors.)

So Max Wall is playing Muggles – and Muggles, by the way, in case you are drawing a blank or perhaps wondering how elements of J. K. Rowling's Harry Potter books got into a panto in 1948, was the name given in this production to the character of Jack's dimmer brother – the Rodney, I suppose you could say, to Jack's Del. And now I mention it, there is quite a lot of the Derek Trotter about Jack in that panto:

stupidly trading a quite valuable cow for some knock-off magic beans, which then get slung out the window in despair, only for the family to get lucky in a very roundabout kind of way. I mean, if you were to throw a Peckham tower block in there and add a Reliant Regal . . .

But I digress. The point is, you may know the character of Muggles better as Simple Simon. Or maybe as Tommy Tucker. Or perhaps as Simple Sammy, Silly Billy or even Miffins. It all depends on what point in the last two and a bit centuries you saw a production of *Jack and the Beanstalk*. And yes, this particular panto really does go back that far – to a time when Christopher Biggins was but the tiniest of twinkles in a pantomime dame's eye.

In fact, some historians suggest that *Jack and the Beanstalk* may have been the first *ever* pantomime, there having been a production of it at the Theatre Royal, Drury Lane, in London in 1819. Allegedly that Drury Lane production boasted a lavish and, indeed, climbable beanstalk. The problem was, the actor cast as Jack – one Eliza Povey, who was arguably the first ever 'principal boy' – couldn't be persuaded to climb it. Too risky, she felt, and she may have had a point. So a stunt double had to be used. I wonder if you could see the join. My suspicion is that you probably could. Even from a seat at the back of the stalls.

I can't quite recall the state of the beanstalk in this 1948 version, or whether any climbing took place on it, either by leading players or their stuntmen. But I do remember the entry of the giant on his stacked heels, which certainly did elevate him slightly above the rest of the cast, but didn't exactly send him up to the lights or cause him to fill the auditorium King Kong-style, which would have been more in line with what I was imagining as we travelled there on the bus. Less 'fee fi fo', and more 'fee fi . . . oh'.

Now, I suppose another child might reasonably have decided, right there and then, to write off the whole idea of the theatre as a swizz – especially a child who had already started going to films with his mum. Call that a giant? How unlike the cinema the theatre turned out to be. When the cinema promised giants – and also ghosts, for that matter – it generally delivered them. The theatre, less so.

The truth is, though, by the time the giant showed up (Act Two, as expected, after the interval), I couldn't have cared less. By then I was having a high old time, swallowed up by the whole experience, agog at the mayhem that was unfolding in front of my eyes. I was rapidly discovering that pantomime was a form of theatre in which the audience had a speaking part. All the call-and-response stuff, the behind yous, the oh-no-you're-nots, the boos and cheers – this was wonderful, inclusive anarchy to my eight-year-old mind, just the very best kind of fun. Amid such bounty, the giant's lack of authentic giantness was a mere detail.

And that's before I even mention the bike they had up there – a ridiculous contraption that Jack would periodically leap astride and on which, as the wheels went round, the saddle went up and down. This, I would later learn, was a Bucking Bronco bike – made by the legendary company Hawtins. I got to know quite a bit about Hawtins later in my life because what they did tied in with a passion of mine. They were a splendid Blackpool outfit, founded in the 1920s by two brothers, Fred and Percy, who devoted themselves for about forty years to making a vast range of mechanical entertainments – jukeboxes, slot machines, miniature train rides, carousels, mechanical grabbers, dodgems . . . When I started reconditioning classic slot machines for fun in my workshop at home, I came to have great respect for Hawtins and their devices and desires, and not a little envy for their operation, actually – this brilliant, maverick business that started out in a shed and grew to occupy a three-and-a-half-acre site employing hundreds of people, all making mechanical amusements. That's my idea of a business worth minding.

And Hawtins' imagination, clearly, had given birth to the Bucking Bronco bike, bolted together so that the forward motion of the pedals caused the saddle to rise and fall – maybe not a major contribution to road safety but without question a major contribution to theatre-going enjoyment for eight-year-olds. As Hawtins' catalogue description of the bike from the 1940s proudly puts it: 'The contortions of riders mounting the machine for the first time provide spectators with an endless source of amusement.' Endless, indeed.

The catalogue goes on: 'The Ride lends itself to competitions, but in our experience we have never found this stimulation to business necessary.' Well, yes, a Bucking Bronco bike race – that I would very much like to see. Over fences, even better. But in the theatre that time it was enough to watch this fantastic machine make its galumphing way across the stage. I had never seen anything like it. I was in stitches.

Funnily enough, not so many years after this, I inadvertently bought a second-hand motorbike that had quite a lot in common with the Hawtins Bucking Bronco. But maybe that's a story for later on. In the meantime, that mad bike was another detail in a riot of colour and licensed foolishness taking place on that Hippodrome stage which seemed to chime very loudly with a certain eight-year-old.

Put the boy off theatre? *Au contraire. Au* very much *contraire.*

*　　*　　*

Now, without changing location, let's get the Spirit to pull his finger out and flash us forward seventeen years, if he could be so obliging – to Christmas 1965. Your author is now twenty-five and once more he finds himself in the Golders Green Hippodrome. But this time he's not in the stalls with his mum, he's on the stage, without his mum, having a Kirby harness fitted.

Now, the Kirby harness is without question a wonderful piece of equipment and a great gift to the world of live theatrical entertainment. It is, to your jobbing actor, what a feather was to Dumbo: it enables him to fly. But that doesn't mean it's comfortable to wear, and certainly not feather-like. Basically, Kirby's patented design is a tight girdle with tethers in the back for the wires that, operated offstage, will lift you aloft. And to prevent you simply sliding out of the bottom of that girdle while airborne, there are two leather straps along its lower edge which fasten extremely tightly around the tops of your thighs. So far so practical. But the effect of the wire taking the weight of the harnessed actor is, of course, to tug the girdle upwards. And, in tugging the girdle upwards, it also, by certain unhelpful laws of physics, brings those thigh straps both up and together at the same time, in a devious scissoring motion, whereupon . . .

Look, I probably don't need to go into detail about the nature of the discomfort this scissoring action in the groin area causes, but suffice it to say that my eyes are watering even to remember it, and the Spirit of Christmas Past, over there by the fireplace, actually just crossed his legs.

Anyway, there's muggins, at twenty-five, getting strapped in for his maiden flight, and about to discover for himself just how painful a Kirby harness can be. Alongside me at this rehearsal for the BBC's Christmas pantomime, which is to be filmed in this very theatre a few days hence and then broadcast proudly to the nation on Christmas Day itself, are five or six other cast members, all similarly wired up and ready for take-off. And though all of us are in civvies while we rehearse this flying ballet, come the eventual shoot we will be wearing police uniforms, because . . . well, because this is a pantomime and policemen who can fly and keep bashing into each other are quite funny, or certainly they are if they suddenly show up unexplained in the middle of *Mother Goose.*

So, assuming I don't reach a shocking end in the Kirby harness during these rehearsals, this will be my television debut, filmed at the very same venue where my eight-year-old self once sat in the stalls and stared agog at Jack and his dumb brother and his equally dumb bicycle, and craned his neck in vain to look up at the very ceiling from which he will shortly be swinging uncomfortably by a wire.

I'll be playing multiple roles in *Mother Goose*, actually. Ever-mindful of the bottom line, the BBC has got me doubling up as a villager in some early crowd scenes, and, later on, as the King of Gooseland, no less. Understandably, news of my involvement in this major televisual spectacular has rocked the world's media. Or, at any rate, my agent has managed to get a little item in *The Stage*, the acting industry's in-house journal, complete with a thumbnail headshot. And, publicity-wise, better a thumbnail headshot, I always say, than a head-sized thumbnail shot. Below a small black-and-white snap of me looking all dewy-eyed and promising, it says:

David Jason, who made the first appearance of his professional career at the New [Theatre], Bromley, as the butler in *South Sea Bubble* last April, is to be King of Gooseland in the BBC TV's pantomime this year. After playing the acrobatic waiter in *Diplomatic Baggage* at the New last July he was signed up as a permanent member of the Bromley company.

All true, that . . . well, almost. I did indeed appear, earlier that year, in John Chapman's *Diplomatic Baggage* at the New Theatre in Bromley, south London, and it did indeed lead me to get a full-time gig with the repertory company there. But I wasn't playing a waiter. I was playing a hotel porter – and for we aficionados of the wonderful world of farce, such distinctions are important.

However, as portrayed by me, this hotel porter certainly merited the description 'acrobatic' – and in ways which, I must sheepishly confess, weren't exactly in the script. I worked up a routine around the pushing of a heavy room-service trolley that lasted whole minutes. Did I overcook it? Well, possibly. But what's a young actor trying to make a name for himself going to do? I saw a chance there, and seized it. My fellow cast members, keen to get on with the play, might have raised a few eyebrows – might even have given me a few frosty looks in the wings afterwards, in fact. But the audience didn't seem to mind. On the contrary, gales of laughter and rounds of applause accompanied me off the stage – eventually – every night. Music to my young and inexperienced ears.

It was a similar story with the butler in Noël Coward's

South Sea Bubble, which had been my very first professional gig since I decided, after months of anxiously mulling it over, to disappoint my parents and abandon my steady and reasonably well-paid job as a self-employed electrician and invite penury by becoming a professional actor. Frankly, as written, the butler was there to serve the drinks and not to dominate the evening. Same goes for butlers everywhere, I guess. But, in collaboration with the play's director, Simon Oates, I managed to get this small part worked up into something a little more, shall we say, substantial.

In particular, there were some ornamental drums on a shelf as part of the decor in what was a rather fancily furnished sitting room, and these caught my eye. What if the butler, passing those drums at one point, noticed them and conceived a longing to have a bash on them? Which, of course, would be right out of order for a working butler. If you played it right, the audience could see him having an amusing little struggle with his conscience – his sense of professional duty tussling with his eventually painful desperation to hit those drums. You knew he was going to succumb eventually and let rip, but you didn't know when, and the time in between the audience working out that this thing was going to happen and it actually happening was, I realised, comedy's playing field. That little number, too, turned into a bit of an item and even got me a gratifying mention in the local paper's review of the show. And, again, while I was busy drawing out this moment as far as it could go without cracking, the other members of the cast were probably surreptitiously looking at their watches, but the audience definitely enjoyed it.

So this was where I was, professionally speaking, going into that BBC pantomime. Now, well may you ask, had eking scraps of off-script comedy from bit parts as waiters and porters always been my grand design since I conceived the idea of turning pro? Was it for this that I junked a company van and a steady wage?

Let me put it this way: just before that first job as a reluctant drum soloist in Bromley, I'd auditioned for a place with a repertory company in Margate. My audition piece? The 'Now is the winter of our discontent' speech from Shakespeare's *Richard III*.

Which, by the way, I could deliver very convincingly – or so I genuinely believed. But the audition hadn't gone well. I was so racked by nerves that my legs shook, causing my heels to beat an involuntary tattoo on the rehearsal room's wooden floor all through my delivery. Consequently, my intense portrayal of a mind riven by bitterness and jealousy was slightly undercut by the fact that I appeared to be tap dancing throughout. A tap-dancing Richard III was not what the panel was looking for. Nor me, really.

I left the room with those famous last words ringing in my blushing ears: 'Thank you very much. We'll be in touch . . .'

But my embarrassment on that occasion is not the point here. The point is, just mere days before taking to the professional stage as a slapstick butler, I had presented myself to an audition panel as a serious Shakespearean. Mark, I pray you, the distance that separates the course we envisage for ourselves and the path we end up taking. You go in thinking, *Richard III*, you come out fooling around with bongos and tea trolleys and move on from there, if you're lucky. But 'go with the flow' was always my motto. And clearly I did.

Incidentally, one other important development took place between those two theatrical roles and ahead of my television debut, which your shrewd eyes may already have noticed: I became another person. Or, at any rate, I ceased to be David White and turned into David Jason. The contract I was offered for four weeks' work in *South Sea Bubble* – two weeks of rehearsal, two weeks of performance – was a ticket I could take to Equity, the actors' union, and apply for membership. And that Equity card would itself, of course, be my ticket to further work – a golden ticket.

I rang up as soon as I could. But there was already a David White registered, the woman on the other end of the phone told me. And a David Whitehead, which was my hastily improvised second choice.

'Would you like to go away and have a think about it?' asked the woman from Equity.

But I wasn't going anywhere. I was in too much of a hurry. As I've explained before, my mind now for some reason turned to fond memories of Miss Kent at primary school, reading the class the story of Jason and the Argonauts, a tale which had really connected with me, and a light bulb went on.

'What about David Kent?' I said.

No, I didn't. I said, 'Is David Jason taken?' And it wasn't, so that was me from then on.

What an opportunity for self-reinvention that was. Just one phone call to an office in central London and I was someone else. I guess it felt a bit odd at first – though not as odd as it would have felt if I had also traded in my first name. Everyone had always called me 'David' and everyone carried on calling me 'David', so to that extent my new persona made no difference. But there were a few early confusions on my part. I remember looking at theatre programmes the first few times and seeing the name 'David Jason' in print and thinking, 'Who's he when he's at home?' and then realising it was me when I was at work.

The main effect of it, though, was liberating – emboldening, actually. The idea that David White the electrician had the nerve to think he might give acting a shot had made me feel extremely self-conscious. By no means the boldest of people, I was ready for people to sneer at my presumption. Auditions in which I tried, and failed, to deliver speeches from *Richard III* over the noise of my own shaking legs didn't exactly decrease that feeling.

But it wasn't David White doing that now – it was this other bloke, David Jason, and maybe *he* had a chance, whatever people thought. The change of name made a clean break with the past and allowed me to think that I was now going forward, away from my old self and into whatever this new life as a professional actor was going to bring me.

Which so far was a rapid acceleration from butler, to acrobatic porter, to King of Gooseland, and all in three short steps. Now that's what I call social mobility.

Reporting to Golders Green for BBC panto duty, I really did feel I had been suddenly thrust up the ladder professionally – far further than I had any right to expect. I was mixing with people who were big stars at the time – among them, Terry Scott, Norman Vaughan and Jon Pertwee, who would soon become, in my humble opinion, the greatest of the Doctor Whos (or should that be the Doctors Who?), but who was already familiar to me as a member of the cast of the radio comedy show *The Navy Lark*, which we always tuned into at home. And I was in a production that had the mighty clout and, at the time, considerable glamour of the British Broadcasting Corporation behind it. The BBC was a bit like Britain's Hollywood in those days – 'star central', in as much as the nation had one. It certainly felt a long way from the New Theatre, Bromley. Filming took place over the course of a week, and one day we all knocked off and headed up the road for lunch – me, sauntering out into the street with Jon Pertwee and Norman Vaughan and thinking, 'Oh, if my friends could see me now . . .' I ended up sitting next to Anna Dawson at that lunch. Naturally, I attempted to play it cool and make it look as though I was out for casual meals with familiar faces off the TV all the time, though my gaucheness and the general quaking in my boots must have given me away.

After the filming wrapped, we didn't have to wait long to inspect the fruits of our labours: just a couple of weeks later, it was Christmas Day. In her address to the nation that year, the Queen turned her thoughts to the various ways in which people might be experiencing their 'first' Christmas: 'It may be the first Christmas for many as husband and wife,' she pointed out, 'or the first Christmas with grandchildren.' Indeed. Or, as Her Majesty might have said, your first Christmas with a son on the telly, which is how it was for Mr and Mrs White of 26 Lodge Lane.

The BBC pantomime, by the way, was a regular TV fixture on Christmas Day even before the reigning monarch was. The Christmas message from Buckingham Palace was an audio-only experience at first, and the Queen didn't start showing up in our sitting rooms until 1957, which was a whole year after Eric Sykes, Hattie Jacques and Spike Milligan had given us their *Dick Whittington*. So by 1965 the Whites had had some time to become ritual Christmas Day panto watchers. I'm pretty sure we sat down in front of *Dick Whittington*, and I know we sat down in front of *Babes in the Wood* with Kenneth Connor and Tony Hancock, and in front of *Robinson Crusoe* with Norman Wisdom. It was just what we did.

And now here we were in front of *Mother Goose*, coming

on at 4.50 p.m., right after *Disney Time* and before *Doctor Who* (played by William Hartnell at this point). Meanwhile, in my first and by no means last personal experience of Christmas Day ratings wars, ITV were doing their best to peel the nation's attention away from me with *Moby Dick*, the John Huston film with Gregory Peck, and, after that, the football results.

Football matches? On Christmas Day? Oh yes. A full programme of them in those days, if that interested you, although nobody in my family was all that bothered. Football was someone else's battle in a far-distant country as far as my dad was concerned, and I'm afraid his indifference got passed down.

Moby Dick, on the other hand, might well have diverted my father, although, thinking about it, a film about whale-hunting would have been a bit of a busman's holiday for a fishmonger. Anyway, in our family, by this point in history, there was no contest: the Christmas panto was on. And so was I.

You had to strain to catch me, though. There were no close-ups. Practically the whole thing was filmed in broad shot, from a static position in the stalls, the idea being, I guess, that you, the viewer at home, would feel like you were experiencing this spectacle as if you were in the theatre. 'Can't get to the panto? No matter – the BBC will bring the panto to you!' As a consequence, though, I was but a speck on the screen of the Whites' black-and-white television set as, just after a dance number and Norman Vaughan's open-ing speech, I stepped forward in my villager's costume and spoke my first televised words:

'*Who comes here?*'

'This is it,' I warned everyone, from my position in the corner of the sofa. 'Wait . . . here it is . . . this is my line . . .'

'That was me!' I said afterwards. 'That was my line!'

Sometime after this, I alerted everyone to my reappear-ance, on this occasion as the King of Gooseland, and now grandly seated on a throne. A throne, I should say, before which Terry Scott, the star of the show, had to kneel at one point and, as memory dimly recalls, plead with me for some-body's freedom – possibly his own. Imagine that! A bona fide TV heavyweight, bowing at my feet. Did I have any further lines at this point? Likelihood would suggest that I did say at least something. I was the King, after all. That said, I suppose I could simply have been entrusted by the director with star-ing silently across the scene in a regal manner. Either way, the soap-engrimed shower curtain of time has long since drawn itself across my recollection of this moment, and the BBC appear to have put the tapes of the show out with the bins, as they so often did before archivists started getting cross about it, so more than this I cannot say.

What I can confirm is that I then appeared for my third stint, this time as the policeman in that flying ballet. And then that was me done.

So, how did all of this sudden national televisual exposure

play in Lodge Lane? Well, if my dad saw a glittering career stretching ahead of me on the basis of these short and blurry moments, he didn't exactly say as much. In fact, I'm not sure that he really offered an opinion of any kind from his traditional place in the armchair that afternoon. But then, just to put some perspective on it, my dad, not long before this, had been unimpressed by the Beatles, a group of moptops from Liverpool that I and a few other people had formed a bit of a liking for.

'Turn that off! Never heard such bloody rubbish.'

So what chance did one humble villager from Gooseland have of succeeding where the Fab Four had failed?

My mum and my Aunt Ede, next to me on the sofa, were, as I recall, a little warmer and more encouraging. But then those two inseparable sisters had loyally come to all the amateur dramatic productions I had ever appeared in, lugging themselves up to the Incognito Group's little theatre in an old bottle factory in Friern Barnet, where, much to my surprise, they had uncomplainingly sat through several extremely angry John Osborne productions and a number of nights of Swedish bleakness courtesy of August Strindberg. By contrast, a few minutes of me swinging from the rafters in a policeman's outfit must have felt like a walk in the park on a sunny day.

So they both smiled as encouragingly as they could at my first broadcast efforts, and, I imagine, silently thanked their lucky stars that it wasn't Chekhov. And then it finished and, without any popping of champagne bottles or smoking of cigars, we all went back to our Christmas.

But I'll tell you who was *really* impressed by my appearances that day: me. That, of course, was the thrill of seeing yourself on the small screen and then watching your name – or, at any rate, your stage name – go by in the credits. As little as a month beforehand, the possibility of this would have seemed vanishingly unlikely. It really was quite something, I thought. Something I would like to do a bit more of, if I ever got another chance. What were the odds of that, though?

*   *   *

Worryingly uncomfortable as it may have been, I understood that when you forced yourself into a Kirby harness, as I did in Golders Green that time, you were strapping on a proper piece of theatrical history. What I didn't appreciate was how relatively lightly I would get off, up there in the skies that time.

George Kirby and his company had been working out ways to get actors off the ground since eighteen-hundred-and-frozen-to-death. Indeed, history relates that it was a fully patented Kirby harness that rendered Peter Pan airborne in the earliest productions of J. M. Barrie's play at the start of the twentieth century. The effect was so uncanny at the time that children had to be discouraged from trying to take wing themselves on the way home – or, worse, while actually in the theatre. Legend has it that a young Prince George, who would later grow up to be King George VI but who was at that point a small boy lost in wonderment at the theatre, had to be restrained one night from attempting to jump out of the royal box and join Peter Pan on a quick aerial tour of the auditorium. This probably wouldn't have ended well, either for the line of succession or for the people in the stalls below.

Kirby introduced all sorts of refinements to his system over the years, including the 'quick release' mechanism, which enabled you to land, flick a switch, seamlessly abandon your wires, and then start walking about nonchalantly as usual with (hopefully) nobody any the wiser. But no amount of perfecting the hardware could ever quite remove the possibility that, like the Icarus of the acting world, you might end up flying too high. 'Getting gridded' was the in-house term for this special indignity – meaning getting accidentally flown up into the lighting grid above the stage, where you would find yourself swinging among hot bulbs and bits of scenery. And as Icarus will tell you, it's no fun up there and also very hot.

I wrote in my most recent book about going on tour in the mid-1970s in Anthony Marriott and Bob Grant's farce, *Darling Mr London*, a feast of intellectual entertainment, it goes without saying, at the deeply moving climax of which I had to be flown up into the rafters clinging to an ornamental light fitting.

Look, I did say it was a farce, didn't I? Were my trousers in place at this juncture in the proceedings? I'm not sure, but you would get good odds, in the context, that they were not.

Anyway, those recollections inspired John Schwiller to get in touch with me with some memories of his own. John was the flyman for that production – the person responsible for tugging the wires behind the scenes and launching me into the air at the appropriate time and in the appropriate manner, and then, of course, ensuring that I was lowered to the ground again when no one was looking – with the curtains closed, in this case, and in time for me to get unhooked and then take my bows in the curtain call. Apparently this stunt went off smoothly on all occasions without fail . . . except for the one night when it didn't.

On that particular occasion, I was hoisted with excess vigour off the stage, got emphatically 'gridded' – and then, just for good measure, became stuck. A wire was trapped somewhere and I was lodged, essentially, in the theatre's attic, with only a small chandelier and the lighting rig for company. And there I had to stay while the fault was rectified.

I'm not sure what's more remarkable: the fact that this thing happened in the first place, or the fact that I can remember absolutely nothing about it. You would think that being obliged to hang from a chandelier in a theatre's roof for a period, until the appropriate measures can be taken and you can be lowered to safety and then hastily do the curtain call with the rest of the cast, might have been the kind of thing an actor would have recalled.

But, honestly, I have racked my brains about it here in the study at Jason Towers – the crucible of this memoir-writing operation – and urged the Spirit of Christmas Past to stop looking at his phone for a moment and help me out. Yet, rather embarrassingly, nothing has emerged. I can only conclude that the trauma was so intense that I have simply blocked it out – and the Spirit of Christmas Past likewise.

Anyway, getting gridded happens to the very best of us, clearly – and some of us really do remember it. My correspondent John also told me that once, when Wayne Sleep was performing as Puck in *A Midsummer Night's Dream*, John had the distinguished honour of flying him. Not a lot of people can say they've done that. Certainly not a lot of people can say they have induced in Wayne Sleep a lasting trauma as a result of their backstage work with the ropes and wires.

It happened like this. For one scene, Sleep, as Puck, was meant to arrive on the stage gently – not from a great height but just lightly propelled into view to give the impression that he was landing softly after a flight: more of a twitch on the wire than a full-strength 'haul away' special, then.

Alas, when the green light came on backstage, which was John's cue to go to work, he inadvertently got his calculations wrong and put too much muscle into it, causing an entirely unprepared Sleep, standing in the wings, to blast off in the direction of the ceiling and then to descend again, coming now into the view of the audience, at a steep angle and with some speed, in the manner of a plunging kestrel.

That kind of move is difficult enough for the flying actor if you're ready for it, but if the flight comes upon you by surprise . . . well, even someone as fleet of foot as Wayne Sleep was always going to struggle. The flustered dancer hit the floor hard and then had to force himself into an upright position and wait for his insides to settle down.

Some considerable time later, John was sitting at home watching Wayne Sleep give an interview on the television to Terry Wogan. His ears couldn't help but prick up when he heard the dancer darkly recount the still fresh tale of the night some bloke had 'gridded' him – an experience that had remained etched upon his memory, clearly, as firmly as any number of dances with Princess Diana.

You should have blocked it out, Wayne, like what I did.

All those exertions, though . . . My current self can only reflect with rueful astonishment on all the flinging himself about that my younger self did in those formative years. These days, even when simply bending over to pick something up off the floor, I'm better off booking in advance. Back then, though . . . well, it strikes me that I was almost as much a gymnast as I was an actor in those early years. It wasn't just the typical farce-led comedy pratfalls, either – falling off sofas, tripping over rugs, getting into a tangle with standard lamps and the doors of wardrobes and so forth. I'd go looking

81

far wider for trouble, seeking even more elaborate ways to, literally, stretch myself.

I remember being in a production of Robin Hawdon's *The Mating Game* with Trevor Bannister. Trevor played a super-smooth bachelor whose flat was kitted out with slick remote-controlled gizmos – light dimmers, electronically operated curtains, a television which rose up out of nowhere. Even the double bed dropped out of the wall at the touch of a zapper. Of course, all these kitsch devices were designed to go wrong at some point during the play, for maximum comic effect.

But I recall looking at that automatically self-concealing double bed and thinking: 'What if I happened to be standing on it when it closed? What if it actually ate me?' Cue extensive discussions with the stage manager and the props manager, followed by experiments to see whether the bed could still operate with my weight on it. It turned out that as long as I was up near the pillows at the time, where the bed met the wall, the lever that sprung the bed back into hiding would still function.

So that's what we started doing. I would jump up onto the bed at one point and the bed would slam shut and my character would disappear into the wall. Once the bed had stowed itself away, I was trapped in a tiny air pocket at the back of the set. Fortunately this gimmick took place at the end of an act, so I could be rescued fairly quickly, coming out the way I had gone in. But clearly in those days I was cheerfully ready to risk my neck and even suffocation for an extra laugh if I felt there was one out there to be had.

But how much being crushed by an automated double bed, or similar, can a person's body sensibly withstand? Quite a lot, it turns out. When I was in *No Sex Please – We're British* in the West End, the show would end every night with me sprinting in a panic across the stage in my boxer shorts and diving through a serving hatch in the wall, supposedly to escape into the kitchen beyond. Except that the audience had been primed to realise during the course of the evening that this serving hatch was treacherous and inclined to slam shut at inconvenient moments. Sure enough, in that climactic moment, as I closed in on it at speed in my underpants, the hatch would drop down of its own sweet accord (ably assisted by someone behind the scenes, of course), and I would end up launching myself, not through the hole, but through the panel, along with the satisfying splintering of balsa wood. Lights out and curtain.

Honed by repetition, it was a smooth little number, though I say so myself, and most nights it could be relied upon to have the audience on their feet in advance of the curtain call. Lord knows how I didn't manage to do myself a permanent mischief, though. Never mind two weeks of wrestling with a room-service trolley: I crashed through that serving hatch six nights a week, plus Saturday matinees, for eighteen months. Afterwards, it was a wonder I could still walk and chew gum at the same time, let alone march forward into a life of rich and varied professional experiences including . . . well, falling through another serving hatch, of course, but many other things besides, let's not forget.

And the seed of all of it, as unlikely as it may seem, was that BBC panto appearance. My work that Christmas gave me a television credit, which was invaluable as a calling card. While acting on a stage and acting in front of cameras are closely related, ultimately they are two different kettles of fish, and not every actor can move naturally from one to the other. A great deal of television in those days was live, so it was a real feather in your cap if you were able to demonstrate that you weren't someone who would lose their nerve when the camera was pointed at them.

The appointment also gave me about £75 for a fortnight's work which was a more than decent amount of bunce for a Bromley-based repertory actor who was at that point on £15 a week.

But probably more important than anything else, it also showed me to be someone who could handle a bit of knock-about physical comedy. And that, for all my lofty dreams of Shakespearean pre-eminence and Hollywood leading man-hood, was where the wind machine of fate seemed to be blowing me.

ON THE FOURTH DEL OF CHRISTMAS . . .

Grapefruits

'Well, you know me. I never talk about my days at sea.'
Uncle Albert, *Only Fools and Horses*

We interrupt this book to bring you some breaking grapefruit news.

Well, you'd be expecting no less from me after my last volume of memoirs, when I outed myself as one of the UK's leading growers of grapefruit trees – or, at any rate, as someone who, over a period of almost fifty years, had successfully cultivated a tall and weighty plant from a tiny grapefruit pip that turned up one morning in his breakfast.

As I told it back then (and please, by all means refer back to that previous book if you feel you want to flesh out what follows here), the story of the growth of my grapefruit tree from its extremely humble beginnings was a classic, uplifting tale of the triumph of hope over adversity – and also of the triumph of plants over neglectful neighbours whom you've asked to water them for you while you were away but who have forgotten.

Perhaps inevitably, then, the story's publication between hard covers in 2020 led to offers for me to appear in all the big grapefruit-related magazines, such as *What Grapefruit?* and *Grapefruit Tree & Grapefruit Tree Owner*, and to go on all the major grapefruit-related chat shows.

Actually, now I think about it, it didn't. Incredible to relate, two whole years on, the producers of Radio 4's *Gardeners' Question Time* have yet to get in touch to pick my brains on all things grapefruit-oriented, and neither, for some reason, has Alan Titchmarsh. He never writes, he never calls . . .

But the tale also had another crucial human-interest dimension to it because the pip in question – the one I planted, the one that became the tree – had once tried to kill me. As anyone with experience around them will know, your grapefruit is one of your more malicious types of breakfast fruit. Oh, they may look harmless enough, halved and lying there silently in your bowl, with their so-called segments. But when you've spent time around grapefruits, you know better than to be deceived. Unlike the largely passive raspberry and the almost completely uncomplaining stewed prune, grapefruits don't always go quietly. They'll look to take you down with them – or, at the very least, inflict some damage along the way. Not for nothing are they known as the absolute hard-nuts of the citrus world.

It's when you think you've got them completely under control that they're at their most dangerous. When you've got them comfortably in the bowl and are casually moving in on them – that's when they're most likely to go for you, responding to the advance of your spoon by sending a high-pressure jet of juice into one of your eyes, where it works briefly like venom. No other fruit, in my experience, has this kind of power in its armoury. The humble orange, under pressure from the peeler's thumb, can only dream of the grapefruit's devastating accuracy and effectiveness as a squirter of its own liquid. And as for the 'easy-peeler' tangerine, which so often makes its way into the fruit bowl at Christmas . . . well, it's not even in contention as a juice-firing combat fruit.

Grapefruits, though . . . well, I still wince to recall the really surly grapefruit that I once got into a fight with in a hotel near Harrogate in the late 1960s, when I was on the road with a production, and which left me seeing double for most of the remaining shows on that tour. I worked through it, of course, like the pro that I am, and in the fullness of time made a complete recovery. But I learned that you mess with grapefruits at your peril.

Which meant that, on the all-important morning in 1973 or so, with spoon in hand in the kitchen of my little bachelor flat just north of Oxford Street in London, I was ready for it. Unbeknown to me, though, the grapefruit that I was about to devour had bigger plans. It wasn't intending to waste its time or energy with any of that low-rent, juice-spraying stuff.

Oh no – blinding me was well beneath its ambitions. This one was going all-in.

This one was going to suffocate me.

Fully closing one eye, and half closing the other in nervous anticipation of the stream of juice that never came, I successfully loosened a segment of this devious grapefruit, spooned it into my mouth, chewed and swallowed – and was on the verge of celebrating a great victory for man over fruit . . . only for a devilishly camouflaged pip to lodge itself directly in my windpipe.

Smart move. My face became purple, my eyes inflated to the size of tennis balls and a whining intake of breath ensued which seemed to last a number of minutes. When that whining eventually stopped, there was a brief and pregnant silence during which the whole of London seemed to fall quiet. And then – kerblam! I went into a coughing fit so explosive that it was impossible to believe it didn't involve actual gunpowder.

Frankly, I was grateful on that particular morning to be breakfasting unaccompanied. There are times when a man is better off dining alone, and one of those times is when he is busy hacking up a grapefruit pip that's got stuck in his throat and, in the process, pebble-dashing the surrounding kitchen with bits of fruit and other parts of his recently ingested breakfast. Overnight guests tend not to enjoy that kind of thing, I find.

Let's be as decorous as we can: the pip was in due course,

shall we say, 'produced', and thereafter lay before me on the table, giving no sign of the true extent of its menace. As I recovered my breath and my composure and waited for my heart rate to return to something closer to normal, I weighed my options vis-à-vis this unlikely assassin's future. Those options seemed to be numerous. More vengeful people than myself, for instance, would perhaps have flicked the offending item out the window and watched it drop, or angrily beaten it to a pulp with the butter dish.

But I, dear reader, as I have related, chose another path. I don't wish to sound pious, but I have always tried to be someone who believes in forgiveness and in the possibility of redemption, and my feeling is that even the very bad grapefruit pips among us probably have goodness in them somewhere, if we only take the trouble to look for it and give it space to flourish.

Plus I needed a hobby and horticulture was suddenly beckoning.

So space is what I gave that pip – specifically, house space. As previously reported, I went out that very morning and bought a pot and some compost and I duly planted the pip. Then I nurtured and watered it and watched it grow, as the days became weeks and the weeks became months and the months became years, pausing only to repot it every time it outgrew its confinement, and carrying it with me whenever I moved home.

Which is why it is now to be found in a giant tub in my

summer house having achieved an impressive immensity, its trunk a pleasingly fat four inches in diameter. Every spring I haul that tree out and place it where it can enjoy the air, and every late autumn I drag it back under cover away from the ravages of the cold for another winter. OK, I can't exactly lie under it during the summer and stare up sleepily into its sun-dappled leaves – or, at least, not without attracting comment. But it's more than big enough to throw shade for at least one of my dogs, and possibly both of them if they budge up a bit.

Here's the thing, though: being written about in 2020 seemed to have a magical effect on my grapefruit tree and force it to new heights of confidence. By which I mean, the following year, to my startlement, a flower appeared among its usual thick clusters of leaves.

And not only did the tree flower. Even more amazingly, it fruited. A little green bud emerged which would, if the stars aligned and the fates conspired, eventually grow up to become a grapefruit.

The tree had done this only once before in its life, shortly after I first moved it out of London, producing, on that occasion, three tiny pods. It was almost as if, freed from the city, it had immediately been driven into overdrive by the richness of the country air. But, sadly, those three pods were incredibly short-lived. Now, after a long break in which no amount of country air could do anything for it, and urged on, it seemed to me, by its new-found fame, it was finally trying again. And this time, more promisingly, it was devoting all its available energy to the one fruit, which duly continued to grow.

I was delighted – and also very impressed. Let me remind you that we're talking about a categorically subtropical fruit. Of all the climates best suited to the production of grapefruits, Buckinghamshire's is not among them, though, likely as not, climate change will alter that in due course. Soon, no doubt, you won't be able to walk ten feet in Buckinghamshire without trespassing on a citrus orchard. On the bits of it that haven't been sacrificed to high-speed railway lines, of course. But not yet. A long history of agriculture amply demonstrates that grapefruits overwhelmingly prefer Barbados to Aylesbury – and in that, I suppose, they are by no means alone. But, look, it's nothing personal. It's just that a grapefruit likes six to eight hours per day of full sun for the whole of its growing life, and you simply don't get that kind of weather in Aylesbury. Not even in Wendover.

Yet here was my tree, somehow inspired by its appearance in print, going into production while being less than an hour from London on the train. I watched in awe as that little bud clung on, and slowly, in a tiny but very definite way, began to swell.

What an exciting development this was. I appeared to have founded a grapefruit dynasty. I was, truly, the UK's Citrus Overlord. Visions began to dance in my head of one day breakfasting on, literally, the fruits of my labour – and, if not choking on one of its pips (too much symmetry there), at least getting squirted in the eye by it. To be temporarily blinded by a shop-bought grapefruit is an ordeal to be wished on no one. But to be temporarily blinded by a grapefruit that you have grown yourself, and on a tree that you personally raised from next to nothing over the course of half a century with your own bare hands – well, that would be something to be proud of, surely.

Alas, though, it was not to be. Only superficially outperforming its three predecessors, my grapefruit grew gradually to the size of a plump pea. And then, perhaps overwhelmed by the effort, or possibly by all the attention it was getting – multiple visits each day from me and Gill, offering encouraging looks and words of inspiration – it dropped off.

I found its little form in the soil one morning – a mournful sight, let there be no question. And thus does this tale necessarily end in sadness and unfulfilment, and not in the blaze of horticultural glory that I had dared to envisage.

Yet, of course, the cycle of life measures out its own consolations and we must be content to understand and accept them. That small fallen bud may seemingly have come to nothing, yet it would now, where it lay, play a small role in replenishing the soil from which it arose. Who knows, it may even have made a hearty breakfast for a family of ants, had they moved swiftly enough.

But they would have had to watch out for the juice, of course. Grapefruits respect nobody.

ON THE FIFTH DEL OF CHRISTMAS . . .

Greasepaint and Pythons

So, obviously, the credits had barely finished sliding across the screen at the end of that BBC pantomime in 1965 when the phone started ringing and the offers of further richly rewarding work began pouring in, directly pointing the way to an unbroken lifetime of high-level cavorting in televisual entertainment's starry firmament.

OK, not really. It was back to the day job, in fact. Which in my case, as a full-time repertory actor, was, of course, mostly a night job. And which, in this instance, meant appearing in Bromley at the New Theatre's 1965 Christmas holiday production of . . . *Aladdin.*

All together now: 'Oh no it didn't.'

Oh yes it did.

From one panto straight to another. What a Christmas that was. As Oscar Wilde so wisely said: to be in one pantomime in a year may be regarded as a misfortune, but to be in two starts to look horribly like carelessness.

Or, as the other old saying goes: out of the frying panto, into the fire. For in Bromley I would have a fortnight's paid labour as one half of a pair of comedy coppers rejoicing under the names Flip and Flop.

Masquerading as a policeman? This was apparently becoming a habit. And the lowest rank of policeman, too. If I'd thought being on television on Christmas Day would earn me instant promotion to a cushy desk job, I couldn't have been more wrong. I was straight back out on the beat.

You'll be bursting to know, though: was I called upon to play Flip? Or was I called upon to play Flop? Or did I, employing my full breadth as a character actor, as demonstrated by my smooth handling of those three very different parts in the BBC's *Mother Goose*, Flip and Flop between the two roles as the mood and the evening took me?

Well, I can tell you: I was Flip, staunchly and solidly and without deviation throughout the night – which, of course, made things very much more straightforward for my counterpart as Flop, who was none other than the Scottish actor Robert Fyfe, a Bromley Rep regular, ten years my senior and a frequent colleague on the stage during my stint with the company. Robert was originally from Edinburgh and had dropped out of university to go to drama school in Bradford. The way it seemed to work for the pair of us at Bromley, Robert got the grander of the lower-class roles on offer, and I got the lower of the lower-class roles. Ah, the wonderfully infinite refinements of the British class system.

Flip and Flop, I guess, at least put us on an equal footing, socially speaking.

Robert would later play Howard Sibshaw in *Last of the Summer Wine* – and do so for twenty-five years, spending an awful lot of that time, as I recall, heading off into the Yorkshire Dales for bike rides with Jean Fergusson's Marina and hoping his wife didn't find out. So both of us, then, Flip *and* Flop, were destined for roles in long-running and much cherished British sitcoms. But I wonder if you would have bet on it from the duff slapstick that we were condemned to in *Aladdin* that year. Let us dwell no longer than we need to on the grinding puns, the overcooked pratfalls, the broad slapstick involving truncheons. Let us simply maintain that south-east London had seen more efficient police work in its time. It had probably seen funnier police work, too.

I don't wish by any means to cast nasturtiums on the team in *Aladdin*, least of all my police force colleague, Robert – but things at the New Theatre seemed distinctly to move up a gear, panto-wise, the following year. Never mind future sitcom stars, in 1966 the theatre managed to attract an actual, already established sitcom star. In a positively glittering production of *Robinson Crusoe*, Wilfrid Brambell from *Steptoe & Son* – and advertised on the posters as 'Mr Steptoe himself' – arrived to give Bromley his Mrs Crusoe. And if that wasn't enough glitter for you, Wally Whyton from the ITV children's programme *Five O'Clock Club* also descended from the entertainment stratosphere, bringing the double treat of himself and his owl-shaped glove puppet, Ollie Beak. Did it get any more starry than that? Well, I suppose it did, yes – but not at the New Theatre, Bromley, over Christmas in 1965.

I, however, did not get to reprise my Flip, nor Robert Fyfe his Flop, massive though the public demand for us to do so must have been. By then, I had packed my bags and moved on to other, less police-oriented theatrical pastures. But those months at Bromley had been enormously valuable for me – the best kind of introduction to the acting business, and a period in my life that I'll always be grateful for, even, in their own way, those weeks of Flipping and Flopping. It was all work, and it was all a learning curve.

Remember, I hadn't been to drama school and had pitched up directly from the ranks of amateur theatre – a self-starter at the age of twenty-five and so wet behind the ears you could have grown cress there. And although I was very determined, I was also very mindful of that lack of formal background – worried that I didn't have the qualifications, that I was always going to be inferior in some way to the 'proper' actors who surrounded me and had studied the craft and been taught how things were *supposed to be done*. I, by contrast, was going on instinct, plus whatever meagre experience I'd been able to grab on the way. The knowledge that I hadn't come through the formal route was always nagging at the back of my mind, ready to jump out and ambush me – almost like I was waiting to be found out.

And you could get beyond it while you were feeling confident, but it was a harder wave to ride in those moments when you were less certain of yourself.

However, what you could always be doing was learning – watching and listening and absorbing. In that sense, for a year, Bromley Rep became my drama school. And because of the way that rep theatre worked, with its fortnightly turnover of productions, the education it offered was fantastically broad, and panto just a tiny – if darkly memorable – fraction of it. One minute I was donning a giant wig and a braided smock and becoming Lord Foppington for the Restoration piece *The Relapse*, the next I was crashing about the stage wearing an eyepatch in *Treasure Island*, and the one after that I was putting on a cardigan and ruminatively picking up a teacup in *Murder at the Vicarage*. I took every part the place offered me and tried to learn as much as I could from it.

Somewhere in the middle of all this, I even climbed back into my waiter's outfit for a bit part in Noël Coward's *Suite in Three Keys*. I fell rather heavily for the leading lady in that particular production, an actor who swept in for the fortnight from outside the company: someone with a few TV credits behind her, but no major player, really, in the larger scheme of things, yet who, from where I was standing, seemed fabulously starry and professional – from another planet, really.

At one point in the Coward play, it was my duty, as the waiter in the Italian restaurant where her character was dining, to pick up the napkin from the table-setting in front of her, unfold it, flap it and lay it across her lap, a moment of intimacy which, given my humble status in the hierarchy, not to mention my smittenness, I was more than a little hesitant about.

'You know what waiters do, don't you, at that moment?' she said to me casually while we were rehearsing.

I said that I didn't.

'Well, of course,' she said, 'you're a man, so you wouldn't have to put up with this stuff. Let me tell you, then. When waiters are putting your napkin on your lap for you, they very often take the opportunity to "accidentally" brush their arm against your breasts.'

I think I practically melted into the floor with embarrassment at this point. But if she really was suggesting that we should incorporate this piece of underhand devilry into the performance, then obviously she was the senior actor with the greater authority and it was my duty as the humble apprentice, looking to learn his craft and advance, to dig deep and do my best.

Actually, she wasn't suggesting that – or not exactly. What she was suggesting was that we develop a little exchange wherein, as I moved towards her with the napkin, she would noticeably snap her body back to prevent any contact from happening, while fixing me with a formidable look to indicate she was wise to waiters and their gropy ways. I quietly thought it might be too small and detailed a thing to come across to the auditorium, but I was wrong. It became a little moment in the play each night. The women, in particular, in the audience got it straight away, and it always got an audible reaction. It was all very illuminating for me – and not just because of what it taught me about what 1960s waiters got up to. I already knew I could find extra places between the lines where I could get laughs by drawing things out. But now I saw how a really clever actor could find a tiny and brief piece of behaviour that's nowhere near the script but which instantly adds something and tells the audience about the kind of characters they're watching. Also, if you make sure the audience is focused on the right place at the right time, you can work on a really small scale, even in the theatre. Again, I'm sure none of this would have been news to the drama-school graduates. But to me, picking it all up like a magnet as I went along, these discoveries were real treasure.

Another day at Bromley someone called Martin Jarvis landed briefly among us, fresh out of drama school – RADA, to be exact, where he appeared to have won all the prizes going and a couple more for good behaviour. Martin would become one of Britain's most popular and recognisable actors – and one of its most popular and recognisable voices, too, the voice of Richmal Crompton's *William* books, among many, many others. Even then, you could tell he was going places. He was six foot tall, blond, handsome, debonair . . . the archetypal leading man, it seemed to me. Splendidly attired in a braided frock coat which he wore as comfortably as if it were his own dressing gown, Martin played Captain Jack Absolute in a production of Sheridan's *The Rivals* in which I was the buffoon Bob Acres. I remember following Martin out of the stage door into the alley at the side of the theatre after one of those performances and watching him move suavely through a posse of women from the audience who had gathered to try and catch his eye. 'Oh, to be six foot tall and blond,' was all I could think to myself.

Much later, Martin and I acted together again when he appeared in an episode of *A Touch of Frost*. That time, in a somewhat different vein, and with no braided frock coats in view, he took the part of a male escort in a story titled 'Fun Times for Swingers'. Which may sound titillating, but this was *Frost*, remember, so the fun times were somewhat undercut, as I recall, by a small number of gruesome suicides in the tale, one of which Jack Frost greeted with the typic- ally dry line: 'Oh dear, oh dear, oh dear. Such a mess on the pavement.'

Anyway, did I take the opportunity, during the filming of that episode, to remind Martin of our previous encounter in Bromley? No, actually. I was such a minor part of the scene at the time that I genuinely didn't think he would recall me even having been there. As time goes on and your career advances, you can't possibly remember the face and name of every single actor you've worked with back in the early days. George Cole used to tell a story about first meeting Dennis Waterman on the set of *Minder* – and then, two whole years later, when the series was in full flow, working out that they'd both met ages before, in a 1971 horror film called *Fright*. But neither of them had realised because Dennis's character had died very early in the film and then lain face down on the set for the most part, and George had spent the shoot stepping over Dennis's prone body. Not the simplest way to get to know someone – or even really to notice them, clearly.

I had a similar experience. When I went along to try out as Del Boy in a read-through of scenes from what became the first episode of *Only Fools and Horses*, I enthusiastically shook the hand of the actor who had come along to read as Grandad.

'Nice to meet you,' I said.

'Nice to meet you, too,' Lennard Pearce replied.

It would be many months later, with our working relationship and our friendship both well established, that someone pointed out to us that Lennard and I had been onstage together before – in 1965, in that same Bromley production of *The Rivals*. We didn't remember each other. But I think we both remembered Martin Jarvis.

So, the New Theatre, Bromley, was my unofficial drama school, the place where my learning got under way – a fact which would no doubt be permanently commemorated with a blue plaque on the outside of the building, but for the small fact that, like 26 Lodge Lane, the building no longer exists to nail a plaque to.

I'm starting to notice a slightly troubling theme developing here . . .

With regard to the sad demise of the New Theatre, here are the facts in so far as we have them. In May 1971, several years after I had packed my bags and moved on, the New was all set to host Cliff Richard in a production of Graham Greene's psychological thriller *The Potting Shed*. I'm not making this up. Stepping into the role of James Callifer, once occupied by none other than Sir John Gielgud, Cliff had appeared in the play in the West End and was now bringing that production to eager Graham Greene fans (and perhaps one or two Cliff Richard fans) in the south.

Coincidentally, I believe the last time Cliff had been on the London stage in an acting capacity, rather than a singing capacity, it had been at the Palladium six years previously in a production of . . . *Aladdin*. Small world, eh? It's one of the things Cliff and I have in common, clearly. Though I don't believe he played Flip. Or Flop.

Anyway, what can I tell you? Cliff's much anticipated appearance in *The Potting Shed* was not to be. With the programmes already printed and tickets sold, my personal drama school burned to the ground on the night of 7 May, just a fortnight before opening night. Cliff was later photographed standing rather mournfully in front of the charred wreckage in a flowery shirt.

Highly unfortunate, that. The theatre burning down before opening night, I mean, not Cliff being photographed in a flowery shirt. Six years later, the Churchill Theatre arose, phoenix-like, from the ashes among a new set of buildings on the site and thrives to this day, so ultimately all was well. But next time anyone tries to tell you that repertory theatre isn't a business fraught with hidden danger and complexities, cite the case of Sir Cliff and my old drama school.

* * *

Right, look lively, Spirit of Christmas Past. Enough of this sitting around over there with your feet up, eating my bis-cuits. Time to earn your corn, son. I need you at this juncture in our tale to sweep us up and carry us forward a couple of years, to the Christmas of 1967.

To Boxing Day, specifically, and to the first edition of an ITV comedy programme for children entitled *Do Not Adjust Your Set*, starring me and my new television teammates, Michael Palin, Terry Jones, Eric Idle and Denise Coffey.

In fact, the episode's full title, in honour of the festive season, is: 'Do Not Adjust Your Set, Or a Happy Boxing Day and a Preposterous New Year', and, on the positive side, that decision to launch the show on Boxing Day, of all the places in the schedules, is a huge vote of confidence in the programme and a major boon in terms of attracting the widest available audience. Our new team can afford to spend Christmas feeling very excited about that outcome.

On the other hand, though, it means our fledgling efforts

find themselves going out opposite the premiere of the Beatles' *Magical Mystery Tour* movie on BBC1, and I don't suppose any new show at this moment in the history of the Swinging Sixties would be entirely happy to find itself fighting the Beatles for attention.

That said, I know which side of that particular battle my dad is going to be on, so we are guaranteed at least one viewer.

Some obvious questions here, though. How have I come to be starring in a children's television show all of a sudden? And how have I come to be teamed up with these young, sharp and rather intimidatingly clever Oxbridge graduates, Mike, Eric and Terry? Well, I can answer all that – which is just as well because when I asked my Spirit of Christmas Past if he had anything revealing to offer in this area, he just looked at me rather blankly and asked me if I wanted him to google it.

I'm a little disappointed with the quality of this Spirit, if I'm being honest. His work seems to fall short of the advertised Dickensian standards. I may have to get on to the agency.

Meanwhile, let me explain to you how this kids' TV opportunity has come about. The man to whom the finger of blame points is a young producer named Humphrey Barclay. Humphrey will have a huge influence on my career, not just here but beyond, eventually pairing me up with Ronnie Barker for some sketch work which will then lead to the pair of us acting together in *Open All Hours*. At this point, though, he is a rising force in TV comedy, who has very successfully produced the satirical radio show *I'm Sorry, I'll Read That Again*, and who, on the strength of that, has now been commissioned to put together a small band of actors who can turn out a comedy programme for children, to be broadcast at teatime on ITV.

Humphrey, Eric Idle, Terry Jones and Mike Palin all know each other from their Oxbridge university days, and have subsequently been involved in various pieces of writing for BBC Radio, so that's all quite convenient and cosy. Humphrey has spotted Denise Coffey, meanwhile, in an Edinburgh Festival production of *A Midsummer Night's Dream*. Like Eric, Terry and Mike, her background is formal and impressive – the Glasgow College of Drama and the Royal Scottish Academy of Music – and while we are making the show, she will get cast in a film production of Thomas Hardy's *Far From the Madding Crowd*, starring Alan Bates and Julie Christie, which I will be deeply impressed by and not a little jealous of, this being the kind of break I was dreaming of.

And me? Well, Humphrey has found me at the end of the pier in Weston-super-Mare. Which I still maintain is better than being found *under* the pier in Weston-super-Mare. I was playing opposite Dick Emery at the time, in a summer-season farce called *Chase Me, Comrade*. Cambridge Footlights, eat your heart out. My CV by this point consists mostly of scraps of TV work, none of it amounting to much: tiny roles in *Z-Cars* and *Softly Softly*. And I have also fallen in and out of the ITV soap opera *Crossroads*. My role there: Bernie Kilroy, a boxing promoter with a shifty edge to him, who also worked as a part-time gardener at the motel. I wonder how often those two professions – boxing promoter and gardener – have been combined. You don't often see Frank Warren doing people's lawns, do you? But then Frank Warren wasn't in *Crossroads*.

Which, actually, now I come to mention it, makes Frank Warren a bit of an exception because an awful lot of people I can name *were* in *Crossroads*, including many that I worked with in other circumstances: Trevor Bannister, for instance, my colleague in the world of rogue stow-away beds, who by the miracles of technology, for which *Crossroads* was by no means famous, played twins in the show; and Bob Monkhouse, with whom I also worked in summer seasons and who was a big enough star that he could simply swan into the motel and play himself.

Then again, would a truly big star have ended up staying somewhere like the Crossroads Motel? Quite the knotty conundrum, that, which I'll leave you to pick away at. It's a bit like Groucho Marx not wanting to be part of any club that would have him as a member.

What I can tell you is that the excellent Lynda Baron did a stint in the motel as a secretary, long before *Open All Hours* encouraged her to go into District Nursing instead. Moreover, my *Only Fools* compadre, John Challis, could also proudly declare himself to be 'school of *Crossroads*', having wandered in for a couple of episodes to appear as a dodgy photographer, many years before he more noticeably became a dodgy car salesman. More on John and Lynda, these sorely missed friends of mine, a bit later.

As for my Bernie Kilroy character, after a six-month stint on the show, starting in the summer of 1966, he ended up having to leave town to avoid conviction on account of some dastardly plot he had concocted to defraud the motel. That should have been the end of him, really, and I certainly assumed so as I caught the train back to London from the ATV Studios in Birmingham. A few weeks later, though, the producers decided that they were prepared to overlook Bernie's problematic past, let him off the hook on this occasion and bring him back into the show as a regular character. There was something about that boxing/gardening hybrid, clearly, that they felt the programme couldn't get enough of.

I, however, saw it differently. And that was nothing to do with boxing or gardening, and nothing to do, either, with the reputation of *Crossroads*, a big red flag though that was for many people, both inside and outside the industry. The show had very quickly become the butt of jokes and used to get kicked about all over the place as a handy byword for the hammy and the clunky. And nobody would deny that it could certainly be both those things from time to time – often gloriously so, but probably no more or less, in fact, than any other televised soap of its era. It was shot quickly and on the tightest of budgets, and that was bound to show from time to time. The walls of the sets were definitely a bit floppy and, wherever you were in the motel, you had to be careful about how you closed doors for fear of giving the impression that the tremors from an earthquake were suddenly being felt in the motel's vicinity. Which would have felt natural in certain parts of the world, of course, but not where we were supposed to be, which was on the outskirts of Birmingham.

But I actually admired the programme – and the more so for seeing how it operated up close. There was no denying the energy around the studio, or how resourceful its production team was – a creative powerhouse, actually, in the sense that at one stage those people were making five half-hour episodes for national broadcast per week, which is an awful lot of drama to be putting together in a hurry. And whatever else you wanted to say about the programme, it certainly knew how to tell a story in a way that made people keep watching.

I should also probably say that I was quite impressed by the wages, too. What ATV were paying their actors – £76 per week in my case – completely outstripped anything I could make in the theatre at that time, which, as I mentioned earlier, was more like £15 a week. And now it was clear that ATV were willing to offer me months and possibly even years of steady employment at these handsome rates. From a financial point of view, I would have been bonkers to leave.

Yet, as new to the business and as unsure of myself as I was, I thought I spotted a trap. What if you made yourself comfy in *Crossroads* for a year or two, and then found you couldn't get out? Because it was clear that roles on long-running and popular television series – especially soaps – could do that to you. You saw it happen to television actors all the time: they would get branded by certain roles, and then discover that nobody, neither casting directors nor audiences, could see past the brand.

I worked out pretty quickly that this was something I would like to avoid if I possibly could. In my youthful and innocent enthusiasm, the whole joy of being an actor seemed to be that you could become as many different people as the world would allow you to be. That was what had been fun about my amateur acting, and that was what my repertory schooling had further instilled in me: that the real pleasure of acting lies in the possibility of ceaseless self-reinvention. Pirate one week, man of the cloth the next, and Restoration-era fop the one after that – that seemed to me the way to go. Finding yourself squashed into one role, or even one type of role, would surely only spoil everything – would defeat the point, even.

Now, it's not always in an actor's own power to save themselves from getting boxed up along the way. Sometimes, as I would discover, it happens through no fault of your own. But for as long as I felt I had the opportunity to keep my options alive, I was determined to do so. Hence my gentle but firm goodbye to Bernie Kilroy, and my fond farewell for ever more to that unique place where boxing had met gardening.

Call me naive, but I had no idea that I would be fighting different versions of that battle for the rest of my life.

For now, though, there I was in Weston-super-Mare. This was where Humphrey found me, driving down from London one night on a tip-off that I might be someone worth having a look at for this new kids' show. And how differently things might have turned out – for this was one of those pivotal career moments, dear reader, at which everything that eventually ensued could have turned out so differently if the scale had tipped the other way, as it so nearly did.

Humphrey had read Classics at Cambridge, was quite a correct, buttoned-up sort of chap with highly intellectual interests, and, as such, he was not really your typical, ticket-holding punter for an end-of-the-pier summer-season farce – even one with Dick Emery in it. Indeed, Humphrey was so unimpressed by what unfolded in front of his eyes that night, that, having somehow made it through the first half without grinding his teeth to dust, he was sorely tempted to cut his losses and leave in the interval.

Which would have been a huge shame for me because my big moment in that production – indeed, my first appearance of the evening – came right at the start of the second half.

Fortunately Humphrey hung on despite the callings of his better nature, and, fortified, I can only imagine, by the stiffest of gin and tonics from the theatre bar, he went back to his seat. And so it was that he saw me do an extended bit of business very much modelled on the Bromley Rep routine I talked about earlier, with the butler and the bongo drums – except that this time I was a man who found himself downstairs in an empty house, weighing up whether or not to inform the residents of his presence by ringing the large ornamental ship's bell that stood in the sitting room.

Different context, different instrument, but same deal, though: as I stood up there, contemplating the bell, in an agony of indecision, the audience knew exactly what was going through my mind, and exactly what was coming – but they didn't know when. With the stage to myself, I could draw that little moment out for several minutes on a good night and have the auditorium in the palm of my hand by the end of it. And luckily, Humphrey came on a good night.

All in all, I've a lot to thank that gin and tonic for.

Flash-forward, then, to the very first episode of *Do Not Adjust Your Set* on that Boxing Day, 1967. We see a mad kind of oompah orchestra, making a horrible but just about coherent racket, with Terry and Mike, Eric and Denise all miming away on various cellos and trumpets and violins, and with me poised at the back, holding a triangle and a beater and clearly waiting for my big moment in this unfolding symphony – my time to shine.

The expression on my face is both expectant and highly anxious. You know that at some point I'm going to hit that triangle, but you don't know when, nor what will ensue when

I eventually do, and in the gap between those things . . . well, we've been here already, haven't we? We are once more in comedy's playing field.

I'm sure I won't be spoiling your fun too much if I tell you that the triangle, when eventually struck, produced the overdubbed sound of a massive, jarring car crash – all crunching metal and breaking glass – to the horrified shock of everyone else in the orchestra. End of performance, end of skit.

And in many ways that was *Do Not Adjust Your Set* in a nutshell, or at any rate in a triangle strike: a cavalcade of absolute and utter nonsense. The show's speciality was extreme silliness, and if it could be swiftly achieved, so much the better. So, for example, in that Christmas launch show, there was a scene in which we all took a moment to display our new Christmas presents. When it was my turn, I looked into the camera with a straight face and said, 'I'm just going to slip on my new shoes.' And then the camera drew back slightly to reveal a pair of shoes on the floor at my feet, which I stepped on and immediately skidded off as if they were a banana skin, landing on my back with a mighty crash.

I had just slipped on my new shoes.

I know: 'sketchy' is very much the right word. But you need to remember that children's television in those days hadn't had much time for the plainly silly, let alone a sense of gleeful anarchy on the part of its presenters. There had always been something rather starchy and upright about it, something responsible – a sense that the grown-ups were always in the room. To that extent, *Do Not Adjust Your Set*, which featured grown-ups but not as we generally know them – the kind of grown-ups, indeed, who were ready to slip on their new shoes – was a giant gust of fresh air.

Each episode, then, was essentially a compendium of nonsense, much of it based on the premise that there's nothing kids like more than adults being made to look foolish. A large percentage of the material was, in fact, parodies of adult television formats – documentaries, news bulletins, discussion shows, all given an absurd twist or made to collapse in some daft or over-literal way. In that, the show very clearly foreshadowed *Monty Python's Flying Circus* – and in other ways, too. Cartoon sequences were dropped in, the work of a big hairy American bloke who used to stomp about the place in a battered Afghan coat – Terry Gilliam. Long before Terry Jones did links between *Monty Python* sketches naked (and seated at an organ), Eric Idle had done the same for *Do Not Adjust* – very modestly shot, of course, given the teatime broadcast slot. The seeds of *Python* are all there, if you want to look for them.

At the time, though, the show seemed – and this was hugely exciting for me – to be drawing tangibly on the influence of *The Goons*, whose radio show, in all its boundary-breaking idiocy, I had absolutely lapped up as a teenager. I had once got a ticket to go and see a *Goons* show being recorded – that's how much of a fan I was. I had sat in awe in the auditorium, watching Spike Milligan, Harry Secombe and Peter Sellers do their thing. To feel that I was now part of something which was working in that same absurdist vein – something that the Goons themselves might even approve of – was truly thrilling.

The absurdity wasn't only what you saw on the screen. It sort of coloured the whole atmosphere in which the show was made. Every episode there would be a musical number by the Bonzo Dog Doo-Dah Band, Neil Innes's highly eccentric pop group, who used to drift around in velvet jackets and silk scarves, smelling of patchouli oil and tormenting the production staff by requesting props for their performances that they didn't actually need or have any intention of using. One time, the band put in a written request for 'a petrol tanker, a plank of wood and a bag of boiled sweets'. Ever obliging, the poor, harried production team solemnly informed them that the plank and the sweets were in hand, but they were having a little trouble securing a petrol tanker; would a large oil drum do?

My favourite slots in the show were the little filmed sequences in which I played Captain Fantastic. A man in a raincoat, with an extraordinary, ferret-like moustache, an oversized bowler hat and a rolled umbrella, Captain Fantastic was intended to be the world's least likely superhero. He, in all his inconsequentiality, was pitted in an endless battle for supremacy with Denise Coffey's Mrs Black, the embodiment of cartoon evil who always had a dark plan up her sleeve to threaten the future of humankind.

Sixties-period surrealism abounded in those skits. Captain Fantastic occupied a world in which alien invaders intent on world domination were best dealt with by engaging them in a custard-pie fight on a deserted train station. I seem to remember getting stuck by my umbrella to a giant magnet in an otherwise empty field at one point, creating an image which Salvador Dalí might have wondered about painting.

At the same time, though, shot properly on film, at a slightly slowed-down rate of frames per second in order to look sped-up when played back at the normal rate, these little pieces were paying obvious homage to the black-and-white comic films that I had grown up with and adored – Laurel & Hardy, Buster Keaton, Harold Lloyd. I got to row a boat across a pond and allude – or so I hoped – to the work of the great Jacques Tati in *Monsieur Hulot's Holiday*, which I had seen in the cinema as a boy and considered for some time thereafter to be the funniest film ever made. It was all great fun, getting sent out into the countryside in the middle of the week and paid to muck about like this. I was living the dream.

Better still, the show seemed to go over well – well enough that a second series was commissioned. It opened in 1968 – with, of course, a Christmas special, 'Do Not Adjust Your Stocking', this time going out on Christmas Day itself. That episode found a moment for me to do my very best impression of Hughie Green, the endlessly sincere television host who was famous for presenting the talent show *Opportunity*

115

Knocks, and then to introduce Terry Gilliam's extraordinary animation, 'The Christmas Card', a piece for the ages,
with traditional festive scenes coming alive in bonkers ways:
three wise men on camels going backwards and forwards in
pursuit of a strangely unpredictable star, ice cracking under a
skater on a pond, a robin on a bough chirruping gaily before
getting picked off by a rifle, clumps of snow avalanching
from a roof to take out some innocent carol singers down
below . . . Christmassy and yet not. In the Captain Fantastic story, I was to be seen rampaging around Gamages,
the grand department store in London, and making a risky
getaway run along the flat roof of the portico above the
main entrance, where the store placed a row of sumptuously
decorated Christmas trees. If you were a London kid in the
forties and fifties, Gamages, with its vast toy department,
held an almost cathedral-like status, especially at Christmas.
I had worshipped at that temple of wonders many times in
the course of my childhood, and pored over the annual gift
catalogue which it issued for convenient at-home brows-
ing, without ever imagining I would one day run amok on
the roof of the place. Clearly, saying you were filming a daft
television show granted you access to places untravelled by
ordinary shoppers.

With the impetus of that big Christmas launch behind
it, the second series really began to gather some steam. It
was still ostensibly a children's programme, broadcast at teatime in among the rest of the children's output, yet, through

no real work of our own, the boundary was blurring. There seemed to be a rising amount of interest from older viewers – slightly bashful about their interest at first, maybe, but then increasingly less so. The story was that people were trying to knock off work early in order to get home and watch it. Adults, too, at this point in history, had not been well provided with surreal madness on television and it seemed that *Do Not Adjust Your Set*, by filling one gap in the market, had exposed another. This was all very exciting. I was involved in something on TV that was getting widely noticed and seemed to have a bit of traction under it.

You'll possibly know what happened next, though. Mike, Terry and Eric decided they didn't want to work on a children's show any more. They had other ambitions for their writing, and they went to Rediffusion and asked if they could make the show exclusively for grown-ups, with a late-evening time slot. And Rediffusion, who understandably thought they were on to a winner with the kids' version, said no. So Mike, Terry and Eric picked up their ball and walked away.

As for Denise and me, we were just onlookers during all this – in fact, not even onlookers. The pair of us did very little writing, so, to that extent, we had no real leverage and, in any case, all these dealings happened over our heads and without our input being sought. When we learned that the plug had been pulled, and the show was over, we were both, naturally, pretty rueful about it.

I was no less rueful a year later when Mike, the two

Terrys and Eric, now joined by Graham Chapman and John Cleese, returned, over on the BBC, with *Monty Python's Flying Circus* – the adult version of *Do Not Adjust Your Set* which they had always wanted to make. You'll see, I think, how, from my point of view, it looked as though the band had split up and then got back together without me, and I don't think I would have been human if I hadn't felt quite wounded by that.

Well, I can see that it wasn't the perfect fit – that I was a different kind of performer to those guys and from a different background. Yet, over the next months and years, as *Monty Python's Flying Circus* shot aloft and became a groundbreaking, internationally renowned and ultimately iconic British television show, diversifying into books and albums and films, while my own career was sputtering along and failing to get very far off the ground, I would start to think I knew how Pete Best must have felt about being eased out of my dad's favourite group, the Beatles, just before they made it, and replaced by Ringo.

Of course, my dad, with his strong views on 'that bloody racket', would probably have said that Pete Best was better off out of it. And I don't know how Pete Best felt about it – you'd have to ask him. But in my case, actually, the way it all turned out eventually, I *was* better off out of it – at least to the extent that all the wonderful opportunities that came my way in the 1980s and beyond would most likely not have done so had I found myself tied up in a successful comedy troupe in the late 1960s. Especially one in which I didn't entirely fit.

So, yes, better off out of it, ultimately. But I can't deny that I had a few long years of chipping away forlornly at the show-business coalface after this, and a few quiet bouts of gnashing my teeth in frustration, before I really began to believe it.

ON THE SIXTH DEL OF CHRISTMAS . . .

Hits and misses

Christmas in the West End of London has a special glow about it, no question. And to be in a successful play at Christmas in the West End of London while it glows . . . well, that's very heaven.

Of course, some of that glow which I mentioned is the result of alcohol, liberally applied, as the season seems to insist. But it has other sources too, as I routinely discovered, stepping out of my flat in the late afternoon in the run-up to Christmas, crossing Oxford Street, and descending down through Covent Garden to the Strand Theatre on Aldwych. It would all be there: the lights ablaze in the shops and strung across the streets; the parcel-burdened shoppers hurrying home; the overstuffed pubs; the liberated office workers falling out of bars – all sources of the glow. It would unfold in front of me on that walk to work like my own personal Christmas movie.

Why, even I become sentimental about this.

You could feel it in the audience, too. It used to fascinate me how every audience had a mood and how you could read that mood almost the moment the curtain was raised. There were audiences that were cold and needed to be warmed up, audiences that came in wet from the rain and needed to be dried out, audiences that had been steaming in the sun all day and needed to be cooled off; audiences that needed to be wound up and audiences that needed to be calmed down. Up there on the stage, I learned that you had to monitor the feeling in the room all the time and adapt to it as best you could. And yes, in that week running up to Christmas, before the theatre fell dark on Christmas Day itself, there was such a thing as a Christmas audience: a conviviality, a communal feel, a willingness to engage, a warm energy that simply wouldn't be there at any other time of the year.

And, yes, a glow – especially after the interval.

So here we are: Christmas 1974. I've picked myself up, dusted myself down and got myself a full-time job in *No Sex Please – We're British*, the long-running farce by Alistair Foot and Anthony Marriott, and I'm pleased as punch about it.* The part of Brian Runnicles in that particular play, at that particular moment, was a big pair of boots for my rather small pair of feet. None other than Michael Crawford had been

---

* Nothing to do with alcohol. The punch in that expression is Mr Punch of Punch & Judy puppet fame, a man famous for his permanently pleased expression. Indeed, versions I have seen have tended to have a rather fixed grin.

in the role directly before me, and his was a name you could genuinely put up in lights without being accused of wasting electricity. He'd been in the Hollywood film adaptation of *Hello, Dolly!*, directed by Gene Kelly and starring Walter Matthau and Barbra Streisand, and he'd acted on Broadway. My claims to fame at this point included two series of a collapsed ITV kids' show, some self-terminated *Crossroads* action, and a bit part in *Z-Cars*. Run this past a reputable comparison website if you wish, but it was hardly a fair contest. The reason Michael was leaving *No Sex Please*, by the way, was because he wanted to do a sitcom the BBC were offering him called *Some Mothers Do 'Ave 'Em*. That didn't turn out too badly for him, either.*

So, some large footsteps to follow in – and a big and established play to enter, too. *No Sex Please* was quite the item at this time. The critics hated it. 'Its triviality is beyond contempt,' said the *New York Times*, in a quote which the

---

* It was clear to those who saw both – me included – that Crawford's Brian Runnicles and his Frank Spencer had a considerable amount in common, not least the same seemingly fragile twitchiness and the same hapless propensity to land up in extreme physical peril, which they then somehow survived, in direct and comic defiance of that very fragility. It was as if all the characteristics of Crawford's Runnicles would find their ultimate and most popular expression in his Spencer, not least when being towed along behind a bus on roller skates in what was arguably *Some Mothers Do 'Ave 'Em*'s emblematic stunt sequence. Point of order: as with Tom Cruise and yours truly (when, of course, the insurers allowed it), Crawford insisted on doing his own stunts. All the truest stars of the silver screen do.

A producer recently told me, 'David, you know what? You would make the most perfect Scrooge.' I'd heard worse, frankly. But Merry Christmas to you, too.

Credit: Lordprice Collection / Alamy Stock Photo

I didn't end up playing Scrooge, but I played Mr Micawber in the ITV series *Micawber*, a comedy drama using characters from Dickens's *David Copperfield*, which debuted on Boxing Day in 2001.

Credit: David Cheskin / Alamy Stock Photo

When I survey the wondrous tapestry of my acting career, it's extraordinary how frequently Christmas comes into the picture.

If only all my Christmases as a theatre actor had been like that West End one of 1974 starring in *No Sex Please, We're British* – spent in comradely warmth, raising a glass with colleagues in a smash hit show after curtain on Christmas Eve.

On set for the 2002 *Only Fools and Horses* Christmas special, 'Strangers on the Shore'. Bon Noël, as they say.

Working has been a very different experience since Covid. Before the pandemic normalised working from home, an appearance on *The One Show* would have been a bit of a day out. Now there's no more professional make-up and no professional camera angles. And certainly no free biscuits. At least the coffee is better.

One of my many lockdown projects. Complete with lockdown beard.

When astronaut Tim Peake offered to take me for a spin in a Gazelle helicopter, I wasn't going to say no, was I?

'Peckham's that way, fellas.'

A bird's eye view of the Isle of Wight.

God bless Derek Trotter. Basically, he launched me into the nation's Christmas tree, and I never came down. It amazes me, the things I now get asked to do simply because I often appeared on the television at Christmas.

Credit: Mirrorpix / Alamy Stock Photo

'Miami Twice', the 1991 Christmas special, would have to feature among my proudest moments from the show. I can vividly recall the Miami hotel we stayed in and drinking cocktails and hanging out in the sun with Nick Lyndhurst thinking, 'Is this actually work?'

Credit: Mirrorpix / Alamy Stock Photo

Bella and Tuffy relaxing after a hard day guarding Jason Towers.

No, it wasn't me. Honest, guv.

The ghostly chair.

From 1991 onwards, after the end of the seventh series, *Only Fools* existed solely at Christmas, the team reuniting only to film extended stories for the holiday period – 'our Christmas present to the nation', as the BBC liked to call them.

Credit: Moviestore Collection / Alamy Stock Photo

Me in my Covid-friendly jumper.

producers decided, on balance, not to put on the posters outside the theatre. But audiences adored it. They came in droves – had been doing so for two years before I arrived, and would continue doing so for ages afterwards, until the show broke the record for a long-running comedy piece: sixteen years and more than 6,500 performances.

And it ended up sort of transcending theatre, in a way. Because of its plot (a young assistant bank manager inadvertently begins receiving a slew of Scandinavian pornography after his wife mis-orders some glassware, and then has to be constantly finding ways to dispose of these growing mounds of illicit material in order to avoid social disgrace and professional ruin), it had a slight whiff of scandal about it, even though, in actuality, it was pretty mild fare and definitely not in the business of frightening anybody's horses.

Yet at the time it obviously provided a talking point and its title was both a gift to headline writers and a phrase that ended up entering the language. (Even now you will see the 'no x please, we're y' formula used: I see someone had a show running in 2021 called *No Sex Please – It's Christmas*.) It was that pretty rare thing: a theatre production whose success seemed to resonate in the culture, far beyond the confines of the West End, and it was fantastic fun to stand at the centre of that for a while – really restorative, actually.

Blimey, it was taxing, though; the most physical role of my life – two and a bit hours of crashing through serving hatches (as previously detailed) and bounding over sofas

123

and swinging from door lintels, with all of the attendant bumps and bruises and strains. It felt less like being in a play at some points and more like being in a bar-room brawl – a bar-room brawl that kicked off six nights a week and with matinees on Thursday and Saturday. But I absolutely loved it. And fortunately there were still some functioning bits of me left to walk away after eighteen months when my contract eventually came to its end.

It also put me in the best cast I had ever worked with up to that point, including Simon Williams and Belinda Carroll and Dennis Ramsden, known to us all as Slim. I consider myself privileged to have shared a West End stage with Slim, not just once but twice (we were later together in the Dave Freeman play, A *Bedfull of Foreigners*, at the Duke of York's Theatre), because Slim was quite simply one of the greatest farceurs of his time. By which I mean, among other things, that if there was anyone in the world who was Slim's equal for working a pair of ill-fitting pyjama bottoms for laughs, then I can confidently say I never met them.

OK, nobody was claiming that this was the most delicate of dramatic skills to be famous for, or the most profound in its effects, and it was clear, even in those days, that you wouldn't automatically get into the Royal Shakespeare Company by doing tricks with your pyjama bottoms for your audition.

And of course, comedy has moved on: these farcical skills can appear antiquated and outmoded now, like thatching or making horse brasses – heritage crafts in our digital world.

Yet my respect for Slim and my abiding fondness for the good old analogue form of comedy in which he specialised means that I will maintain staunchly until my dying day that it took a special kind of comic brilliance to be able to yield gales of laughter from a pair of ill-fitting pyjama bottoms.

And to be able to do so six nights a week and with two matinees . . . well, again, let's try and show some credit where it's due.

Also in that *No Sex Please* cast was Richard Caldicot, another vastly experienced British theatre and film actor. Richard played Leslie Bromhead, the bank manager, my character Brian's boss, who at one point catches Brian alone among the recently arrived pornography stacks. I remember the pair of us working up a nice moment out of that encounter.

'Runnicles, what do you think you're doing here?' was Richard's line.

Then there would be a standing face-off between us, with me trying hard to hide a guilty expression, but saying nothing at first. We found we could hold it for ages, staring each other in the eyes. And as long as neither of us cracked up, the audience would frequently come right along with us, their expectation building for whatever it was I was about to say to burst this moment of embarrassment for my character.

On a good night, as we stood there, I was aware that if I just very slightly twisted my hand slowly inside my shirt cuff, it would start a laugh going in the auditorium. That would be the licence to build it, maybe shoot one cuff, and then put my arms back down by my sides, and then, in the fullness of time, shoot the other – all while holding Richard's gaze. As long as the audience were on board and in the right mood for it, we could draw this moment out for a whole minute before I eventually let it go and spoke my line.

'I beg your pardon, sir?'

And that would get a belter – a belter so long that we'd have to go back to staring at each other just to wait for the laughter to clear.

Not for nothing, dear reader, was I known in the cast of *No Sex Please* as 'the milkman'. There was *nothing* – and I mean nothing – that I wasn't prepared to milk if I thought there was a laugh to be found there.

But even the milkman got a day off at Christmas.

Ah, happy times. If only all my Christmases as a theatre actor had been like that West End one of 1974 – spent in comradely warmth, raising a glass with colleagues in a smash hit show after curtain down on Christmas Eve, exchanging a few small gifts and then walking home through the festively inebriated streets of London, with a bed awaiting and Santa on his way.

But no. Alas, 'twas not ever thus. Far from it. By way of acute contrast, permit me to ask the Spirit to show us one last Christmas scene, before I close out this chapter and we leave the theatre behind us for the greener pastures of television.

And perhaps, in fact, this scene can explain *why* we'll be leaving the theatre for the greener pastures of television. Or certainly why I was lucky to do so.

Actually, so deeply etched on my memory is this particular Christmas, and so apt is it to revisit me at random moments of its own accord, that I don't really need the help of a hired ghost for this one. Which is just as well, because he left the room a couple of minutes ago, saying he was going outside for a vape.

I don't want to sound unpleasantly confrontational about it, but I really am going to have to have a word with someone.

Anyway, as I say, I'm fine to fly solo here, because this is a scene that stays vividly with me – too vividly, in fact. Join me, if you will, in Newcastle in the north-east of England, on Christmas Day 1979. And let us arrive, specifically, in the deserted dining room of a determinedly uninteresting three-star business hotel in the city centre – deserted, but for a solitary 39-year-old actor, seated at a table, disconsolately using his fork to nudge a few bits and pieces from the hotel fridge around the plate in front of him. On this great day of convivial cheer and joy to the world, when loud hosannas rend the air and angel voices are heard on high, along with that of Noddy Holder, the occasional scraping of the fork on the plate is literally the only sound in the room.

Merry Christmas to me, then – in town to play Buttons in *Cinderella*, and now well and truly on my Jack Jones on

Christmas Day.* We don't need to spend long gazing upon this mournful picture. I've written about this low point in my career before. But essentially, Christmas has come, the rest of the cast have sped off to their families and loved ones, as recommended in all the Christmas guidebooks, and muggins here has been left to celebrate the birth of the Saviour entirely by himself.

Should I have been driving home for Christmas? History indicates that that's certainly what Chris Rea would have done in my position. Chris, presumably, would have been down to London like a shot, with a full tank of petrol and a bag of wine gums in the glove compartment.

Then again, he didn't have to be back for a matinee of *Cinderella* on Boxing Day. Or if he did, he never mentions it in the song.

Also, unless, again, he thought better of singing about it, Chris Rea didn't have a stonking head cold. That didn't help. Having dragged myself through the Christmas Eve performance like the peerless professional that I was, I had spent most of Christmas Day locked in my room in an unsuccessful

* Jack Jones: imperfect cockney rhyming slang replacing the word 'own' or 'all alone' – and nothing, by the way, to do with the smooth, middle-of-the-road American singer, Jack Jones, and everything to do with a music hall song from eighteen-hundred-and-frozen-to-death, entitled ''E Dunno Where 'E Are', concerning a former Covent Garden market porter, Jack Jones, who has come by some money and suddenly developed some snooty and aloof ways, much to the disgust of his former pals. It happens, you know. But no names, no pack drill.

attempt to sleep off the lurgy. Which meant that, having ascertained from the hotel manager the night before that 'Christmas dinner' would indeed be available in the dining room, I then discovered that 'dinner' in these north-easterly parts actually means 'lunch' and I was too late.

Hence the 'cold collation', pulled together by a kindly and sympathetic member of the hotel's skeleton staff but which only had the effect of increasing my self-pity on that day of days, as I suppose a portion of actual, literal hard cheese served in an empty room was always likely to.

Oh, the misery, dear reader – and how efficiently Christmas can magnify it, if you're not careful, just by being there. According to the posters, I was 'TV's David Jason'. Was I really, though? None of the TV I had been in to this point had amounted to much. And anyway, whatever else it meant, being 'TV's David Jason' didn't spare you, clearly, from spending Christmas on your own in a closed hotel dining room.

In short, there I was, a single man, soon to turn forty, finding consistent success a little hard to come by and starting to wonder, in fact, whether he ever would find it; staring out of the window at the dark and deserted centre of an unfamiliar city, and asking himself just what he thinks he's playing at and whether this acting lark is ever really going to be worth the candle.

Still, cheer up, eh? Only six more weeks of playing Buttons to go.

Six weeks!

Christmas bells? Hell's bells, more like.

They weren't all easy, then, those years of itinerant thesping, when I was an actor of no fixed production, constantly moving on, simply in order to keep working. Those were the years in my life when I became deeply familiar with our nation's railway network and all its less than lovable foibles, and especially sensitively attuned to that instruction, so well known to all who were condemned to travel the length and breadth of the country in this manner: 'Change at Crewe.'

Just as the country's travelling rock bands would, in the early hours of Sunday morning, collide with one another at motorway services, so the nation's roaming actors would, of a weekend, find themselves rubbing shoulders at Crewe. That station was almost like our clubhouse. You would know it was Sunday afternoon because there would be all these luvvies calling out to each other as they breezed past on the platforms.

'Where are you headed, darling?'

'Off up to Middlesbrough, love. What about you?'

'Bournemouth for me, darling!'

And because it was Sunday there would frequently be engineering works and the timetable would be up the spout, meaning that a lot of sitting around and waiting was going to be done.

What are the three most heart-sinking words in the English language? That's an easy one: 'replacement bus service'.

And more often than not the station cafe would be closed, so you couldn't even get a cup of tea and a dead sandwich to insert between you and your wandering thoughts.

So you would end up sat on a bench with your suitcase, staring across the tracks, watching the trains come and go – or not, as may be – and you would find yourself, perhaps, with just a little bit too much time in which to think about things and to start wondering what, if anything, was the meaning of it all. Were you living, or was life passing you by? You could feel very detached at those moments, disjointed and uneasy, as though your life was a bunch of unrelated fragments – literally, an assortment of different parts – and you were waiting for something or someone to come along that would link them all together, yet you had no idea what or who that might be.

In 1994, when I was asked to do *Desert Island Discs* – a rite of passage, if ever there was one – I picked among my eight recordings for castaway usage Simon & Garfunkel's 'Homeward Bound', which history relates was written by Paul Simon while he sat on Widnes station in Merseyside, waiting for a train (or possibly a replacement bus service) to take him back to London.

OK, Paul Simon probably wasn't heading for Weston-super-Mare to start a summer season with Dick Emery like some of us were at such times. But for the travelling musician, the feelings of rootlessness and disorientation and all the longings that come with them were, I'm sure, very

131

similar, and the song always and instantly transports me back to those strange and lonely Sundays in transit.*

Incidentally, on that castaway show, I also convinced Sue Lawley, who was then the presenter, to let me have, for my chosen book, a boatbuilding manual, and, for my luxury, a full set of carpenter's tools. It's called planning ahead. I don't think she twigged. But I had no intention of hanging around on my own for any longer than I needed to. What would I do for work?

Oh, and would you care to guess when the BBC chose to broadcast my *Desert Island Discs*? You're probably ahead of me. It was Christmas Day. It could have just been coincidence, of course, but I don't think so. By 1994, this whole 'Mr Christmas' thing had already taken hold.

And I think I know who to blame – for this and many other changes in the shape of my life. It was a bloke called Derek Trotter.

* For the record, my other chosen discs were: Phil Harris, 'The Darktown Poker Club' – a novelty song from my childhood (the chances are you know Harris better as the voice of Baloo, singing 'Bare Necessities' in Disney's *The Jungle Book*); 'Help!' by my dad's favourites, the Beatles; an extract from *The Goon Show* episode entitled 'The International Christmas Pudding'; Rita Moreno and George Chakiris performing 'America' from *West Side Story*; Dean Jones and Susan Browning performing 'Barcelona' from Stephen Sondheim's *Company*; Simply Red's 'Holding Back the Years', for its *Only Fools* connotations, of course; and a quick blast of 'Mars' from Gustav Holst's *The Planets* suite, because you can't beat a bit of Holst.

ON THE SEVENTH DEL OF CHRISTMAS . . .

Hauntings and phone-ins

The Spirit of Christmas Past has just rung in. Would it be OK if he worked from home today?

He assured me that he would be attending to business just as dutifully as if he were 'in the office' – and possibly even be 'able to get more done', what with saving the time from the commute. And he said that if I needed haunting in a hurry, I could always Zoom him during the afternoon – although if I could leave it until after five, when *A Place in the Sun* finished on Channel 4, that would probably be better.

Is this OK? I appreciate that we're all in a new 'world of work' as we emerge slowly from the two years of disruption visited upon us by the pandemic. And I understand that people are taking this period as an opportunity to reassess their priorities and perhaps reach a new accommodation with the age-old balancing act between work and life.

But to be honest, I'd hoped for a bit more, now the restrictions are off, from someone employed in what we might think of as the 'spiritual hospitality' business – the personal touch, and all that. As an employer – and certainly as someone writing up their memoirs – you want to be in a position to look the ghosts of your past directly in the eye, don't you? To knock a few things back and forth in person? Dickens, I feel sure, would back me up here. I certainly don't remember any of the ghosts in *Scrooge* phoning it in – not even in the Ross Kemp-led 2000 remake.

Ah, well. So be it. It seems I'll be working solo this morning at the memory coalface. And that's OK, as it turns out, because the story I want to tell you now is spooky enough on its own. Indeed, consider it, if you will, my own modest contribution to the venerable tradition of Christmas ghost stories. Except that I'm not making it up. It's about something seriously occult and profoundly unsettling that genuinely happened the other night in the kitchen. And no, it's got nothing to do with my cooking, thank you for wondering.

As I may already have made you aware, parts of my humble home here at Jason Towers – though fortunately not the plumbing – date back hundreds of years. Indeed, a dwelling on this site is apparently recorded in the Domesday Book of 1086, so the house has had a while to accumulate some previous owners. As such, there have been times before now when I've had cause to wonder whether some of those previous owners might still be around – whether the place might actually be haunted. By authentic ghosts, I mean, rather than ones I've ordered in for work purposes from Spirits R Us.

There was, for instance, that episode I recorded in my last volume of reminiscences, involving a moving chair which, in a frenzy of terror (and while, I should probably add, driven quietly nuts by self-isolation during lockdown), I interpreted as poltergeist activity . . . but which actually turned out to be one of the dogs who had crept into the room silently and guiltily (knowing she was not really meant to be there) and who had slid under the chair's legs and was trying to get comfortable there, as subtly as possible.

That incident came on top of a whole period, not all that long ago, which must have gone on for a couple of years at least, when bottles of Diet Coke would keep appearing and then disappearing from the fridge, and mugs and other bits of crockery, similarly, would vanish from the kitchen and not reappear for ages, and when I would sometimes be convinced that I had heard the front door opening and closing and the eerie sound of footsteps on the staircase in the middle of the night.

But then I realised that wasn't ghosts. That was having a teenage daughter.

There was always a gratifyingly reassuring explanation in the end, then. But this new episode seemed to me to be of a quite different order – activity of a kind which only a supernatural presence could explain.

It was the end of the evening, the house was quiet, and I

was out in the kitchen doing a bit of washing-up. You'll be telling me, perhaps, that people have dishwashers for that kind of thing these days, and indeed, many do. And so do we. But I'm old-school: when it comes to washing-up, I prefer to roll up my sleeves and get my hands dirty. Or clean, actually, which is what happens if you're doing it properly.

As I washed and then wiped, I found myself, as so often at such times, free to meditate upon life, the state of the world and the meaning of everything, which I would suggest is one of the great advantages of doing the washing-up manually – that space for reflection. I mean, you could stare ruminatively out of the kitchen window while the dishwasher was going through its cycle, I suppose. But it wouldn't be quite the same, and very few people, so far as I know, take the opportunity.

On this occasion, after scraping some persistent and rather ugly food scraps off a plate, I was thinking, for some reason, about Vladimir Putin, the Russian president, who had recently chosen to celebrate the general easing of restrictions around the pandemic by invading Ukraine and releasing another prolonged bout of suffering and anxiety upon the world.

Thanks a bunch, Vlad. If there was ever a person for whom social distancing was invented . . .

In particular, I was wondering about the origins of the name 'Putin', which you don't seem to hear a lot, outside of conversations about Mad Vlad, of which there have been rather too many lately. And . . . well, this may not do me much credit, but into my casually drifting mind came the thought that maybe, back when Vladimir was just a young lad and restricted, presumably, to invading neighbouring gardens rather than neighbouring whole countries, he had found himself growing up in a remote Soviet-era household without sanitary facilities.

And maybe the rudimentary nature of this accommodation had obliged him and the rest of his family to do their fundamental human business in a large metal can – perhaps a catering-sized baked beans tin, if Soviet-era Russia ran to such a thing – which they stood outside the back door. And maybe this improvised arrangement had gone down badly with the neighbours, causing them eventually to become known widely in the area as the Poo Tin family. And it had stuck. The name, I mean.

Yes, yes – a childish digression, I know. But I swear this was the branch line down which my little train of thought was chuffing as I stood there, staring blankly through the window into the dark garden and slowly rotating a sponge scourer on a dinner plate.

And what do you know? Clearly I wasn't the only person whose mind had gone down that track. At any rate, not long after the evening in question, some simple, home-made signs appeared overnight on the sides of the bins for dog waste on a common in London. They showed the head of Mad Vlad under the legend 'POO TIN'.

Not guilty, your honour. And I have a solid alibi. I was all in favour of the gesture, though. As a child of the forties, I remain a big fan of what I guess we could call the 'Hitler has only got one ball' school of political commentary – the urge to send all puffed-up tyrants into oblivion where they belong by the means of good old schoolyard mockery. And it worked back then, so who's to say it might not work again now?

So there I was, in the kitchen, exploring my feelings about the president of Russia, when I first heard . . . the noise. Actually, it was a sequence of noises. First came a short series of soft taps, four or five in total. And then, more eerie still, came a strange, keening moan.

I paused from my labours and listened. Nothing now. Only the gentle popping of the Fairy Liquid suds in the sink. Had I imagined that other stuff? I must have done. I picked up another plate to dry off the draining board and resumed work.

Hang on, though: there it was again. Exactly the same thing, coming from the hallway just outside the kitchen – a series of gentle knocks, like somebody feebly trying to attract attention, and then that shuddering, baleful moan.

Again I froze. Again it stopped. Again I resumed work, but much more stealthily this time, with my ears fully attuned.

And once more the noise came, unmistakable now – the knocking followed by the eerie moan.

I felt my insides turn cold. I'm not generally given to jumping to conclusions, but as someone who has watched simply hundreds of horror and ghost movies down the years, I would recognise a keening, moaning sound like that anywhere. It was the noise of a lost and tortured soul, condemned to roam the earth in search of ease. Stands to reason, doesn't it? It was the totally distinctive sound of a restless spirit – and not the Spirit of Christmas Past who, needless to say, had knocked off many hours earlier, mid-afternoon, citing a dentist appointment.

And, typical: the part of the earth this particular lost and tortured soul was condemned to roam was apparently the bit of it right next to my kitchen.

It seemed to me that I had two options at this point. I could exit in a hurry in the opposite direction, via the back door, before all the cupboard doors started flying open, the lights started flashing on and off, and it all properly kicked off, *Poltergeist*-style. Or I could head towards the noise and bravely confront the source of it, perhaps with a weapon in hand – possibly a piece of newly rinsed cutlery – thereby doing my manly bit to protect my home and loved ones.

I know which approach I felt more inclined towards: bolting into the garden. Yet something – call it the innate heroism for which television actors and theatricals in general are famous – seemed to be drawing me, almost magnetically, in the opposite direction: drawing me towards whatever this thing was.

I slowly crept to the threshold of the kitchen, braced myself, and peered out into the adjacent hallway, wondering what I would see there – wondering, indeed, if what I saw there would be the last thing I would *ever* see.

Leaning against the wall was my wife Gill's guitar. And below the guitar, stretched out on the floor, was . . . a dog.

A hound of hell?

No. A hound of ours. Tuffy.

Who didn't get up, but who did at least, upon seeing me, offer a small, lazy tail-wag by way of greeting. 'Thump, thump, thump' went the tail, quite softly, on the body of the adjacent guitar. And then, as the tail settled down again, into its reclined position, it passed, on its way, across the guitar strings, like a bow across a cello, thereby producing an eerie moan of the type a person might associate with . . . I don't know – a lost and tortured soul, condemned to roam the earth in search of ease maybe?

The dastardly Tuffy. Spooked yet again by that devious mutt. It took me a while to thread it all together, but I eventually did so. The sound of me moving plates around in the kitchen had, in full accordance with Pavlov's famous old theories on dogs and their associations, triggered in the nearby, half-asleep Tuffy the thought of food. And the thought of food caused the dog's tail to wag involuntarily in anticipation; and thence the thump and the moan, each time another plate moved. I don't think I could have set this effect up if I'd tried. I don't suppose Pavlov could have done so either, and he had more experience of this kind of thing than I did.

So, haunted once more by my own pet. Humiliating, really, and it's turning into a theme. But I have to say, this was another level of haunting. It utterly trumped the poltergeist impression with the dining chair from the lockdown period of 2020. Now deploying musical instruments, the dog had really upped her game, and all credit to her for that. I can't say I'm not worried about what this development portends for even more sophisticated hauntings in the future – and, by extension, the state of my blood pressure. On the other hand, what's that line of Terry Pratchett's? 'Every dog is only two meals away from being a wolf.' So I always think, with dogs, that for as long as I retain ultimate control of the dog food, all should be well.

I should say at this point that Tuffy's record on haunting is almost as impressive as her record on food clearance, a vocation which she shares with our other dog, Bella. When the two of them work together as a team in this area, it's something to witness. In fact, if Crufts wasn't so hung up on trifling things like pedigrees, well-brushed coats and obedient behaviour, and if it had a segment where dogs competed to clear a floorspace of toast crumbs with the maximum efficiency in the quickest time, I think I could be looking at an award-winning pairing and every-thing that follows in terms of publicity, sponsorship and free bags of Winalot.

Consider this. Quite recently, thanks to the operation of

the principle known to science as Sod's Law,* I managed, while reaching into the fridge for something else entirely, to dislodge a large carton of cream from the shelf, and then watched it drop to the ground, burst open and create a significant lake of double-thick dairy product across much of the kitchen's tiled floor.

I closed my eyes in exasperation, as you do, already entertaining a heart-sinking vision of the practically *Exxon Valdez*-scale clean-up operation that I knew was now upon me. Well, OK, a job that would take up more of the rest of the evening than I wanted it to, and involve, no doubt, the repeated and unpleasant wringing out of cream-soaked cloths, the spreading of the offending liquid even further in the attempt to absorb it, thus making the problem look several times worse before it even began to look better, the likely noticing of deficiencies in my work by my wife a little later on, etc.

* The law which states that if something can go wrong it will do. Sod's Law dictates, among many other things, that wherever you stand in relation to the bonfire that you have just lit, the smoke will end up blowing directly in your face. It also ensures that the final tiny screw that you require to complete a complex repair job will, exactly at its moment of need, slip from your hand, drop to the floor and disappear down a crack in the floorboards. The expression is believed to date back to the ancient Egyptian monarch King Sod of the Sodomites (1570–1544 BC), who was the first person in recorded history to get all the way through bagging up a weekly shop at the supermarket checkout and then discover that he'd left his wallet at home. (I may have made that last bit up.)

However, when I finished wincing and disconsolately opened my eyes, I could hardly believe what I saw. The lake of cream had already practically vanished. Like first responders at a warehouse fire, Tuffy and Bella had instantly arrived at the scene, and they were already close to solving the problem the only way they knew how – by eating it. I could only look on admiringly, and with the deepest gratitude. In due course, not only was there not a drop of spilled cream to be found anywhere in that kitchen, but the tiles were so shiny you could see your face in them. The dogs looked pretty happy about their work, too. Indeed, this will have to go down as a rare instance of a dog looking like the cat that got the cream.

Now, before you get on the phone to the RSPCA, I fully appreciate, by the way, that cream is not a recommended foodstuff for dogs. At the same time, frankly, by comparison with some of the other things those two have found to eat in the course of their lifetimes . . . well, let's not go there, apart from to say that I'm not sure how long something would need to be dead and buried before my dogs would fail to dig it up and find it appetising. In that context, cream practically qualifies as a health food – one of their five-a-day: not so good fibre-wise, but high, at least, in calcium. And if it's only (Sod's Law permitting) once in a lifetime, then, really, I don't think there's cause to worry too much.

The point is, when they're not scaring the living wits out of me, I'm extremely grateful for the work these dogs do. They pay their way, I would say. Tuffy isn't merely in the mess-clearance business; she's actually in the mess-prevention industry. She doesn't just hear food when it hits the floor – she somehow, through some kind of sixth sense available only to certain highly attuned canines, becomes aware of that food in the split second before it leaves the plate. Consequently, she's more than capable of taking any remotely edible morsel out of the air during its descent from the table and she will have chewed up and fully digested it well before it would have hit the ground in a Tuffy-free household. Again, Crufts is missing a trick here.

Meanwhile, in terms of her hoovering abilities, she is practically unparalleled in my experience, getting deep into corners and those hard-to-reach areas, completing the job in no time at all and with no operator effort, and requiring no mains or battery power. I should probably license the patent for her to James Dyson and make myself a few quid.

Mind you, she won't do dust – or certainly not dust without a fairly prominent food component. And, in fact, she moults. I guess both of these things would have to be accounted a disadvantage in a household cleaning device. Back to the drawing board, maybe.

* * *

Anyway, where was I? Oh yes: rueing the temporary absence of my hired spiritual help on this current writing project and raising my eyebrow slightly about his decision to work from home. Yet, for better or worse, remote working is now officially with us, and has touched even my humble trade in ways it would have been impossible to imagine as recently as two years ago.

Indeed, there have been quite a few occasions since the pandemic descended on us when I have found myself phoning it in – in the modern sense, obviously, of using Zoom or similar, rather than the old sense of not being all that bothered. And perhaps most prominent among those occasions was the time when Gill came into the study and broke the exciting news to me that *Strictly Come Dancing* had been in touch.

I know what you're thinking: what kept them? I was thinking that, too. But here at last, clearly, was a chance to show the nation the full glory of my paso doble, perhaps in the arms of Oti Mabuse, or maybe Karen Hauer, although, between you and me, both of them would need to up their game a bit, dance-wise, because I wouldn't intend to be messing about.

Looking across at my shelves that day and narrowing my eyes slightly, I took a moment to clear a little space, mentally, between the BAFTAs and the National Television Awards for the fabled *Strictly* glitterball trophy. I have to say it looked pretty good sitting there among the accumulated silverware of a lifetime in show business – maybe almost the crowning glory. It seemed to fit.

'Do you think I should press for something dynamic and

Latin-based in week one?' I mused aloud, sitting back from my desk and sucking ruminatively on the end of my pencil. 'Or do you suppose I should ease myself in gently, and go ballroom – offer them a simple but beautifully executed American Smooth, perhaps? Either way – best book an afternoon at the tanning salon, pronto.'

'Actually,' said Gill, 'they want you to read out the terms and conditions.'

With an almost audible 'pop!', the virtual glitterball on the mantelpiece disappeared and the BAFTAS and National Television Awards shuffled sheepishly back into their places.

The terms and conditions? The yards of obligatory rigmarole relating to the viewers' phone-voting process? 'Calls will be charged at your standard rate' and so on? So much for my shot at dance-floor glory. You can't dance to the terms and conditions. Quite the opposite, in fact. As a long-time viewer of the programme, I knew that for quite a while Claudia Winkleman, *Strictly*'s co-presenter, had had the unenviable weekly task of ploughing through that paragraph of deathless legalese, and even in her terrifically capable hands it had always been a tricky moment for the energy of the show. And also a tricky moment for her, I can only assume. There was certainly one occasion when she completed the job, looked into the camera wanly and uttered the immortal concluding plea: 'Fire me.'

Then at some point the producers realised that it would be an idea to get a guest to perform that function each week and make a little feature out of it. A very smart move: people like Brian Cox and Peter Kay stepped up. John Cleese, as I recall, amusingly read out the rules while unsuccessfully stifling a number of yawns.

Some elite company there, and I suppose I should have been honoured to find myself in the frame for the job. But what about my paso doble? My cha-cha-cha? Overlooked, spurned, cast aside, it seemed, and left to moulder in the darkness of destiny's fitted wardrobe, along with my spangly outfits and my finest slashed-to-the-navel shirts.

In truth, this may not have been an entirely bad thing. And I'm not just referring to the slashed-to-the-navel shirts. All bluffing aside, when it comes to dancing, I make a very good singer. And when it comes to singing . . . well, we'll get on to me and singing in a little while, but suffice it to say for now, it's a somewhat delicate matter.

Anyway, as it happened, some overcrowding in the diary meant I never did get to delight the nation by bringing my very best, theatre-honed tones to the *Strictly* terms and conditions – which was a shame because I had a secret plan to break off, somewhere between 'calls cost 15p from a landline' and 'your vote will not count and you may still be charged', and execute a perfectly timed reverse fleckerl, just to show the producers what they were missing.*

---

* As any aficionado of the Viennese waltz will tell you, 'fleckerl' is a word meaning 'small spot' and denoting a step in which the dancers cease

However, by way of consolation, I did appear on the show's 2021 Christmas special edition – in keeping, yet again, with the puzzling televisual law that seems to say, 'It's Christmas, so let's see if David Jason wants to be involved.' And again, for some reason my red-hot samba did not seem to be required, but neither was I in the 'terms and conditions' role. This time I was there as . . . well, what I suppose you would call 'an emotional support actor'.

That year, Jay Blades, the presenter of *The Repair Shop*, was taking part in the competition, carefully steered, of course, by a professional partner, Luba Mushtuk, and, I was told, the music they were intending to dance to was the closing theme from *Only Fools and Horses*.

Yes, I know: in all these years of hearing that tune and thinking about its half-price cracked ice, its David Bowie LPs, its pool games, gold chains, wosnames, etc., it never once occurred to me that it was a dance number – any more, frankly, than *Strictly*'s terms and conditions are a dance number. I've heard of people playing the *Only Fools* closing theme at weddings, and I've heard of people requesting that it be played at funerals, and I'm sure an excuse may have been found to play it at all kinds of gatherings in between.

---

travelling across the floor for a few beats and rotate on the spot instead. But, of course, *Strictly Come Dancing* has made us all experts in this area. Never mind fleckerls, I thought a Viennese waltz was a luxury ice-cream dessert made by Wall's until I started watching *Strictly*.

But I'd never heard of people wanting to dance to it in a formal, competitive ballroom setting, and I'm pretty sure John Sullivan never envisaged such a thing when he wrote and recorded it.*

But what do I know? You'd struggle to tango or waltz to it, possibly, but it turns out that, if you know what you're doing, you can get a competition-standard jive going to the sound of John hymning 'Hooky Street', in what music critics and aficionados of the genre such as myself now solemnly regard as one of the earliest recorded examples of UK rap. Try it at home in the privacy of your living room.

So, that was going to be Jay Blades's mission on the Christmas special: a jive to 'Hooky Street'. What the *Strictly* people wanted to know was: given his choice of music, would I be prepared to record Jay a little message of encouragement

---

* Just for the avoidance of doubt, John wrote and sang two themes for *Only Fools* – the one for the end credits, which we're talking about here, and the Chas & Dave-style, rolling-piano one for the opening titles. The opening number was requested by the BBC for series two to replace the original instrumental Ronnie Hazlehurst theme, in the hope that it would explain the show's title. Hence that opening theme comes with the emphatic pay-off line: 'Why do only fools and horses work?' It took the BBC a long time, and several million viewers, to stop feeling anxious about the oblique nature of the show's title, but you could argue – and John did argue – that that oddness was exactly what made it stick in people's minds. Anyway, for what it's worth, after much tapping on the table, I've worked out that, if the closing theme lends itself to a jive, the opening theme would more or less furnish a cha-cha-cha, if you fancy a shot at it. I'll just watch while you do it, though, if it's all right with you.

with which they could ambush, and hopefully inspire, him during the show?

Now, I'm as regular a viewer of *The Repair Shop* as I am of *Strictly*. A show set in a workshop where people take things apart and fix them up again could have been designed with me specifically in mind. In fact, that's not really a TV programme, as far as I'm concerned: that's most of my weekends. And it's always seemed obvious to me – even without meeting him in person – that Jay is a good thing. So I said I would certainly be happy to cheer him on.

It was time to dive deep into the wardrobe, then, and pull out what I think of as my ghost's uniform, or alternatively my resurrection outfit – the clothes with which I can bring Derek Trotter back to life on the occasions that I need to. Chief among these is a leather bomber jacket which I actually wore while playing Del on the show but which seemed somehow to make its way home with me when the show finished. I'm not quite sure how that happened, but I assume there is an entirely innocent explanation . . . Anyway, the jacket is in a shade which I think, if it were a car interior, we would be calling 'oxblood', and I feel fairly certain its value has always been more emotional, shall we say, than financial. It was all about the style, really. In the true Trotter tradition, that jacket looked a million dollars but only cost a fiver.

Along with the jacket, I retrieved a bright red pullover and a tweed flat cap – both model's own, let me be clear, and neither of them palmed off from the BBC's ample wardrobe stocks on the quiet. And by the simple application of these three items, and with a few preliminary flexes of the neck and rolls of the shoulders by way of a warm-up, I was more or less ready to stop being David Jason for a couple of minutes and start being Derek Trotter.

You'll imagine, I'm sure, the disruption here at Jason Towers on the day my message for Jay was filmed: the arrival on the drive of various lorries and vans; the offloading of cameras and lights and stands and reflector screens; the wardrobe and make-up teams going about their work; the script people doing last-minute edits; the *Strictly Come Dancing* production staff dashing around with clipboards and earpieces.

And if you imagined any of that, you'd be completely wrong. This was 2021, don't forget. I can list the people and the equipment involved in getting me onto the screen in that *Strictly* Christmas special very swiftly indeed. The people were me and Gill and the equipment was Gill's phone. The whole item was written, produced, directed, lit, filmed and edited by my wife, on location in front of a conveniently blank portion of wall in our house.

Watching the show at home on Christmas Day, my informed opinion was that Jay, bless him, is a better repairer than he is a dancer, and, even allowing for the generous spirit of the season, the judges seemed to agree with me: Jay got turned over by the singer Anne-Marie in the final scoring.

My informed opinion about my own contribution to the show, however, is that it looked . . . well, a touch underlit and a bit . . . *home-made*. Which I guess is hardly surprising in the circumstances.

This is simply where we are nowadays. The same thing happened not long ago when *The One Show* got in touch. As part of BBC 100, the BBC's centenary celebrations, viewers had been voting for their most loved BBC TV programme and . . . far be it from me to shine my own buttons here, but *Only Fools and Horses* had come out top, just ahead of *Doctor Who*.

It's extraordinary, really, and extremely gratifying. It feels like hardly six months goes by without me hearing about the success of *Only Fools* in a public poll of some description. If I had a pound for every time the bar-flap sequence has been voted people's Funniest Television Moment, or similar, I'd probably be able to afford to hire a Spirit of Christmas Past permanently and not just while writing this book. The point is, forty years after our show first went out, and the best part of two decades since its last new episode, people are still talking about it and making clear how fond of it they still are, and that's not something I can ever quite get my head around.

And now here were the viewers of *The One Show* offering the programme another show of confidence and sitting it on top of what, on closer examination, proved to be an extremely distinguished pile, featuring not just sitcoms but BBC-made programmes of all kinds. Just to put this in perspective, *Blackadder* and *Fawlty Towers* were a little way back on this latest list, and Sir David Attenborough's *Planet Earth*, which, whatever else you want to say about it, covered a lot more ground than *Only Fools* and was probably a bit trickier to film, was languishing somewhere down at number 12.

Should have put a few more gags in it, Sir David.

Anyway, the question from *The One Show* was: would I come on the programme and, in this moment of triumph for *Only Fools* and everyone connected with it, say a few words of thanks on behalf of the team?

Now, before the pandemic normalised working from home, an appearance on *The One Show* would have been, for better or worse, a bit of a day out. It would have required a journey to London, for which they probably would have sent a car for you. You would have spent some time behind the scenes in the green room where you would have mingled with the great and good and chatted to your fellow guests, all the while enjoying generous access to the BBC's normally quite challenging coffee and probably some free biscuits.

And then, after having a light dusting of make-up applied to your better side by a professional make-up artist, you would have been ushered by professional production staff into a professionally lit studio to be filmed by professional camera operators – with the result that you might, if you're lucky, end up looking quite professional yourself in the segment that eventually went out into people's sitting rooms.

But of course none of that applied this time. It was me, Gill and Gill's phone all over again, doing our best to put

153

something together and then crossing our fingers that the show would be able to use it. Working from home, in other words. No car, no green room, no day out. More importantly, no professional make-up and no professional lighting and no professional camera angles. And certainly no free biscuits. I suppose at least the coffee was better.

And although I can see there's plenty to recommend this method, it does seem, from the point of view of the finished product, a slightly retrograde development to me. We appear to have gone directly from the pin-sharp, slickly produced, Ultra HD broadcasting era to calmly accepting smudgy and shaky videos off people's iPhones or shot through the slightly dusty lenses of the cameras on their laptops. It's like certain kinds of television programmes are now patchwork quilts, with people working on their own little square of the design at home. And nobody minded during the drudgery of lock-down, because we were all doing our bit and we were just grateful to see faces, no matter the quality of the imagery. But for obvious reasons, relating to convenience and budget, among other things, this approach has continued beyond the pandemic. The self-shot TV appearance seems to be here to stay, smudges, shakes, dust and all.

Of course, that it's possible in the first place to make broadcast-ready images of any kind without leaving your own armchair and employing only a standard-issue phone is pretty remarkable. Why, it doesn't seem all that long ago that I was appearing in adverts for a marvellous technological breakthrough and a dazzling new contribution to freedom and convenience which was about to be unleashed upon the Great British public and which was to be called . . . the British Telecom Phonecard.

Honestly, what would those amazing people in the lab coats think of next? First a man on the moon, and now this. Here was an ingenious, plastic, credit-card-shaped device which, if slotted into the appropriate receptacle near the handset in a public call box, would enable you to – as BT boldly trumpeted – 'buy your phone calls in advance'. The brave new world was truly upon us.

No more fumbling about with coins and frantically feeding the machinery bits of silver to keep the call alive! We were all pinching ourselves in disbelief. Could you even imagine such a time would ever come, let alone in your own lifetime?

This was in the early 1980s, though apparently it was almost a decade before, in 1974, that British Telecom first set up (I'm not making this up) a 'Coinbox Study Steering Group', charged with exploring the future of the coin-less payphone and, by extension, the future of the phone box. Oh to have been a fly on the wall – or even a fly in the phone box – at the proceedings of the Coinbox Study Steering Group. Oh to have been a member of it, actually. I think I missed my vocation.

Of course, history will now demonstrate that the ultimate future of the phone box turned out to be providing storage space for emergency defibrillator equipment or becoming an improvised lending library for the neighbourhood's old paperback books. But I don't suppose anybody on the Coin-box Study Steering Group was predicting that in 1974. And that august committee's big idea, at the conclusion of its doubtless long hours of steering? The phonecard. Because, as the voice-over accompanying my advert for BT patiently explained: 'There will be times when you need to make dozens of calls from a public phone.'

To be perfectly honest, with the benefit of hindsight, I'm struggling to think of a single situation in which you might have needed to make *dozens* of calls from a payphone – unless, I guess, you were doing something like organising a wedding and wanting to save on paper for invitations.

But practically speaking, making dozens of calls from a phone box was never going to work out for you, because, quite apart from anything else, after about call number four, and most likely much sooner, you'd have had a waiting customer tapping agitatedly on the glass with a coin – or with the leading edge of their phonecard – and asking you whether you were planning to be in there all night. There was an unwritten but strictly applied code of conduct around payphone usage, as I recall, and a strong sense that these were shared, public facilities which were to be treated as such. Gumming them up by blathering on for hours on end was very much frowned upon, however much BT might have been trying to encourage it.

On the other hand, quite by contrast, smoking in phone

boxes appeared to be entirely acceptable – indeed, almost obligatory. Some of them even provided an ashtray for your smoking convenience, and in the absence of that, there was always the floor. Or the little metal-lined cubbyhole into which rejected coins dropped. Consequently, there was a long period in the seventies and eighties when the mouth-piece of any public phone had a distinct whiff of smoke and ash about it, as if it had recently been set fire to. Ah, how the memories linger. I can almost re-summon that stale odour of nicotine-impregnated plastic to my nostrils now.

Anyway, in 1982 or thereabouts the all-new British Tele-com Phonecard was obviously going to be an absolute boon to you, especially if, for example – like me in the advert – you had broken down in a remote spot and a cloud of smoke while driving a lorry-load of fresh eggs and needed to get a repair service out in a hurry.

I don't mean to ruin the suspense for you, but the gag was that my lorry driver had to place countless calls from a phone box before he could find a garage that was willing to come out to him, with the result that all his eggs had turned to chicks by the end of the ad.

No CGI in those days, by the way: those hundreds of chicks seen spilling out of the back of my lorry were truly hundreds of chicks spilling out of the back of my lorry – imported from a nearby farm for the purposes of our film-ing. And I probably don't need to say, as extras they were a right old handful. Several hundred right old handfuls, in fact. Never work with children or animals, they famously say, and newly hatched chicks amount, in a sense, to both those things at once – a perfect storm of things you shouldn't act with. I've performed with dogs, who can be bad enough when it comes to responding to cues – and even worse when it comes to learning their lines. But let me tell you, getting hundreds of newly hatched chicks to sit where you want them . . . It was anarchy.

Still, I was proud to play my part, however incidental, at what was clearly such a revolutionary moment in the history of personal communication. It's amusing to reflect, though, that just a few years after making that advert, I would be standing in the Nag's Head as Del Boy, in that episode from the sixth series of *Only Fools* entitled 'Sickness and Wealth', trying to persuade Mike the barman, played by wonderful Ken MacDonald, to part with 'forty nicker' for what Del proudly – indeed, cockily – described as his 'executive mobile phone'.

This was 1989, and you can conclude that a mobile phone was clearly a) still something cutting-edge enough to merit the glossy adjective 'executive', and b) still something that needed to be explained in a sentence or two to the casual observer. Alas, as you may recall, this particular model of which Del was an early adopter, and in which he now tried to interest Mike, came complete with a radio-style aerial that shot upwards during his big sell and nearly took Mike's eye out, causing Mike, understandably, to become sceptical.

As Mike says, after reeling back: ''Ere, that aerial's a bit urgent, isn't it?' Incidentally, I love the word 'urgent' in that line. It's not technically even a punchline, and there's barely any time for the audience to pause and take it in, but there is still something so instantly funny about it. And it's very John Sullivan, of course: the poetry of the pub, for which he had such an acute ear.

And that same urgent aerial would, later in the very same episode, shoot up my nose and become lodged there at an inopportune moment while a bunch of us were trembling behind a curtain, hiding from members of the menacing Driscoll family. And that, I can tell you, was one of those moments where the absurdity of what you have ended up doing for a living comes home to you: during the making of that scene, I found myself devoting a significant portion of my working day to seriously addressing the issue of how best to get a mobile phone to dangle by its aerial from my left nostril. It's very hard to take yourself too seriously when this is what you hesitantly define as 'work'.

A typical Sullivan plot development there, though: the thing that Del is most inclined to be swanky about early in an episode – the thing that gives him new reason to be con- fident about himself and his place in the world – will be the thing that ultimately undoes him in the most embarrassing way. Developments like that were seeded and knitted into the script so many times along the way, and it was always done so deftly that you wouldn't see it coming.

However, the point is, Del's newfangled yuppy apparatus didn't come across as something that was going to be utterly life-changing any time soon. In fact, as you possibly remember, it merely appeared to be utterly channel-changing – switching the programme on the Nag's Head's telly, to the irritation of Boycie and some other customers, who were trying to watch the horse racing. 'I think I'll stick with the phone in the public bar, Del,' as Mike says – probably speaking for the majority of people in 1989, at that point when mobile phones were first moving among us and looking almost comically unpromising: bigger than house bricks, unreliable in a built-up area, likely to change the channel in the Nag's Head, etc.

Yet before long, of course – literally within a couple of years of that episode – absolutely *loads* of people would be walking around casually with these devices, albeit made a touch smaller and shorn of the urgent aerials. And now look at us all – pretty much in thrall to our handsets and carrying them with us everywhere we go.

Well, I say 'all' of us: to be perfectly honest, my mobile phone tends to live on the windowsill in our kitchen where most of the time it makes me slightly more difficult to reach than our landline. But I know I'm not typical in that regard and for most people now the mobile phone has become a constant companion and, it would even appear, a comfort in times of need.

Which is fine, by the way. Each to their own. However,

I'm not saying near-instant, twenty-four-hour connectivity hasn't been a blessing to our world in so many ways, but I *am* saying that it has brought its own unique inconveniences, too, which sometimes we prefer to overlook. Consider, for example, the amount of communication which is now typically involved when a friend arranges to have lunch with you. There'll be the call, obviously, to make the appointment in the first place. But then there'll be another call, the day before, to check you're 'still on'.

To which my reaction is always: 'Well, why wouldn't I be? If anything had come up, I'd have rung you, wouldn't I? But it hasn't. So I didn't. And I am.'

And then there might be a further call on the morning of the lunch to say your lunch companion is 'running a little late, but just setting out now'. And there will almost definitely be a call, or at the very least a text, to say he's struggling to find a parking space and may not be with you for another five minutes . . .

Which probably, now I come to think of it, explains why my mobile spends as much time as it does on the kitchen windowsill. In many ways, I think I preferred it when people were simply late and you didn't know why. At least there was a bit of mystery and suspense to cling to. And the phone rang less often.

Still, such is the march of technology – and consider how far we have come on that march, and how fast. First came the miracle of transporting our voices from one room to another down a wire – the telephone! Then we found a way to send our voices through far greater distances across the airwaves – the miracle of the wireless! Then we found a way to send pictures, first in black and white, and then in colour – television! And now we think nothing of sending live, moving images of ourselves in real time to and from little handsets that we carry with us everywhere like religious tokens.

What next? we may well ask. Well, as Derek Trotter's representative on earth, I'm here to tell you. Teleportation, that's what's next. Trust me on this. It's coming soon. Scotty on *Star Trek* has been beaming people up and down for years, and only occasionally had a problem with the nuts and bolts, so why not here on earth?

Don't the boffins tell us that we're just a mass of vibrating atoms? They'll find a way to shift those atoms wirelessly from one place to another, sure as my eggs in that British Telecom Phonecard advert were eggs – or eventually chicks. No more shuffling off to the airport and subjecting ourselves to air travel's myriad inconveniences and indignities. Say goodbye to National Express coaches, too, and cars, also, electric or otherwise. Teleporting is the future. Give it a short while, and we'll all be saying: 'I'll be with you in a shimmer.'

Does this sound a touch unlikely? Reflect on this, then. Imagine if you had been around in Victorian times and someone had told you that one day you would be able to make an appearance on a *Strictly Come Dancing* Christmas special via your mobile phone and without leaving your own sitting room. You would have laughed until your top hat fell off. And then you'd have had that person carted away to an asylum.

A couple of boxes at home on the shelf in the hall: an ARRIVA box, and a SENDA box. That's all you're going to need. Straight after breakfast you'll be dissolving yourself in Taunton and reconstituting yourself three seconds later up at your brother-in-law's in Scarborough. And you won't even need to add water.

But you'll still be phoning ahead to say you're just setting out, of course. That goes without saying.

It's the future of personal transport, and I'd be willing to bet good money on it, were I a gambling man. And I'd also bet good money on the equipment being with us about five minutes after they've finished destroying whole swathes of the UK's most beautiful countryside to build the HS2 railway line, instantly rendering that whole project obsolete.

Because technology, as we well know, is temporary. But Sod's Law is forever.

* * *

Our good deed producing and delivering that video message for Jay Blades on *Strictly Come Dancing* did not go unrewarded. Seven months later, Gill and I received a guided tour of the *Repair Shop* barn in West Sussex.

'Wait until the summer,' Jay had said, 'because the barn can get a bit cold in the winter.' So we hung on until July, and ended up going on one of the hottest days of the year.

Good plan. Instead of freezing, we all melted instead.

What a fantastic day it was, though. It was officially Jay's day off and he should have been out basking in the heat somewhere, but he came into work specially to meet us and look after us. As anyone who watches the show knows, Jay is great fun – just a bundle of positive energy and enthusiasm, committed to showcasing dying skills and trades and utterly determined to promote the value of restoration and recycling in our throwaway society. Amen to that. I share his belief in the increasing importance of mending stuff, and it's how I try to operate in my own life, too.

Most of Jay's team was there that day: Suzie Fletcher, the leather expert; Steve Fletcher, who does clocks and watches; Will Kirk, the woodwork man; Dominic Chinea, the metalwork man; Lucia Scalisi, the art restorer; Sonnaz Nooranvary, the upholsterer; Jayesh Vaghela, the milliner; and Richard Biggs, who turns his expert eye to telescopes, and both his expert eyes to binoculars.

I got to chat with every one of them and was so impressed by how much they know and how passionate they are about what they do. I had the chance to watch them at work, too, performing challenging, delicate, sympathetic repairs, all helping each other out and chipping in with their individual expertise when problems arose. A proper team. I'd been slightly worried that getting a peek behind the scenes might spoil my enjoyment of the show, letting light in on the magic in some way. On the contrary: *The Repair Shop* is as you see it. My enjoyment and respect for what that team do and the way they do it only increased.

What a great place to go to work each day, too, in a truly beautiful country location. You could feel how the environment was feeding everybody's enthusiasm and general demeanour. We had a lovely lunch brought in by a local chef and ate under a tree in the fields, and, with the sun shining, it felt like there was, at that moment, no finer place to be.

By lunchtime, I have to confess, I had developed an advanced case of extreme tool envy. The barn inevitably houses an astonishing collection of really quite wonderful tools and I found myself lusting after many of them and wishing I could take them back to my own humble workshop. Dom the metalwork guy, in particular, had this utterly marvellous toolbox on wheels which seemed to contain every single tool one would ever be likely to need, plus a couple of others just in case.

Oh for one of those on the numerous occasions when I have found myself trudging back disconsolately from a job at the bottom of the garden to fetch the single tool which Sod's Law (see earlier) has belatedly revealed I need. Actually, when Sod is *really* going for it, that can happen three or four times on the same job. A toolbox like Dom's could take whole miles off my working day.

I took along a video to show everyone of Marvo the Mystic – the old, end-of-the-pier, coin-operated fortune-telling machine which I restored with my great film-making friend, Brian Cosgrove. I took it mostly because I thought they would be interested in it, but there was also a little part of me that wanted to make sure they all saw that I know one end of a screwdriver from the other. I'm well aware of the public image we thespians frequently labour under: that we're a bunch of highly impractical, out-of-touch luvvies who couldn't put up a shelf if our parts depended on it – and I suppose, yes, I have met one or two like that, but it's certainly not the whole truth and it's definitely not the case with me. Had the cards fallen differently, maybe I could have been an expert on *The Repair Shop*. Now, that I would have loved. Probably specialising in motorbike restoration, or metalwork like Dom.

Instead, I'll just have to be content to be inspired by those guys, and get on with the work as it arises in my own somewhat scruffier home workshop. Gill has made me a wooden sign to hang on its door: 'Sir DJ's Repair Shop'. But I know that I can only aspire to operate at the level of skill found in the barn. In my case, it's more like 'The Despair Shop'.

ON THE EIGHTH DEL OF CHRISTMAS . . .

Parties and oil rigs

I'm going to talk in this chapter about when the *Only Fools and Horses* Christmas specials properly took off, but before I do that I want to tell you about a picture I own.

Some while ago I was at a dinner where, after the food had been served and gratefully demolished, they held a charity auction – all sorts of desirable items and opportunities getting flogged off, and all in a good cause, but one of those events where you have to be very careful what you do with your fork or else you go home having accidentally dropped fourteen grand on two tickets for a Spanish cookery weekend and a signed photograph of Alan Titchmarsh.

However, on this occasion I seemed to be managing to keep my fork under control and stay out of trouble. One of the lots, though, somewhere around the middle of the auction, was a giant portrait painting of the late John Sullivan – an excellent likeness of him, my artistic eye told me, with, around the edges, little painted scenes from some of the shows John wrote: *Citizen Smith*, *Just Good Friends* and, of course, *Only Fools and Horses*. Within the spirit of the evening – and indeed, perhaps a little under the influence of the spirits on offer *during* the evening – I felt something of an acquisitive urge come upon me. It would be nice for me to own that picture, wouldn't it? Perhaps I would wave my fork after all.

At the same time, though, somewhere inside my head, a sensible voice which hadn't been entirely doused in the evening's freely flowing refreshments said to me: 'But where would you put it?'

I had to concede, it was a good point that my sober self was making, and he was making it well. This was a properly big picture, the portrait element of it being at least life-size, and there are no rooms in my house that have high enough ceilings to hang a painting like that without it looking . . . well, a bit overpowering, shall we say. A bit urgent, even.

You know that thing which is always said about really good portraits, and in particular about the *Mona Lisa* – that the eyes seem to follow you around the room? Well, in this case, if I'd tried to hang that picture at my place, it wouldn't just have been John's eyes that were following me around the room, it would have been the whole of him, and he would have been practically tapping me on the shoulder and breathing down my neck. And much as I loved John – and as amusing as John would no doubt have found that outcome – I felt it was one I could probably get along without.

So I kept my fork to myself and simply looked on as the picture attracted some hectic bidding and went for a decent sum to somebody on the other side of the room. The auctioneer moved on to the next lot – possibly a Spanish cookery weekend, or maybe a signed photograph of Alan Titchmarsh, I now forget – and I thought no more of it.

When the evening eventually came to an end, I got up and began to leave. As I was on my way out, though, a man whom I didn't know approached me, carrying that large painting.

'Here,' he said, 'I saw you were here tonight, and I really want you to have this.'

This man was the successful bidder for the painting of John, and now he was trying to give it to me.

I was really taken aback and didn't quite know what to say. He'd just paid a fair bit of money for that picture. It was his. I said I couldn't possibly take it off him – that I wouldn't feel right.

Plus – though I didn't say this – the ceilings in my house are too low for it.

But he was really insistent. He said that *Only Fools* had given him a lot of pleasure down the years and had made him laugh a lot, and had also moved him, too, and he felt it was his way of repaying all of that and saying thank you.

'Really, I want you to have it,' he said.

Obviously, I was flattered and touched by his insistence, not to mention his generosity. And he was so sincere about it that I felt I had to accept the painting. I thanked him warmly for his kindness and told him how moved I was that he had done that, and I took the picture from him, got it outside and into the car somehow, and then took it home.

It was all extremely touching. But, of course, none of this meant that my ceilings were any higher.

My quandary now, obviously, was that I was the proud owner of a giant portrait of John Sullivan with no wall space on which to hang it. A number of potential solutions to this problem immediately presented themselves and I mulled them on the journey back that night. The most obvious tactic would have been to quietly pass on the artwork to someone with more suitable ceilings – or perhaps even to put it on eBay and trouser a few quid. But neither of those things would have seemed quite right given the sentimental, and not to mention charitable, circumstances in which I had acquired the painting. Plus I really did like the picture . . .

I continued to mull.

'Move to a bigger house' was, I suppose, an option, but that did seem a bit extreme, not least given that we're very happy where we are, actually, and have spent so many years getting the garden the way we like it.

Another possibility might be to get a special extension built on the side of the house in order to provide some extra exhibition space for the painting, like the National Gallery in London did a few years ago – the Sainsbury Wing, as I believe they call it – albeit, in their case, not just for paintings of John Sullivan, but for other ones too. Maybe I could commission a Sainsbury Wing for Jason Towers. Maybe Sainsbury's would be interested in funding it: they've had enough of my money down the years.

Then again, wasn't the extension to the National Gallery exactly the project that Prince Charles famously described, when it was originally proposed, as 'a monstrous carbuncle on the face of a much-loved and elegant friend', causing the original design to be scrapped and the architects to go spinning back to the drawing board? I wouldn't want to court controversy in that way. You have to be so careful, clearly, when you try and make alterations to precious and historic national monuments, such as the National Gallery and my house. The last thing I'd want to do is get the windows all wrong and have Charles turning his nose up every time he dropped round for coffee. (First Thursday of every month, in case you're wondering. And he sometimes brings a bag of washing.)*

Maybe a less controversial – and, indeed, practically invisible – solution would be to dig out the basement underneath the house and create space for the painting in a whole new multi-purpose environment down there. Isn't that what we're always reading about the oligarchs doing to their Kensington town houses? Or at least we used to read about them doing it, when oligarchs were still allowed in the country.

* Just joking. He never brings a bag of washing.

No such problem for me in leafy Buckinghamshire, though, where I still seem to be welcome. So maybe I could call in the diggers, carve out a whole new cavern beneath my house, and create room for the painting, along with a swimming pool, a bowling alley, and parking for fourteen cars.

That would be expensive, though – and extremely disruptive for those of us living upstairs while it was being built. It might just be me, but I find it to be a rule that, the more one can minimise building work in one's house, the more one's quota of happiness rises.

Maybe the simpler and more economical option was to get the scissors out and cut the painting into manageable pieces – bite-size morsels, if you will – and distribute them on various walls around the house, thereby ending up with bits of John in different rooms. But that, too, didn't feel quite right, somehow: it would have seemed like an insult to the fundamental integrity of the artwork, and indeed to the fundamental integrity of John.

Then I had a light-bulb moment. I could put the painting on the back wall of my garage.

Now, I need to be careful about how I explain this because I'm aware that when you say you're sticking something out in the garage, it doesn't necessarily sound like you're offering that thing the warmest of welcomes to your home. I mean, it's not something you find yourself saying to someone when the Christmas presents are getting opened, is it? 'Ooh, how kind of you! And I know exactly where I can put this:

straight out in the garage.' A bit like putting someone's book in the downstairs loo, shoving someone's painting out where the car goes could be interpreted as a mixed compliment.*

But hear me out. The back wall of my garage isn't a place where I stack unwanted Christmas presents and things which have lost their claim to a place in the house – far from it. In fact, it has become something of a . . . well, 'shrine' would be too strong a word for it. But maybe 'wall of remembrance' is closer.

At any rate, it's where I've hung a large picture of Ronnie Barker, my inspiration and mentor and eventually my partner in comedy and close friend. It's a painting based on a photograph taken at the BAFTA ceremony in London in 2003, when Ronnie did me the honour of presenting me with the BAFTA Fellowship award, and, of course, it's a picture of a moment that means an enormous amount to me.

In the compilation of clips from my career that BAFTA screened at that Fellowship presentation, there's a glimpse of a two-man comic play that Ronnie and I did together, right back at the beginning, as part of the LWT series *Six Dates with Barker* – a loopy, quite dark but very funny piece

---

* Incidentally, dear reader, if the downstairs loo is where you choose to store this particular book, then I assure you that I have no problem with that whatsoever. On the contrary, it's your book to do with as you will, and I am flattered that you should consider giving it house room of any kind. Indeed, if the loo is where my book is currently in front of you, I couldn't be more honoured. As long as it won't shortly be behind you.

about a depressed husband hiring a hit man to finish him off but then, when the hit man shows up at the front door as requested, going cold on the whole idea. So then it's the hit man's job to persuade the husband that, no, the notion is still sound and he should go ahead with it. After all, the hit man has come all this way, given up his precious time . . . Ronnie played the husband and I played the hit man. The clip at the ceremony was my line to Ronnie: 'Lucky we met, isn't it?'

Lucky we met: indeed it was. How different the whole path of my career would have been if I hadn't had the great good fortune to meet Ronnie Barker. And the same goes, in equal measure, for John Sullivan, too. Which is why, next to the painting of Ronnie, I now hung the painting of John. So every time I come home in the car from wherever I've been and switch off the engine, I'm looking directly at John and at Ronnie – the two people in my career to whom, by any reckoning, I owe the most. Lucky we met. And they hang together in my private rogues gallery as a constant reminder of those two pieces of amazing, life-altering chance.

However, I have to tell you that, of the two of them, Ronnie is very much the more stable. By which I mean his picture never budges. He just sits there on the garage wall, completely still. John, on the other hand, can't seem to stop fidgeting. At any rate, every week or so, I'll look at that painting and find it's not hanging straight. Which, I confess, is something I'm rather fussy about. It's the legacy of my time as an electrician's apprentice, I suppose – the inheritance from all those days spent running electric cables down walls, stepping back and saying to your mate, 'Does that look right to you?' And he'd give it his best appraising look and say, 'Nah, it's pissed.' And then you'd have to do it again. So even now I can spot a mis-hung picture from a mile away, and if something around the house is on the skew, it offends my eye, and I won't be happy until I've straightened it up.

And so it is with John. I'll come in sometimes and he'll be drunk and I'll have to put him right. A week later, despite my best efforts, he'll have shifted to one side again. It's like he's constantly giving me a gentle reminder as I go about my business: 'Excuse me, don't forget where this success of yours came from.'

And I haven't. And I won't.

* * *

Spirit of Christmas Past! Why do you torment me all of a sudden with this image of a care home and elderly heads in paper hats? What's your point here?

Oh, wait – no, I see where we're going with this. This is 1983, isn't it? That's Russell Harty's care home.

Well, not literally Russell Harty's care home. It's the care home in which, for one night only, Russell's early-evening BBC chat show, *Harty*, has chosen to film its Christmas party – its 'Harty Party' as the producers have by no means resisted the urge to label it, and at which Nick, Lennard and

175

I must now mix and mingle in costume and character as our *Only Fools and Horses* selves.

Ah, the sweet joys of publicity. That said, though, it is at least a positive thing that we have been given some publicity to do. We've been grumbling quite regularly up to now that the BBC aren't pushing us forward for magazine stories and newspaper profiles and appearances on other shows to the extent that they could be doing – things which might put the show under a few more people's noses and expand the audience faster than it seems to be expanding under its own steam.

Sometimes we have even wondered whether the BBC is a touch embarrassed by our little working-class show with its working-class characters and its working-class settings – inclined to sweep us under the carpet a little, in favour of other, less working-class shows. Maybe that was just insecurity on our part. But we did wonder.

Not right now, though. Here in 1983, with the show three series old, the PR machine finally seems to be clicking into gear. Me, Nick and Lennard have already posed for a spread in the Christmas *Radio Times* dressed up as dopey choirboys, in cassocks and white frilly ruffs.

And now here we are, the three of us, with just four days to go until Christmas, in Woking, in Surrey, at the former Railway Orphanage, a giant Victorian building, latterly, as mentioned, a care home. The plan is that, in a large hall filled with tables and chairs and decked for the season, amid plates of sausage rolls and mince pies, Russell and his guests will mingle with residents of the home in party hats. And here, over by the BBC band, which has also been imported into the care home for the evening, Nick, Lennard and I will do our best to drum up some interest in the upcoming, third *Only Fools* Christmas special which, for the first time in its history, has been scheduled to go out to the nation on – trumpet fanfare here – Christmas Day.

Quite late on Christmas Day, it must be said: at 9.35 p.m., to be exact, after *All Creatures Great and Small*. What might be regarded as the season's golden slot – Christmas night, 7.15 p.m. – has gone to *The Two Ronnies*, and we are by no means in a position to argue with the pre-eminence of those two titans at this still young moment in our show's life.

Nevertheless . . . Christmas Day! This is without a doubt the most prominent billing the show has received and we are all, inevitably, highly excited about it, and what it will mean for us and specifically for the chances of our show getting commissioned by the BBC for another series, the possibility of which somehow always seems to be agonisingly in the balance, at every step of the way.

This will also be the first time I have made it onto the nation's screens at the very apex of the holiday period since a certain BBC pantomime almost two decades ago now – and whatever else occurs, it will, at least, be a darned sight easier for my parents to pick me out this time.

So here I sit, in the 'Harty Party' care home, ready to do my promotional bit at this potentially pivotal moment for the future of our show. And, not to put too fine a point on it, I'm a little on edge.

For one thing, Russell Harty and I have, shall we say, some history. Nothing too serious – but definitely some history.

It happened a little while before at an event we were both at, the exact nature of which, I'm afraid to say, has long since boarded memory's barge and floated up the dank canal of yesteryear. What I do recall about that event, though, was that Russell, acting as, I believe, the night's compère, was required to introduce me onstage in front of a quite substantial audience.

What was I going to do when I got out there in front of that audience? A stand-up routine? The 'dogs of war' speech from Shakespeare's *Julius Caesar*? A spot of balloon-folding? Again, memory completely fails me.

But what I do vividly remember is standing in the wings, readying myself to go out, and hearing Russell say the following:

'Ladies and gentlemen, please welcome ... DAVID JANSSEN!'

At the side of the stage, I looked back over my shoulder, just in case. Nope: no sign of David Janssen, the American television actor, best known for starring in the sixties series *The Fugitive*. No sign of David 'Kid' Jensen, the Radio 1 DJ, either. By David Janssen, Russell must be meaning me.

A slip of the tongue, then, on Russell's part? Well, we all make them, if so. But take it from me, it's quite wince-inducing to walk out in front of an applauding audience to whom you have just been introduced as someone else, and try to carry yourself as normal. You feel pretty . . . foolish.

Could I have handled it better? Probably. Should I have handled it better? Most certainly. But with ill-concealed irritation, I took the microphone and spoke as follows:

'Thank you very much, Russell Farty.'

Not very grown-up of me, I'll admit. Neither big nor clever. But at the same time, looking back . . . well, kind of funny. And certainly satisfying as a piece of payback at the time. I believe it even earned me a round of applause.

Still, you know what they say: be nice to people on the way up, in case you should meet them on the way down – or, in my case, here in this care home turned TV studio in 1983, still on the way up.

So, that little incident is hovering, a touch unsettlingly, in my mind. Then there's the set-up for this piece we're about to do, which I'm not altogether happy about. The idea is that the cameras will eventually find the three of us seated at our table among the throng, and, on cue, we'll go into a short, scripted sketch, which John Sullivan has written for us. And then, when we're done, Russell himself will appear at our table and conduct an interview with us, during which we are to remain in character.

That last bit is the part I'm dreading, to be honest. Not that riffing for a few minutes in the character of Del doesn't come easily enough by now. And I don't suppose Russell is planning to spring any particularly devious questions on us in this context. Most likely he'll just ask us what we're getting each other for Christmas and lob us a couple of other fairly soft ones, and we'll be out of there.

No, what's bothering me is the potentially awkward transition from the scripted phase to the unscripted phase. That, for me, has the shape of a moment which could go either way. Frankly, I'm worried it's going to look as naff as hell.

And all of this live on one of the biggest and most-watched shows currently on television.

Anyway, stiff upper lip, and all that. Stiff drink, too, wouldn't go amiss, but that's not going to happen, and not just because we're in a care home. 'No drinking on duty' has long since been a mantra of mine. The two don't mix – or not for me, at any rate. I'm very much like a policeman in that respect, or a vicar – and very much unlike someone who works in Downing Street. The stiff drink will have to wait until afterwards.*

So, the big moment arrives. Russell, on the other side of

---

* I'll tell you someone who wasn't with me on the 'no alcohol while performing' rule: Charles Dickens. When the author did his famous reading tours, knocking 'em dead with extracts from *A Christmas Carol* on a nightly basis all over the provinces, he apparently adhered to a strict pre-performance routine. Breakfast: two tablespoons of rum with cream. Supper: a pint of champagne. Half an hour before curtain-up: a glass of sherry with a raw egg beaten into it. I feel sick already, but for Dickens that intake would power a high-intensity three-hour performance that would have them either rolling in the aisles with laughter or convulsing

the room, introduces us for some reason as 'Grandad, Rod and Del Boy', thereby becoming possibly the only person ever to abbreviate Rodney's name in a public setting. And also, I'm fairly sure, the last. And then the camera swings over, and finds the three of us, getting seated at our table, hunched among the studio guests.

The scripted bit doesn't go too badly: a couple of stumbles, maybe, but nothing to get us hauled up in front of the union. A couple of decent laughs from the assembled care home residents, too. John's script doesn't take a vengeful pop at Russell on my behalf over what we should probably now be calling 'Janssengate', but it does loose off a nice one in the direction of one of Russell's BBC colleagues in the interviewing game.

Del is trying to explain to the other two that he's getting them a Christmas on the cheap by bringing them here, to Russell Harty's party.

'Who's Russell Harvey?' asks Grandad.

'No, you know him,' says Rodney. 'He's like that Michael Parkinson, right, but he's got O levels.'

And if the pace lags, I at least have my cigar to fall back on. When acting, on a Russell Harty show or anywhere else, something to do with your hands is always welcome, and I can report that the cigar delivers exceptional versatility in

---

with tears, depending. I would love to have seen it. But if it's all right with you, I'll still just have a glass of water.

this area: you can put it in your mouth, chew on it, take it out, examine it, wave it about . . . It's altogether a cracking distraction. And on this occasion I'm more than commonly grateful for it.

With the sketch done and dusted with no noticeable casualties, Russell, as planned, comes into shot rather awkwardly, and, as not planned, blows a squeaky toy at Nick. Well, I guess it is a Christmas party . . . He then asks us a few questions, including what we'll be getting each other for Christmas. Again, we just about get away with it, but it's all a bit nervy, not quite natural. Nick and I both seem to be trying to fight a combination of irritation and embarrassment. The only one of us who appears completely at ease with the situation is Lennard, who, with supreme Grandad-style bluntness, solemnly tells Russell, apropos of nothing at all: 'I don't like you. You're not as good as Parkinson.'

Ah, dear old Lennard, bless his memory. There weren't many situations involving *Only Fools* where he didn't seem to be enjoying himself enormously. The whole experience appeared to come as a fantastic gift to him at a point in his career when he had begun to think he was edging towards that state nearly every actor dreads: retirement. He really relished it.

Actually, now I come to think about it, there was ONE time when Lennard wasn't entirely buoyant about the way things were going, and that was when Nick and I crept into the dressing room, where his costume was laid out ready for him, and nailed his shoes to the floor. That really didn't go down well. Normally Lennard would see the funny side of a prank very quickly – which was a highly necessary attribute to have on the set of *Only Fools*. But with this one I think we must have just got him at the wrong time or something, because he absolutely lost it. At one point he was even threatening to get the police involved. Which, of course, only made Nick and me laugh harder. But I swear it was the only time, while working with Lennard, that I saw him looking anything other than cheerful with his lot.

It's all the more poignant, then, to think of how much lay ahead of the show at this point in 1983 – and yet the Christmas special we're promoting, 'Thicker Than Water', will be Lennard's last appearance. A year later, in December 1984, just after we've started filming series four, Lennard will suffer two heart attacks, three days apart, and die at home in his flat. The news will hit us like a sack of bricks. We'll all pack up and go home bewildered at the loss of our friend. And we'll also assume the show is finished. Because how can it possibly withstand the loss of Lennard? But obviously we will not be anticipating how John Sullivan will fold Lennard's death into the storyline, allow us to mourn and celebrate him there in the show, introduce the character of Uncle Albert, and take the series forward.

But I'm getting ahead of myself. For now, at least, in this

vision from 1983, Lennard is magnificently alive, and baiting Russell Harty like a good 'un. The three of us get through Harty's Party and withdraw for that self-promised stiff drink before heading off to our respective homes for Christmas. It's not, perhaps, been the smoothest promotional appearance that any of us will make. But at least the name of David Janssen never came up.

'Thicker Than Water' goes out on Christmas Day. It's the one where Del's long-since vanished father, Reg Trotter, played by Peter Woodthorpe, walks into the flat on Christmas night, eighteen years after he abandoned the family. It's nicely set up and maybe we think we know which way this is all going, Christmas being, of course, a time for reconciliation, and especially in Christmas specials on television. But John's interest once again is in subverting the form, and he isn't going to let the audience have it quite so easy.

Reg is essentially how Del would be if you stripped out all the nice things about him. There isn't much there for an audience to like – or for Del to like, you would think. The pair of them row quite bitterly and Del feels able to dispense some home truths. Yet before he leaves, Del will end up quietly slipping his dad a bit of cash to ensure he's OK. For all that Del can't stand the man and resents the fact that he walked out on them, that's still his father, when all is said and done, and he's not willing to think of him suffering. It was, I think, another of those poignant passages where you see a deepening of Del's character, and it was certainly a very touching moment to play.*

That Christmas Day slot and our promotional efforts earn the show 10.8 million viewers. That's a million and a half more people than watched 'Diamonds are for Heather' the previous year – so, heading in the right direction. Unfortunately, though, it's a million less than watched the final episode of series three just three days earlier.

So, heading in the wrong direction, actually.

We all feel a bit flat. So much for the power of the Harty Party.

* * *

And then, really, the biggest shift of all – the quantum shift: the 1985 Christmas special, 'To Hull and Back'.

Transport me, Spirit – when you've finished taking your cycle clips off, obviously – to the deck of the good ship *Inge*, as it ploughs its way across the choppy North Sea in the general direction of Holland.

Actually, don't. That little tub was like a scene from Dante's *Inferno* most of the time we were on board it. The good ship *Inge*? The good ship *Chunder*, more like. I,

---

* As with a tender hinterland, mentioned earlier, there is no reliable over-the-counter cream for dealing with a poignant passage, but your GP may be able to prescribe something stronger that works, so do consult them – especially if you find you are repeatedly having touching moments.

fortunately, was pre-fortified with seasickness tablets, but practically everybody else, cast and crew, really struggled during those water-borne scenes, and that alleged old seadog Uncle Albert more than any of us. The shade of green that Buster Merryfield turned that day has yet to be seen on any manufacturer's paint chart, and what ended up going over the side of that boat during the making of this film doesn't bear thinking about.

However, on a happier note, I am using the term 'film' advisedly here. For that's exactly what 'To Hull and Back' was – a ninety-minute film, shot over six weeks with a budget that ran to location shoots on the North Sea and in Amsterdam. Unimaginable luxuries. I remember John's script coming in the post. The story was great, of course – a mad caper about the Trotters agreeing to smuggle some diamonds to Holland for Boycie and deciding to go in the back way, by sea. But what really struck me about that script on arrival was the sheer size of it. It was three times as thick as the ones we normally got. You could have used it, rolled up, to beat back a charging elephant. Moreover, it contained no studio sequences in front of an audience, and the whole thing was going to be shot on film stock, rather than on video.

We all went around saying it to each other: it felt like we had graduated to the movies.

And that meant a whole new way of operating. Without the studio audience to think about, the show could work to a completely different set of beats. You weren't needing to hit a laugh every few lines – things could develop much further, gags could evolve over much longer time frames, with the consequence that the clinching laugh, when it came for the viewer, could be that much stronger.

And, of course, this was the point at which the show could have got utterly lost – more lost than Del, Rodney and Albert on the North Sea, so lost that it might never have come back. We've all seen film-length versions of television sitcoms which simply haven't come off. To pluck one out of the ether at random, I don't think anyone regards the *Dad's Army* movie as among that show's finest hours. (I mean the 1971 film version with the original cast, not the 2016 remake which was a different thing yet again.) Even the makers of *The Simpsons*, a programme which I regard as a work of genius, failed to make a movie version quite click. You can't fit a quart in a pint pot, people like to say, but a pint can also look a bit lost in a quart pot, and that so frequently tends to be the case when sitcoms are offered the bigger scope. The extra length and the different story demands don't always suit what was originally there and what people warmed to in the first place.

The good news for us was that *Only Fools* clearly could survive the transition; 'To Hull and Back' ended up proving it beyond a doubt. There was enough in the writing, and enough in the characters, and enough in the direction (by Ray Butt) to sustain that much bigger act of storytelling. Indeed, the show clearly rejoiced in the freedom and the extra space, as did all of us who worked on it.

Lots of scenes stay with me from that episode, but I particularly enjoyed doing that bit when the motion of the boat on the waves causes Del to be abruptly overcome with a surge of patriotism and to step across the deck with some declamatory oratory in celebration of 'this septic isle', while Rodney is in the background, trying to hold on to the contents of his stomach. That was great fun to do, although Nick barely needed to act at that point.

And then, of course, there was the now famous sequence with Del shouting up to an oil worker to be pointed the right way. We all loved that gag and thought it was an absolutely brilliant piece of imagination by John, as well as a defining Trotter moment. Getting lost in the North Sea and stopping to ask directions from an oil rig? It doesn't really get much more Trotter than that.

That said, Nick tells a story about explaining to one of the oil rig guys how this joke was going to play out, and being a bit disappointed to get no real reaction from him at all, and certainly not the belly laugh Nick had been hoping for.

'Yeah,' the guy eventually said, matter-of-factly. 'You'd be surprised how often that happens.'

So, why this access all of a sudden to time and locations and budgets and film stock – this new 'whatever the show needs' attitude on the part of the BBC? Well, blame Arthur Daley, I guess. The story is that Michael Grade, who had just become the Controller of BBC1, got wind that ITV's big Christmas number for 1985 was going to be a film-length episode of *Minder*, the channel's popular and well-established (it had been around since 1979) comedy drama. Worried that 'Minder on the Orient Express', as this special edition seemed to be called, could come to dominate the season over his first Christmas in charge, and determined to make sure that ITV's Christmas tree got well and truly stuffed up its chimney, Michael scanned the weaponry available to him and decided that *Only Fools and Horses*, now four series old, was the tank in the BBC's armoury to take *Minder* on.

And when I say 'take it on', I mean properly take it on: head-to-head, at 7.30 p.m. on Christmas Day.

Now, Michael Grade was a superb broadcasting executive – one of the finest, with a real feel for what people wanted, expected and needed from television shows. And don't get me wrong: I love a ratings battle as much as the next man. But I have to say, I thought the scheduling aspect of this was madness.

Whoever ended up benefitting from plonking the shows down directly opposite each other, at exactly the same time of night, it wasn't going to be the viewer. Remember that this was 1985, well before the age of streaming and catch-up TV, and even video recorders were still quite a rarity in the British home. Basically, if you missed a programme back then, you missed it for good, or at least until such time as the powers that be saw fit to repeat it, which would normally be a year later if you were lucky. In the case of *Only Fools* and *Minder*, it was self-evident that large amounts of people liked both shows – they had a few things in common, after all – so you were only cutting off your own nose, surely, by forcing them to choose. Cutting off everybody's noses, in fact.

Still, the papers loved it, building up the rivalry between Arthur Daley and Derek Trotter like it was the Beatles v. the Rolling Stones. And we all played along with it, on both sides, because it was obviously gold dust, publicity-wise, and also because, I can't deny, it was quite a buzz, after twenty years of trying, to find a piece of your work at the heart of the national conversation all of a sudden.

Did dirty tricks feature anywhere along the line? Well, far be it from me to accuse anybody of outright lying, but the *Minder* team put out the rumour that this might be the last ever episode of their show. Very crafty – the old Frank Sinatra 'retirement' gambit. Guaranteed to put bums on seats. But if 'Minder on the Orient Express' genuinely was meant to bring down the curtain, then can I just gently point out that the show was around for another nine years after this, until 1994? That's an awful lot of comebacks.

I fought back by giving an interview to the *Mirror*:

'It's got to be us, innit. We will be funnier and better, no doubt about that, my son.'

Did I really put it like that, or did the newspaper automatically hear the tone of Del in my voice and decide that a touch of poetic licence wouldn't go amiss in the circumstances? No matter: all is fair in war. I also seem to have accused *Minder* of only having three viewers.

My honest feelings? I was a huge admirer of George Cole, who, of course, played Arthur Daley – and had been a huge admirer since I'd stared up at him in *Scrooge*, on that formative Christmas trip to the cinema that I wrote about earlier. I thought Dennis Waterman, who played Terry McCann in the show, was a brilliant actor, too – one of those people who makes a lot of difficult things look easy. And I was altogether a huge fan of *Minder*, which made my remark about the three viewers a bit rich. I *was* one of those three viewers. I watched it at home and thought it was a fantastic piece of entertainment. I wished the show nothing but well.

And I hoped to heaven that we would beat it to within an inch of its life in those Christmas ratings.

The final score? When the smoke cleared from the battlefield and all the bodies were finally accounted for, *Minder* had got 12.5 million viewers that Christmas night. *Only Fools* had got 16.9 million. A decent victory for the right team, then, and some payback for all that seasickness, and we were all very pleased with ourselves, especially Michael Grade. Looking back now, though, with the benefit of maturity and sweet wisdom on my side, it all seems a bit bonkers. Again, you don't need to be Rodney to do the maths: there were at least 29.4 million people sitting in front of their television sets looking for something to watch that Christmas. What numbers might both our shows have achieved in 1985 if they had been separated instead of being sent into the field to lock antlers with each other?

191

Dennis Waterman died while I was writing this book – in May 2022, at seventy-four. Another good one gone. I knew Dennis, and he was a lovely man. He told me how, in bars occasionally, people with a bit of drink inside them would take him on. Well, he was that tough bloke from *The Sweeney*, wasn't he? That plain-clothes cop who fancied he could handle himself in a ruck. So lairy blokes would have a go. When he told me all this, part of me thought: what gets into people? Can they really not separate the actor from the character he plays? Don't they realise this stuff is made up?

But another part of me thought: blimey, though – that's some tribute to Dennis's acting and the degree to which he inhabited the role. Not only could people not see the join, they forgot there was a join there in the first place.

And then yet another part of me (for I am a man, clearly, of many parts) thought: I'm so glad I never played a tough guy. I've had all kinds of public reactions to Derek Trotter, and Pa Larkin, and Inspector Frost, and Skullion, and Granville. But I can honestly say that nobody has ever wanted to sort anything out with any of them in a car park. Not once has anyone fronted up to me in my local Harvester and said, 'Let's settle this here and now.' I guess I got lucky.

Also, I don't go to my local Harvester. But that's beside the point.

As for where all this high-profile action in 1985 put *Only Fools* in the general scheme of things, perhaps you can get a sense of that from the fact that Nick, Buster and I were asked to represent the BBC in a trailer for the broadcaster's Christmas output that year. It showed us flicking through the Christmas double issue of the *Radio Times*, picking out the highlights.

Del, naturally, seems to be looking forward to watching some of the season's cultural offerings, in particular 'the Royal Ballet doing *The Nutcracker*'.

To which Rodney, drawing the magazine slightly closer to his eyes, replies, 'I ain't surprised in those tights.'

So, not subtle, no: but certainly prominent. (I'm referring to our burgeoning presence on the screen here, not to anything concerning the Royal Ballet's tights.)

And on the cover of the Christmas *Radio Times* which we were consulting in that teaser? Us three, that's who.

Now, that felt like a genuine and unignorable statement about the giddy heights to which we had ascended. People talk about the cover of *Rolling Stone* and the cover of *Vogue* as the twin pinnacles of magazine-based exposure and the surest indications of a person's arrival at the heart of Western culture.

But, dear reader, you and I both know that not to be true. It's appearing on the cover of the Christmas double issue of the *Radio Times* that *really* announces to the world that you've made it.*

---

* These days the cover of the Christmas *Radio Times* tends to be a generic illustration of some kind – a Christmassy cartoon, probably featuring

In that cover shot, Buster, pouring Nick some champagne into a half-pint glass, is in the obligatory Santa outfit, already having the beard for it; Nick is looking cheerful in a knackered camouflage jacket; and I am modelling an exquisite black polo shirt with ultra-suave white detailing, from the Derek Trotter festive-appropriate leisurewear range, and raising a glass of bubbly and a cigar in the general direction of the camera. Cheers!

And frankly, along with the daffy smile, that was a pretty accurate reflection of how I felt about life at that point in the show's history. After all these years of slogging away at it, I was finally part of a truly successful, much-loved show – one that, with Lennard's passing, had weathered a storm that would have finished almost any other programme, yet whose team had pulled together and come through as strong as ever; and, to cap it all, a show that could now attract the best part of 17 million viewers on Christmas Day.

It simply wasn't going to get any better than that. Was it?

Father Christmas, or a snowman, or even The Snowman (as in Raymond Briggs's *The Snowman*), or potentially all three of them. Which no doubt spares the magazine from having to deal with hordes of thwarted, big-star egos, but something – as those of us who are, ahem, multiple recipients of the Christmas front-cover accolade tend to feel – is lost.

ON THE NINTH DEL OF CHRISTMAS . . .

Choppers and gliders

Mission complete and day over. As our two helicopters, blades clattering, rose above the airfield and separated – his heading east, mine pointing west towards the setting sun and home – a voice crackled in my headset.

'Nice to have met you, David,' said Tom Cruise. 'Take it easy and have a nice flight.'

'Good to meet you, too, Tom,' I replied. 'Safe journey and see you somewhere down the road, I hope.'

None of which, dear reader, is invented. None of it. And yes, I'm aware that this tale is something of a digression from the main thrust of our narrative at this point and has nothing whatsoever to do with Christmas, but, frankly, I think I've done pretty well to hold off this long into the book before bashing on about this.

I mean, how often does a person end up chatting, helicopter to helicopter, with Tom Cruise?

Well, I can only speak for myself in response to that

question, and the answer is: once, so far. And I fully intend to tell you about it.

So obviously I'm going to need to explain to you exactly how I came to be in the skies with an open radio channel to the Hollywood A-lister and star of *Top Gun: Maverick*. But in order to do that I'm going to have to tell you first about some work I've been doing recently, exploring the comedy potential of helicopters.

Again, bear with me: I am not inventing this. And I won't be inventing the bit where Tim Peake walks into this story, either. But let me just try and do this one step at a time.

Here's how it panned out. Late in 2021, I found myself invited to attend a meeting with members of the military's Gazelle helicopter display team. They were wondering if it might be possible to create a show involving skilfully flown helicopters which wasn't the usual military display of closely coordinated manoeuvres – as impressive as that is – but was a piece of family entertainment that might be suitable for the Royal International Air Tattoo at Fairford, the world's largest military air display, where helicopters would normally get a bit overshadowed by the Red Arrows doing their business or by fighter jets screaming overhead at Mach 3 and tearing everybody's ears apart.

I was asked to be involved because I am a proud patron of the RIAT, and because I guess, as a pilot, I am known to occupy, somewhat unusually, the ground where entertainment and helicopters meet. So I set aside my labours on this book, picked up a sketch pad and began to come up with some ideas for Olly the Heli – a young helicopter with a friendly face who responds to instructions from the tannoy, does tricks, plays football, helps out around the place, misbehaves a bit, seems reluctant to have a bath before bedtime . . . something perhaps on the Thomas the Tank Engine lines, if you will pardon me that actually rather deft pun.

And then I headed again down to an airfield in Hampshire to explore how this show might work, and what exactly it's possible to do, technically and safely, when you've got helicopters in the air and a crowd on the ground watching. Which is how, among other things, I came to spend a morning in an army airfield in Hampshire, carefully scrutinising ways in which the downdraught from a helicopter blows an enormous ball around.

It's dirty work, I admit. But someone's got to do it.

As I quickly discovered, the guys from the Gazelle display team are a great bunch. Experienced servicemen with serious campaigns behind them, they have that military-bred camaraderie which I can only assume comes from being together in situations which bring you close to your own mortality, and so becomes all the more life-affirming for that. At any rate, their constant piss-taking of each other was a joy to behold and their love for flying was off the charts.

It was suggested that it might be useful for me to see what their standard display looks like.

'Excellent idea,' I replied, thinking: what a treat – my own private air show from a front-row seat on the ground.

In fact, they thought I should experience it from a little closer than that – from a seat in the cockpit.

I think I might have swallowed hard at this juncture.

But . . . play it nice and cool, son, nice and cool, as someone once said. So, buckled up tightly, I sat in one of the army Gazelles while the lads ran through their repertoire of tricks – doing formation flying in amazingly close proximity to each other, their skids almost touching, and then going up in unison, practically vertical, before dropping the nose and plunging downwards through the air, prior to rescuing the descent and pulling out horizontal again.

What can I tell you? It was quite a ride. To witness the precision of those manoeuvres from on board was absolutely breathtaking. This stuff requires such faith – faith in your own abilities and the abilities of everybody else in the team, and also faith in the machine you're flying. If you did these kinds of things in my little helicopter, the blades would fall off.

And, of course, it takes a strong stomach, among other strong things. But I emerged in one piece, managed to walk in a fairly dignified manner across the grass with the chaps afterwards, and thanked them all warmly for an experience that I will never forget.

Only the laundry basket knows exactly how frightened I was, and the laundry basket is sworn to secrecy.

Along with us that day was Tim Peake, the astronaut, who

retains strong connections with the Army Air Corps from his time in the military, and was also consulting on this potential display project. Our paths had crossed once before, in a radio station where we were both promoting books, but I will happily confess that I am more than a little in awe of astronauts. Indeed, I have probably never been as discombobulated as I was when I got the chance to shake hands with Buzz Aldrin at a Buckingham Palace charity garden party one year. I'm not much of a person in general for forelock-tugging and standing on ceremony except where it's absolutely necessary, but I am very much of the opinion that one should rise when an astronaut walks into the room. It's just a matter of the respect that's due. Either that, or the lack of gravity.

I have to say, though, that this did not seem to be an attitude obviously shared by Tim Peake's chums in the Army Air Corps Gazelle display team. The liberal amounts of piss-taking I previously mentioned very much extended to include the first British astronaut to walk in space, who was the constant butt of his colleagues' jokes while I was with them all, and continually roasted for being 'a spaceman' – all of which he took in extraordinarily good part and even seemed to enjoy.

When, in a break, Tim offered to take me for a spin in a Gazelle, I wasn't going to say no, was I?

'Let's go and have a look at Downton Abbey,' said Tim. So we did, flying over the Hampshire countryside until we found Highclere Castle, the monumental dwelling where the television series was filmed – all two hundred rooms of it, sat in five thousand acres of carefully tended land, and therefore pretty hard to miss from the sky. It was something special to fly with Tim. This is a man who has jumped on board a rocket, lived in space for six months, and flown home again in a tiny Russian capsule which, he told me, actually had paper maps of the world in its glove compartment. Before he did all that, he was a military and commercial helicopter test pilot. It was literally his job to take helicopters into the sky and see how far you could push them before they broke. His perfectly normal morning at work in those days would involve flying helicopters up to a couple of thousand feet, switching off their engines and seeing what happened.

Suffice it to say, then, that you feel pretty confident when the helicopter you're sitting in is in the hands of Tim Peake. You also get to feel somewhat humble about your own skills as a pilot. Tim handed the controls over to me at one point, which was a bit like being asked to sit down at the piano and bash out a tune straight after Oscar Peterson has just stood up and left it. No pressure or anything. Still, I flew us for a while, without any tricks, fortunately.

'Do you want to land it?' Tim generously asked as we returned to the airfield.

I wasn't going to push my luck.

'I think I'll leave that to you, Tim,' I said.

So, that was how the idea of Olly the Heli got going – a little production journey that's still in development at the time of writing. We'll see where it ends up.

After that initial meeting, though, I flew with my good friend and esteemed business partner, Leon Harris, to Duxford Aerodrome in Cambridgeshire to do some further research there. The staff member who met us when we landed by the control tower pointed down the airfield where, way off in the distance, a large black helicopter was dimly visible.

'That's Tom Cruise's helicopter,' he said.

Which, of course, was exciting to hear. But it was a long way away and we had some business to do, so, to be honest, we didn't think much more of it. Instead, Leon and I had coffee and got on with our work in the officers' mess.

In due course, a guy came up and introduced himself.

'My name's Jack,' he said.

'And I live in the back of the Greta Garbo Home for Wayward Boys and Girls,' I replied, without hesitation, deviation or repetition.

Jack looked at me in stunned silence. Several awkward seconds passed. Beyond his politely puzzled expression, I could sense him thinking: what's he on about?

And fair enough, really. I mean, the guy was about twenty-five. How could he be expected to be familiar with the lyrics to 'My Name Is Jack', the Manfred Mann hit from 1968?*

---

* If you know, you know. For some of us, it's impossible to hear the name Jack without it automatically triggering the next line of the chorus. I guess the guy got lucky, though: at least I didn't try and sing it to him.

Look, just occasionally my flashes of comic repartee are doomed to wither on the stalk, but what can you do?

Fortunately, this sticky moment passed and Jack got back in his stride. He was introducing himself, he said, because he worked over at the Duxford Imperial War Museum, also on the aerodrome site. The museum was closed to the public at that point, but he wondered if I fancied a little look around.

Ah, the advantages of having a known face. It's a pain sometimes, I'm not going to deny, but just occasionally it works out in one's favour – as for instance when someone is offering you a private tour of the country's finest collection of historic aircraft.

Leon and I were delighted to accept, and Jack organised a car to take us all on the short drive across the aerodrome to the museum. It turned out the car's driver, too, was called Jack. Two Jacks now, then. This was turning into a promising hand in poker.

I decided not to repeat the Manfred Mann line.

Touring the museum was a real privilege. I'm always incredibly moved by the sight of World War II aircraft. It's the product of being a war baby. I feel I grew up with the Spitfire and the Hurricane. They're such powerful, beautiful machines and knowing what our freedom owes to the job they did only increases one's sense of awe. We took a good look at the restored Spitfire, discovered in the 1980s where it lay in Normandy, having crash-landed, and brought back

Here I am with my co-pilot Leon Harris and some other guy who photo-
bombed us.

My sister June and me, standing where our front room used to be . . .

On set for the 1986 Christmas special for *Only Fools*, 'A Royal Flush'. I never win lucky dips.

Credit: Moviestore Collection / Alamy Stock Photo

Jay and Daryl, my twin bodyguards for the *Only Fools* convention. Dedicated to their duties and, if the situation arose, selflessly prepared to take if not a bullet then at least a thrown Kylie Minogue album for me.

Had the cards fallen differently, maybe I could have been an expert on *The Repair Shop*. Instead I'll just have to be content to be inspired by those guys, and get on with the work as it arises in my own somewhat scruffier home workshop.

How different the whole path of my career would have been if I hadn't had the great good fortune to meet Ronnie Barker and John Sullivan. The back wall of my garage has become something of a shrine to them.

Not guilty, your honour. And I have a solid alibi. I'm all in favour of the gesture, though.

We interrupt this book to bring you some breaking grapefruit news. Buoyed by its new-found fame last year (mentioned in my last book), my humble grapefruit tree attempted to bear fruit. Needless to say, it got as big as a pea and then dropped off.

Me with my wife Gill, who puts up with the *occasional* 'Bah! Humbug!' outburst from me.

Credit: Fiona Hanson / Alamy Stock Photo

Me with Gill, Sophie and her friend Esther on our annual trip down the red carpet.

Credit: David Bennett / Getty Images

All things considered, it was no real surprise to me that, when the BBC brought back *Open All Hours* as *Still Open All Hours* in 2013, they chose to make a Christmas thing out of it and launch it on Boxing Day.

The Platinum Jubilee. One moment the crowds feasted their eyes on the gold state coach, the next they were watching a yellow Reliant Regal Supervan III puttering in the same direction. New York, Paris . . . Buck House?

Credit: Jonathan Brady / Alamy Stock Photo

Merry Christmas.

SCROOGE AND THE TURKEY.

From A Christmas Carol.

I look like Scrooge? Who, *moi*? I hope they mean this warm-hearted geezer and not the sour-faced tight-wad from the beginning of the tale.

Credit: Mary Evans Picture Library / Peter & Dawn Cope Collection

to Duxford to be revived and proudly displayed – a truly stirring sight.

In the same hangar as the Spitfire was a bright red biplane. It was being fitted with cameras, after which, apparently, a middle-aged guy called John, who was said to be able to fly anything with wings, was going to take it out and test-fly it. There was a bright blue biplane, too, the wings of which had been reinforced with fibre glass, so they could support somebody's weight. There was also an area of the hangar which had been set aside for desks and computer screens and where people were checking bits of film. It was the *Mission: Impossible* production office. They were working on flying sequences for the next movie in the series.*

As Jack was explaining all this, there was a loud buzz outside and a yellow biplane rolled into view by the hangar's open door.

'Oh, that's Tom coming in,' said Jack casually.

We looked around for a little longer and then Jack offered to show us the place where the museum does its restoration work. We left the hangar and walked out onto the tarmac. There, near the now parked-up yellow biplane, stood a small group of people, including the somehow unmistakable figure of Tom Cruise.

'David!' Tom called out as we passed, a look of disbelief on his face. 'Unbelievable!'

* *Mission: Impossible – Dead Reckoning Part One*, due out in 2023.

He left the group and came barrelling towards me.

'Man, I absolutely LOVE your work. All of it! But who would have thought I would ever get to meet you?'

OK, none of that happened and he didn't say that at all. In fact, I'll be eternally grateful to the woman who, just as we came near, was getting a photograph taken with Tom, but who spotted me and said, 'Ooh, my lucky day! Can I get one with you both together?'

Excellent timing. Tom must have been thinking, 'I might not know who this guy is, but these other people seem to, so . . .'

Anyway, I moved in for the picture, and, when that was done, Tom and I were introduced to each other and fell to chatting. Of course, as I was able to inform him, he and I share many things: a seemingly effortless sex appeal, a long string of leading roles in blockbusting action movies, and a widely remarked longevity at the very top of the global entertainment business. Plus, of course, that famous sun-kissed glow.

What is perhaps less remarked upon in the glossy magazines, however, is that we also happen to share, more or less, a height. Standing with him, eye-to-eye on the tarmac, I had a light-bulb moment.

'I could work as your stunt double.'

Because Tom famously does his own stunts, of course. Absolutely insists upon it, as much as he possibly can. Me too, down the years. Dangling off a ladder, dropping off a bike, falling sideways through a bar flap, bursting through a closed serving hatch . . . As we've amply seen during these pages, whenever the script called for it, I've been happy to put my body on the line. For one thing (and Tom will back me up here), it always looks better if you do it yourself. Nobody gets to see the join. And for another thing, it's good fun.

Or it is if you're the kind of person who, like Tom and me, is drawn to stunt work. Maybe it's genetic. Maybe we just can't help it. Maybe it's just who we are. I certainly enjoyed that line that Tom came up with at the Cannes Film Festival in 2022 when he was doing press for *Top Gun: Maverick*. Somebody asked him why he does so many stunts.

'Nobody asked Gene Kelly, "Why do you dance?"' Cruise replied.

Say it loud, Tom. Say it loud, my friend. I believe I uttered something very similar on the set of 'Tea for Three', in the fifth series of *Only Fools*, when my pleas to do the scenes in which Del gets sent on a madly out-of-control hang-glider journey across the English countryside seemed to fall on stony ears.

I was serious, though. That sort of thing was right up my street – or rather, right up my runway. For a good while in the late 1970s and early 1980s, whenever I got a Sunday off, my idea of getting away from it all was to drive to Northolt Airfield and take up a glider for a few hours. I absolutely loved it: the silence, the isolation. It took me right out of myself. That was where I first got the flying bug which in due course led to me learning to pilot a helicopter.

So, a spot of hang gliding? I was rubbing my hands with glee. Nothing like combining work and pleasure.

No go, though. The show's insurance wouldn't allow it. Too risky, allegedly. And fair enough, I suppose. If I had fallen out of the sky midway through shooting, it could have had some rather nasty consequences for the rest of the series, not to mention for anyone who had the misfortune to be underneath me at the time. So, reluctantly, I stepped aside and let the professionals take over.

In fact, as it happened, the wind was so blustery on Butser Hill in Hampshire on the day of filming that even the stuntman they'd brought in, a guy called Ken Barker, wasn't allowed to get off the ground. Ken, you should know, was a highly experienced stunt double who had worked on *Superman III* and *Labyrinth*, so had definitely seen some major action in his time. Yet donning the camel overcoat of Derek Trotter proved to be more dangerous and problematic, I think, than any of them.

We had to rig it in the end. For me it became a hang glider in the most literal of senses: I hung from it, roped to a crane which lifted me just a couple of feet off the ground. There, buffeted by the breeze but otherwise stationary, I was a sitting target for the cameraman just below me, who could film me, as if airborne, against a background of pure sky.

Once more, as I dangled there, waiting for the shot to be

set up, I had cause to reflect ruefully how much of my career had been spent, quite literally, hanging about – from that initial BBC pantomime in 1965 to this, some twenty years later. I came in on a harness; it seemed quite likely that I would be carried out on a harness.

Tom Cruise, clearly, would have shared my frustration at being thwarted on Butser Hill. But now, face-to-face with him on the tarmac at Duxford, I sensed an opportunity. Maybe I could ease some of his workload, stunt-wise – take some of the pressure off, make those *Mission: Impossible* movies just that little bit less impossible. I tried to explain to him that he knew it made sense . . .

'If you break an arm or something, the whole production comes to a halt,' I said. 'I could save the producer a fortune here.'

'But I am the producer,' Tom said.

'Then I'm talking to the right person,' I said.

'I'll bear your suggestion in mind,' Tom said.

'Well,' I said, the light going on in my brain again, 'perhaps I could be your double in the love scenes, leaving you free to do the more arduous stuff.'

Tom again said he'd think about it.

We then talked a little about helicopters and flying, before bumping fists and moving on. What an affable and warmly approachable chap he seemed – quite strikingly so for a Hollywood superstar.

Leon and I returned to the helicopter late afternoon, with

the light fast fading. It was as we were talking to the control tower directly after take-off that we heard Tom call in and ask for permission to taxi to the end of the runway for his own take-off. He must have heard us, too, because that was when we had our little exchange of farewells across the air-waves. And with that we went our separate ways.

Probably only a matter of time before I hear from him on that stunt-double proposal, though. All very exciting.

ON THE TENTH DEL OF CHRISTMAS . . .

Cocktails and riot shields

I am often asked which of the *Only Fools* Christmas specials is my favourite, and it's always a question I slightly struggle with. For one thing, there's a lot of riches to pick from here. For another, the shows lodge in my head for different reasons, and often for quite personal or particular reasons.

From my own private perspective, very often I find I am quietly proudest of the moments where playing Del pushed me as an actor. Those aren't necessarily the big showpiece moments that people love and celebrate, like the Batman and Robin chase sequence in 'Heroes and Villains', though I'm inordinately proud of that too, of course. But often what my memory tends to alight on seem to be the much smaller, more nuanced things.

For instance, there's a tiny bit in 'Dates', the 1988 special. That was the one that brought Tessa Peake-Jones into the show as Raquel, changing the whole game for Del, and therefore, by extension, changing the whole game for me, portraying Del. After this there were all these new realms that the character would need to go into – finding love, moving in together, becoming a father . . . There were whole new emotions to explore and whole new layers of detail to find.

But on their first date, Del chooses to go upmarket and takes Raquel to a restaurant at the Hilton Hotel on Park Lane, where the table is very poshly laid. I suggested doing a bit where both of us would get in a muddle about knowing which pieces of cutlery to use – a moment of social anxiety which turns into a bonding moment between them.

Now, I know that's never going to get the big laughs and reruns like falling through a bar flap, but, truly, that's a moment in the show that I'm abidingly proud of. As I tried to explain earlier, finding those little pieces of character-defining behaviour has been what I've loved about acting since the first day I walked into a theatre, and the satisfaction of happening on one that absolutely works is, for me, as good as anything the job offers.*

---

* 'Dates' was the episode that John Sullivan often said was his favourite. It won the BAFTA for Best Comedy the following year. By the way, some eagle-eyed clever clogs claim to have spotted a 'continuity error' in this episode in the fact that Del is seen reading a newspaper in two scenes which are meant to be whole weeks apart – but it's the same newspaper. Well, did you never, at a bored moment, pick up a paper that's been left lying around, find it's days old, but read it anyway? That was no mistake: we were just trying to be true to life as people actually live it. That's my story, anyway.

Similarly, 'Miami Twice', from 1991, would have to feature among my proudest memories of the show, but maybe not exactly for the reasons that other people like it. Yes, obviously I vividly remember that episode for the opportunity it gave me – not one which had come up before in my life, I must say – to shout across the water at Barry Gibb of the Bee Gees, and then, later, take tea and a piece of cake at Barry's gaff overlooking the water.

Where I learned, incidentally, that he was a) admirably down to earth and b) just the most enormous fan of our show. As an ex-pat, Barry apparently used to insist on having two things flown out to him from the UK that he couldn't get in the States: Jaffa Cakes and tapes of *Only Fools and Horses*. Ah, that rock'n'roll lifestyle.

And I vividly recall the Miami hotel we stayed in and drinking cocktails and hanging out in the sun with Nick and mucking about on boats in the Everglades, and thinking, 'Is this actually work?'

I also vividly recall the looks on the faces of some of the cast when the scripts were handed round and they realised that they weren't in those scenes.

But the actor in me likes 'Miami Twice' most for the opportunity it gave me to play two parts – Del, of course, and his mafioso doppelgänger, Don Occhetti – and to try and pull off the scenes they have together, which is a technically tricky thing to do. Another different experience, and another stretch.

I also remember the madness of the press around that trip. Antoni Corone, who played Occhetti's son, Rico, was an American actor (he'd been in *Miami Vice*) who didn't really know how big a deal *Only Fools* was in the UK until he suddenly found himself being taken aside by a reporter from one of the tabloids and offered $500 in used notes for his script.

Antoni, being a man of high principle, declined. Or, at least, I think he did. But that was the level of the temperature around the show at that time. The press were determined to get the scoop on what we were up to, to the point of tailing us all the way across the Atlantic. Whenever I moved around the set in costume as Don, I had to be accompanied by guys holding up blankets to conceal me from view. If a photo of me dressed up like that had leaked out, it would have blown the story and spoiled our Christmas surprise.

Similarly, I feel very fondly disposed towards 'Modern Men', the middle episode in the 1996 trilogy, and in particular the scene where Del and Rodney get stuck in a lift and talk through Cassandra's miscarriage. (It emerges, of course, that Del secretly sabotaged the lift in order to bring about the circumstances in which this difficult but necessary conversation could take place – a highly Sullivan-esque twist.) That was a scene that even John said he was nervous about putting in, and it's one I'm fiercely proud of, and I know Nick is, too. Somehow it makes me love it even more that it comes in the episode directly after the one with the Batman and

Robin scene. That we were now part of a drama that could range within an hour of its lifespan from daffy costumed hilarity and caped superhero high jinks to sincerely addressed issues of birth and death spoke volumes about the journey the show had been on and what it had become. 'Christmas Crackers' this was not.

Questions about acting aside, though, if I was picking episodes on the basis of 'moments that made me laugh then and still make me laugh now' . . . well, again, I'd be a long time getting to the bottom of that particular pile, but Buster Merryfield's gasp of horror in 'Rodney Come Home', the special from 1990, will always rank highly with me in this category – and not just because I actually DID laugh at the time.

The set-up is that Rodney and Cassandra are, yet again, having some relationship difficulties, and this time Rodney seems to be planning a crafty date with another woman. Del, who is appalled, instructs Uncle Albert to assist him with the talking-to that he is about to give his brother by injecting an expression of shocked moral horror into the conversation at the appropriate moment. The gormless intake of breath that Buster came up with for that moment is rightly treasured – BAFTA-worthy on its own, if you ask me.

But when Buster produces that gasp for the third, entirely incorrect time, I'm afraid I go. As I swipe at him with the newspaper and deliver the line 'I'll whack you one in a minute, believe me', there's a smile in my eyes that strictly

213

speaking ought not to be there. Simply couldn't help it, though.

Corpsing, dear reader: it happens to the best of us.

In this line, everything about the Peckham Spring Water ruse in 'Mother Nature's Son' continues to amuse me very strongly, too. Or I might go for 'Fatal Extraction' and the scene where Del's late-night, over-refreshed and altogether utterly terrible singing of the Barry Manilow ballad, 'One Voice', starts a full-scale riot on the estate which the police will eventually have to deal with using shields and horses. That seems exactly as funny to me today as it did then, if not a little more so. And finally I had found a part in which my singing voice – never the strongest weapon in my acting armoury – could be used convincingly.

Initially a professional singer was brought in to cover for me. I thought about this development for a while: the implicit assumption was that my voice was so bad that I couldn't even be trusted to sing badly. Was I a little hurt by that suggestion? I may have been. And did I feel a small but satisfying burst of vindication when the singer's recording was dubbed onto the footage and it didn't really sound right, obliging them to come back to me and ask if I could step in after all?

No, actually, because I *really* don't like singing.

Also, talk about up against it. Barry Manilow, I'll have you know, layered his voice forty times for his most famous recording of this song, so he had thirty-nine more chances than I did to make a splash. Hard enough for someone like me to go up against one Barry Manilow, but forty all at once? Not a hope. Anyway, I couldn't help but laugh when, several years later, in 2010, I saw that Manilow had performed this song at a special concert in Oslo to mark the awarding of the Nobel Peace Prize.

Peace? Depends where you sing it, Barry. And who sings it.

On the other hand, if I was picking out episodes on the basis of sight gags, I might go for 'The Frog's Legacy', the 1987 special, which contains, in my humble opinion, one of the absolute classics: Rodney, in the job that Del has found for him as chief mourner at the local funeral directors, leading the hearse the wrong way down a one-way street. John told me he had actually seen this done, in south London. Oh, to have been a fly on that chief mourner's Victorian-style top hat.

But when I think about that episode I also think about how it was the last to involve Ray Butt, who was leaving to take charge of comedy at Central Television. Ray had been on board as producer and director from the start and he was a lovely, easy-going guy who set the tone around the place. His departure caused John Sullivan to wonder about packing up. The show had run for five series at that point, and the Christmas episode had done some tying up of what had been one of the big narrative strands since the beginning – the mild but persistent mystery of Rodney's paternity. It could have felt like a decent enough place to stop. Maybe if 'The Frog's Legacy' hadn't gone down well, John would have gone

215

through with it and the show would have ended at Christmas 1987 – before 'The Jolly Boys' Outing', before 'Miami Twice', before 'Time on our Hands' . . .

Our dear pal Fate may be said to have trembled in the balance here.

But that special did go down well, and John's faith was restored. So, did a mad tale involving a former navy frogman, an explosives expert called 'Jelly' Kelly and a bungled post office raid actually end up saving *Only Fools and Horses*? Well, you could argue the case, and stranger things have happened. Certainly, Tony Dow, who had been production assistant, moved up to replace Ray and the show set off again, bound for its highest heights.

*   *   *

And then there's the one I remember because it almost didn't get finished . . .

John Sullivan was one of nature's more voluminous writers. He couldn't help himself. When he got going, the ideas flowed and the pages accumulated. I have letters from John that run to a side and a half of A4 and they're just an invitation to lunch. So it didn't really surprise any of us when, asked to come up with a three-minute *Only Fools and Horses* sketch for the Royal Variety Performance in November 1986, John wrote a first draft which was twenty-five minutes long.

Who knows? Maybe the Queen Mother would have enjoyed an almost episode-length edition of *Only Fools* staged in her honour that year. But unfortunately the producers of the Royal Variety Performance had a few other acts to squeeze in as well: Bob Monkhouse, Ken Dodd, Rory Bremner, Victoria Wood, Aled Jones, Nana Mouskouri, Petula Clark, Victor Borge, Lulu, to name only those. Oh, and also Paul McCartney, no less, appearing at a Royal Variety for the first time since being there with the Beatles in 1963, when John Lennon had instructed the people in the cheaper seats to clap along and the others to rattle their jewellery.

Possibly even topping that, in my humble opinion, Angela Rippon had apparently agreed to join us at the Theatre Royal Drury Lane to reprise the high-kicking dance routine she had debuted for the Morecambe & Wise Christmas show in 1976 – regarded as an iconic and vanishingly rare public appearance by a newsreader's legs, which were normally kept entirely below desks in those days and were therefore a closely guarded secret.

And also on the guest list, it seemed, was my old pal Ronnie Barker, who had been given the job of greeting the royal party – the Queen Mother, accompanied by Sarah Ferguson – at the door of the theatre, dressed in a liveried frock coat and in character as Arkwright, the stuttering shopkeeper from *Open All Hours*.

Brave man. And to think I blanched at doing a bit of

in-character improv with Russell Harty. I could only admire the seeming ease and aplomb with which Ronnie would eventually pull this off, handing the Queen Mother a bunch of flowers and then saying, 'That'll be one pound fifty, please. Oh, no, you don't carry money with you, do you? Like Granville.'

So, a crowded bill, all things considered, and, at the end of the day, only space enough in there to treat the Queen Mother to the three minutes of *Only Fools* which John eventually, reluctantly, whittled his script down to.

And just as well, really, because we were busy enough at this point, without landing a whole extra episode on our shoulders. Beyond busy, in fact. We were making what would become the 1986 Christmas special, 'A Royal Flush' – or at least it would become that if we managed to finish it in time, an outcome which was looking terrifyingly unlikely as the shoot wore on and the deadline approached.

That shoot was six weeks long, in various locations around Salisbury and in Derbyshire, and intended to wrap in mid-December. And it had some lovely stuff in it. This was the one where Del ends up chaperoning Rodney at a posh weekend shooting party – and turns out to be rather good at the shooting. That scene contains one of my favourite moments, an instance of what I suppose we can only describe as 'cockney glue ear' – a mishearing by Del which is entirely dependent on London pronunciation. It occurs as Del is preparing to shoot.

'Ready when you are, John.'

'Do you mean "pull"?'

'Oh, sorry, Paul. In your own time, my son.'

It only works if, like Del, you instinctively pronounce 'Paul' as 'pull'. But if you do, it works very well indeed.

That show also gave me the chance to act with the great Jack Hedley, who played the wonderfully scornful Duke of Maylebury. Jack wasn't all that long off the set of *For Your Eyes Only*, the James Bond movie, but I'm sure that experience paled into insignificance for him beside the high glamour of a couple of days' work on an *Only Fools* Christmas special shoot.

But oh, the problems that shoot endured. It was utterly plagued by delays and slippages and outbreaks of our old friend Sod's Law. We fell behind schedule very early on and kept going from there. One step forward, three steps back. When the schedule starts to fall apart on a shoot, a very different kind of energy comes over the place – a sense of growing panic which isn't always the best to work under.

Nick and I didn't help matters by falling ill on a rota basis. I woke up one morning and found I had no voice. You can push through quite a lot of things on a shoot, but when you sound as though you've been gargling nails and paraffin for a fortnight, it doesn't leave you very much wriggle room. My absent voice took me out of commission for three days, following which, with perfect timing, Nick went down with the flu. That was a week lost in total – about a sixth of the available time. I don't think either of us had missed a day's shooting through illness before this. But that was the kind of shoot it was.

As Christmas loomed ever larger on the horizon, we started to wonder whether we would ever get the whole script filmed in time. It reached the stage where the idea was floated that maybe, with at least the location material in the can, we could act the studio scenes in the Trotters' flat live, at the time of broadcast, on Christmas Day itself. Could we not play the recorded material off-tape and then cut live to the studio in between, like on a current affairs show?

This would have been a first in so many directions. I'd spent numerous Christmas Days watching telly. I'd never spent any Christmas Days *making* telly.

Mind you, think of the overtime we'd have been able to ask for. Double time? Triple time, more like. Plus a big fat tip.

Fortunately for our nerves and our Christmases, and almost certainly the show, that particular spare-parachute rip-cord never had to be pulled. Everything we needed did get filmed in the end, including the flat scenes. But it all happened so close to the wire, doing nobody's blood pressure any good. The show was still frantically being edited late into the night on Christmas Eve, with the broadcast slot just hours away. It was skin-of-the-teeth stuff.

So, in many ways, the distraction of a live appearance at the Royal Variety Show bang in the middle of all this chaos was the last thing we needed. But it didn't seem to be an offer the show could really refuse. People fall over themselves to give a performance 'by royal command', as the rather intimidating phrase has it, although, to be honest, I think in our case it was more Michael Grade's command than anyone's specifically at the Palace. But anyway. When you are called . . .

So Buster, Nick and I found what time we could to rehearse John's script, which was very little time, and then, in the middle of the shoot, feeling badly underprepared in one direction and badly behind schedule in the other, off we went to London.

Ah, the unique buzz of the Theatre Royal on a Royal Variety Performance night, with the cream of British show business in attendance and curtain-up nearing. I wish I could tell you something about it, but I can't because we were nowhere near the place at the time. The three of us arrived in the West End to find that we had been – or so it seemed to us – carefully corralled where we couldn't do any damage. The aforementioned cream of British show business was applying its slap in the illustrious, and above all convenient, dressing rooms of the Theatre Royal; we, meanwhile, were among a batch of acts – including, oddly enough, Tyne Daly and Sharon Gless from the US cop show *Cagney & Lacey* – who were stationed over the road in the Fortune Theatre, which had been requisitioned for the afternoon and evening as a kind of overflow car park.

The poor relations again! We stayed in our dressing room for the whole show until our call, at which point a production assistant wearing a headset led us over the road into the theatre, via the stage door, and guided us into the wings. And there we all stood in the dark until she got the signal in her earpiece and we heard her say, 'Go.'

I believe that was the most anxious I had ever felt while waiting in the wings of a theatre. Take it from me, it puts you on your mettle when you know you're about to walk out in front of a packed house containing royalty and a full selection box of la-di-da types to perform an under-rehearsed piece that you've never done publicly before. Everyone else, all those big stars on that bill, seemed to be doing slick routines that they had already honed. Only we seemed to be going where we had never gone before – and doing so in an underprepared and slightly chaotic way which seemed to be entirely typical of our seat-of-the-pants operation.

Still, out we went, fumbling our way onto the stage in the semi-darkness, pretending to believe that we were in Chunky Lewis's nightclub in the West End, dropping off a dodgy consignment of whisky, and only belatedly working out where we actually were. Entirely fitting, of course, that when the *Only Fools* team finally got to join the black-tie-wearing elite of British light entertainment, they would do so in a scenario that had them arriving in the room entirely by accident. The story of our show, you could almost say.

At the peak of that scripted confusion, I found myself squinting up at the royal box and declaiming the immortal line:

'Hello, Chunky – is that you?'

And, as has now gone down in show-business legend, the Queen Mother – working entirely without a script, let's not forget – responded by smiling and giving a regal wave. (I guess any wave given by the Queen Mother was a regal wave. But you know what I mean.)

Now, to be honest, this moment in the skit was a bit of a no-no. Long-standing protocol insisted that none of the performers onstage at a Royal Variety Performance were meant to engage with the royal guests of honour, or bring them into their act in any way. Like speaking to the Queen before she has spoken to you, or stubbing your cigarette out in a Buckingham Palace teacup, this was simply regarded as bad form. At the Royal Variety, any attending royals were to be left entirely alone to enjoy the show, and if you were looking to the audience for a willing assistant for your magic juggling act, or somebody to hypnotise, or whatever, you were under strict instruction to look anywhere other than the royal box. Those were just the rules.

To put it in theatrical terms, it was like a royal version of the fourth wall – a fourth wall with, if you like, metaphorical soldiers in bearskin hats standing guard in front of it – and you were not supposed to break it, even for dramatic effect. In fact, especially not for dramatic effect.

And what had I just done? Well and truly broken it. And for dramatic effect.

Still, if you don't have a little push at the boundaries every

223

now and again, you won't ever change anything, will you? And let's just lend our so-called rebelliousness that night a bit of perspective here. The word was that Max Bygraves had been utterly determined to keep in his routine a pungently fruity joke about Princess Michael of Kent and had only been narrowly persuaded to leave that pungently fruity joke out after some probably equally pungently fruity toings and froings with the producers. In the wider context of what Max seemed to be hoping to get away with, my little exchange with the Queen Mum was surely among the very mildest of indiscretions.

And Ronnie Barker had already asked her for a quid fifty!

Well, whatever the Queen Mother may have felt about it, and whatever discomfort I may have inadvertently caused her, it didn't stop her daughter knighting me, as you may know, in 2005. And closer to the offending moment, Sue Lawley certainly didn't seem to be sucking her teeth too hard about it, either. Sue was doing the commentary for the BBC broadcast, which went out a few nights later. After the show there was that traditional moment where the cast lined up backstage to be presented to the royal party. Nick, Buster and I were graciously allowed to come over from the other side of the street again for this, and at the moment when the Queen Mother was introduced to the three of us, Sue said: 'It used not to be done to incorporate the occupants of the royal box into your act, but I think they got away with it tonight.'

Indeed. In more than one sense.

Afterwards, a car took Nick and me back down to

Salisbury. Slumped in the back seat, relieved at having got through that sketch without drying or otherwise making undue idiots of ourselves, we uncapped a half-bottle of whisky. A little while later, the whisky began to take effect in more ways than one and we asked the driver to pull over.

Standing a touch unsteadily in the bracingly cold, late-November air and looking out across a dark field, I took a little moment to reflect on the great swings and roundabouts of life and how randomly they transport us on this earthly journey. One minute you're performing by royal command, the next you're emptying your bladder in a lay-by beside the M3.

By the time we reached Salisbury, the whisky bottle was empty. Yet somehow the next day we were up at the crack of dawn and back at it on the set. I was running on pure adrenaline in those days. The whole show seemed to be.

* * *

Of the tips I can offer, based on my long and esteemed years at the coalface of nationally broadcast light entertainment, being extremely wary of working with children and animals would be right up there, of course. With a special mention, as we have seen, for recently hatched chicks.

But also prominent would be avoiding filming in a moving coach.

Nothing to do with carsickness, although that could be an issue. No, it's the continuity problems. It stands to reason, really. If your coach is moving, then so is the view out of your coach's windows. And that means that, as you cut backwards and forwards between various shots of people inside the coach, the stuff that can be seen over the shoulders of those people is going to be jumping around all over the place, and a long, sticky and altogether nightmarish session in the editing suite can only ensue.

Another tip: if your plan is later to blow that coach up in front of the cameras, then make sure you get the shot right first time. The same, I can attest, very much applies to shots involving dropped chandeliers. Expensive things, coaches and chandeliers.

This important wisdom about coaches comes to you courtesy of my experiences making 'The Jolly Boys' Outing', the *Only Fools* Christmas special for 1989, where we did indeed manage to blow up the coach correctly first time (admittedly an already wrecked, substitute coach, and not the one we'd been driving around in all day), and where cutting the moving coach sequences was indeed a nightmare. But it was worth it. A Christmas special about an August bank holiday? This was John Sullivan at his most confrontational in terms of the traditional expectations. How far away from stuffed turkey and paper hats could you get? No further, surely, than Margate beach in August.*

---

* It was August in the story, but we filmed it in May, just in case anybody's wondering. A sunny May, thankfully.

So, yes, as I was saying when we came into this chapter, my favourite *Only Fools and Horses* episode is a question too knotty to be resolved: too much choice, too much baggage, too much history.

But if I could only keep one . . .

And yes, it's partly the exploding coach, because that's such an enormous comic moment – wonderfully framed by the conversation that Rodney is having with Cassandra from the nearby phone box, defending his brother against Cassandra's accusation that something always goes wrong when Del is around.

'I agree that Del gets a bit out of hand. But I think it's unfair to say that everything he touches goes wrong.'

Kaboom!

Nick's reaction shot with the phone receiver still at his ear is one for the ages. But the shot of the rest of the cast, looking on in shock, bathed in an orange glow, will also tickle me for ever more.

But more than that, even, it's the 'Everybody's Talkin'' sequence – the aerial shot of Margate seafront from the camera in the helicopter, which picks up the coach, bringing everyone down for this day at the seaside. And then we go on board with the cast and start switching between interior and exterior, the day's high jinks starting to unfold. And Harry Nilsson's 'Everybody's Talkin'' is playing, setting the mood for what's to come, and it just flows.

Today you wouldn't allow the sequence to do that: you'd

come in and out on the beat, puncture it with lots of shots – cut, cut, cut – and totally destroy the mood. But the director, Tony Dow, had the courage and the sensibility to let the scene run and play itself at length, to take its time, allow us to be in the moment and enjoy it.

And I hate to say it, because you risk sounding like some old fuddy-duddy, but actually, in this case, I don't care because I think it's true: they just don't make them like that any more.

I struggle to write about the way that sequence works on me now. It's a rush of pure nostalgia. Such powerful emotions, so much sentiment, such a massive tug on the heartstrings. Nowadays it reads to me like a cine film of a family holiday. I know we're all acting, all playing characters that aren't ourselves. But it's different from any of the scripted sequences, because it's an assembly of clips of us simply mucking about – charging around on the beach, larking about in the shallows, and so on. And, of course, we're doing it in character, and in costume, and we're making a television programme, not having a holiday. But the way that film gives you the interaction between the cast, it feels to me now like candid shots, as if the camera had just been left to run and caught us being ourselves.

And yes, the show would get bigger than this: the trilogy for Christmas in 1996 would rise to its giddy heights, the 'Time on our Hands' episode would find that 24.35 million audience and break records for good and practically set fire to the National Grid, which, of course, would have been a very Trotter-y thing to happen. And yes, all of that was obviously just the most astonishing and exciting thing to be a part of.

Yet, for me, it's all here already, really, compressed into this single sequence from seven years earlier, down there in Margate – the gang of friends that the cast had become, and the sheer fun of it all. And so many of those faces no longer with us, of course. Nowadays the glimpse of John Challis reaching across to swipe my hat off is so poignant that I practically have to close my eyes, and the whole thing is a world that's gone.

So if someone were to ask me to sum up what, at its very best, it felt like to be in the cast of *Only Fools and Horses*, I would say to them, 'Look, I can't really tell you, to be perfectly honest. Because I've tried many times and I never seem to have the words to do it justice.'

And then I would say, 'But I *can* show you this . . .'

And I would play them that 'Everybody's Talkin'' sequence from 'The Jolly Boys' Outing'. Because that's what it felt like to be in *Only Fools*. That's what it felt like, right there.

ON THE ELEVENTH DEL OF
CHRISTMAS . . .

Tattoos and Kylie albums

Hindi, the official language of India, has no word for 'plonker'. How do I know this? Because I went to a conference centre in a hotel near Bedford in May 2022 and it turns out that it's the kind of thing you learn when you do that – if you go on the right day, anyway – along with a thousand other things including, overwhelmingly, how much people still love *Only Fools and Horses*.

I mean, *really* love it. And not just for Christmas.

The conference centre in question was in the Sharnbrook Hotel, and the occasion was the Only Fools and Horses Appreciation Society's 40th Anniversary Convention, marking forty years since the show's launch, in 1981.

Now, you don't need to be Rodney and have the relevant GCSE up your sleeve to be able to do the maths here and to find the numbers slightly wonky. Don't blame the organisers, though. This anniversary event was originally booked in for

2021, which qualified mathematicians will confirm is properly forty years on from 1981, the year *Only Fools* first appeared on the nation's screens – on Tuesday 8 September at 8.30 in the evening, to be precise, in between *The Rockford Files*, starring James Garner, and *The Nine O'Clock News*, read by John Humphrys. (Television really did boast some mighty stars in those days. And James Garner wasn't exactly a nobody, either.)

But, as with so many carefully planned events at that time, the pandemic got in the way. How often was that the story across the country, as we all did our best to pull together, abide by the rules and put our lives on pause for a while in a unified effort to contain the virus and protect the vulnerable? It seemed the only way you could carry on socialising as usual during those lockdowns was by getting a job in Downing Street.

But the situation eventually began to ease, and in May 2022 we were able to get together and, forty-one years after *Only Fools* was born, celebrate the show's fortieth birthday. I know it wasn't quite what everyone was originally intending, but, on the consolation side, there was at least something rather satisfyingly Trotter-like about that outcome. Indeed, as birthday commemorations go, you might almost say it had a touch of the chunky gold 'Rooney' ID bracelet about it.* It felt somehow right, in other words. Wrong, but right.

* Del's birthday gift for Rodney in 'Heroes and Villains' in the 1996 Christmas trilogy – 'Twenty-four-carat gold, no rubbish – it's

Incidentally, were I a less easy-going kind of person, and more swift to take offence, I might have had cause to remark that it was nice of *someone* to make an effort to mark the show's fortieth anniversary. I don't mean to sound touchy, but others – such as, for instance, anybody in any kind of position of eminence at the broadcasting corporation which commissioned the show in the first place – had shown strangely little inclination to mention it. At least, if there was a note or a card or even a one-line email sent out from anywhere in the BBC's upper echelons, saying, 'Blimey, doesn't time fly? Forty glorious years!', or, better still, 'Here's an evening of commemorative programming on BBC2', I certainly never saw it. And when I talked to Tessa Peake-Jones and Gwyneth Strong and Sue Holderness, all of whom also came along to the 2022 convention, they didn't seem to have heard a peep, either.

And now I'm on the subject, neither did we hear anything when *Only Fools* was voted the favourite BBC programme of all time by *The One Show*'s viewers. I sent a

---

even got your name on it, look . . . No, that's a "d" – it's just, like . . . copperplate writing.' And, of course, as with the 'urgent' mobile phone aerial, it's another one of those lovely 'plants', setting up the moment at the end of the story where Albert reads aloud the local newspaper's report on Del and Rodney's inadvertent crime-busting activity, and the part played in the apprehension of the muggers by Mr Trotter's 'younger brother Rooney'. It's just so nicely stitched together, and something which was a great gag in itself ends up paying off all over again.

note about that to John Sullivan's son, Jim, and the rest of the Sullivan family, because it felt like such an honour to the memory of their beloved John. But gone, alas, are the days when BBC bigwigs such as David Hatch and Mark Freeland would send an immediate note of encouragement or congratulations when something happened around the show. David's notes became known as 'Hatchlets' and I have a file full of them. Mark was instrumental in bringing back Granville and Arkwright for *Still Open All Hours*, along with all the energy and enthusiasm to the project that the BBC used to have.

No matter. We took a little time to celebrate the fortieth anniversary for ourselves, near Bedford that weekend.

I had darkened the door of the Sharnbrook Hotel – not to mention its towels – once before this, in February 2020. That was when I went along to 'The David Jason Exhibition', organised by the Only Fools and Horses Appreciation Society, which featured a display of props, scripts, costumes and pictures, and which also featured me, making my first appearance at any kind of fan convention. And, of course, looking back, it could so easily have been my last appearance at one as well – and possibly my last appearance anywhere, in fact.

That February, this thing the scientists were calling Covid-19 was still a gathering threat, somewhere out on the horizon – something which, it was becoming apparent, we would have to confront eventually, but whose exact shape was as yet uncertain and which, for now, seemed to be happening elsewhere.

Now, within a month, of course, the entire country would be under government-issued lockdown orders and we'd all be learning to socially distance from one another and discovering what life was like when you took away, not just *Only Fools and Horses* conventions, but pubs and restaurants and cafes and cinemas and sports events and most kinds of shops and even the chance (No. 10 Downing Street excepted) to have a few people inside your own house.

Back then, though, as I installed myself at that 2020 convention, all that stood between me and a long line of people waiting to come and shake my hand was a single bottle of hand sanitiser, placed on a shelf at the head of the queue. And I remember looking at that bottle and thinking how unusual it seemed – almost exotic. None of us really had any idea how much a part of our lives bottles of hand sanitiser were about to become. Nor how much a part of our lives shaking hands with people was about to unbecome.

As for wearing paper face masks in populated places, we hadn't even begun to think about those at that stage. And therefore it follows logically that we hadn't begun to think, either, about what it would be like to wear a paper face mask during the hay fever season and endure a sneezing fit on a path up to a dentist's surgery – which I only mention because it seems to have become one of my own most enduring memories of mask-wearing during the pandemic.

Without wishing to go into too much detail, it was one of those pollen-led sneezing attacks that comes out of nowhere, ambushes you from all sides and triggers five or six rapidly consecutive explosions, leaving you a dizzy and watery-eyed shell of your former self. You certainly don't want to be holding a tray of crockery when one of those happens, and neither – I can vouch wholeheartedly for this – do you want to be heading into your dentist's with a face mask on. By the time I gingerly opened the door and entered that surgery, I was wearing a mask so heavily weighted with the expelled contents of my sinuses that it was beginning to sag slightly and gently bounce on its ear elastic.

The receptionist was good enough to respond to my muffled and slightly sticky request for a new mask and I quickly adjourned to the bathroom area to sort myself out – but too late, clearly, to prevent the mortification of this moment from staying with me in perpetuity in the form of a muscle memory. Another of Covid's little gifts.

In February 2020, however, delights like these were all off in the mists of our collective future. And, just to recap: I had cheerfully signed up to do the first large-scale meet-and-greet event of my life, one which brought me into close contact with eight hundred people in four separate sessions across two days, just as a rapidly spreading and cunningly mutating airborne virus was working out the best way to shut us all indoors and make sure we saw nobody we weren't living with for whole months on end.*

Again, if you're not seeing a slight trace of the Derek Trotters in that plot development, I would gently suggest you're not looking closely enough.

But I lived to tell the tale, and I also lived to go back for another helping, a little over two years later, walking up to that perfectly innocuous-looking hotel early on the

* I don't know about you, but I remained confused about the nature of the Covid-19 virus all the way through lockdown and beyond. We knew that it was capable of mutating in order to stay alive so it seemed to have some kind of purpose, or at any rate a driven ambition to exist. But what did it actually want? What was it after? What were its hopes and dreams and what was it hoping to achieve by messing us all up like this? Had anybody sat down with it and asked it these questions? If it was just money that it was looking for, could we not have had a whip-round, got a couple of hundred quid together and sent it on its way? It was all very puzzling. At one point during my vexed thinking about these matters, I developed a kind of 'inverse Trojan Horse' approach to battling the virus. On the understanding that the virus was desperate to attach itself to humans, the idea was to wheel giant, laboratory-made and utterly convincing human-a-likes – Trojan Humans, if you like – into deserted town centres around the country to attract all of the virus in the area and then, once the bugs were inside, to tow the human-a-likes out to sea as quickly as possible and dump them. I thought this was a pretty neat solution – classical but with a twist. Oddly, though, nobody at Pfizer or Astra-Zeneca seemed interested in following me down this route. But fair enough, I suppose: the boffins found their own way and had some success, it can't be doubted, with the vaccines. Next time, though, I'm suggesting we go 'inverse Trojan Horse' on the problem. You read about it here first. And yes, don't worry: I've patented it. I wasn't born yesterday, you know.

Saturday morning, where there was nothing to announce to the outside world the full nature of what was unfolding within, unless you count the yellow Reliant Regal Supervan parked by the front door, which, I suppose, now I mention it, was quite a big clue actually.

If I was in a subdued and more than commonly thoughtful mood as I entered the building that day, it was for one reason. No John Challis this time. John, who had been an absolute stalwart attender of these conventions, died in September 2021. He was seventy-nine. We've suffered so much death around *Only Fools* – more than any show's fair share of untimely earthly departures, surely. Lennard Pearce at sixty-nine, Ken MacDonald at fifty, John Sullivan at sixty-four, Roger Lloyd Pack at sixty-nine . . . Buster Merryfield lived to be seventy-eight, which is more like a decent score, but he died while John Sullivan was still alive and the show was still running and there were episodes still ahead of him, so even with Buster there was a sense, among us, of a life cut short.

In the spring of 2022, the world lost Lynda Baron and Denise Coffey, too – two more enormously talented colleagues of mine and greatly cherished companions on the voyage. And not long before that, Terry Jones had passed, also. All these people that I have come through with, now dropping off the perch . . . I find it so hard to reckon with and really difficult to process. I just really wish they wouldn't. I'm starting to feel a little bit exposed up here.

John's death hit especially hard. He had been ill with

237

cancer since 2019, but was doing OK, it seemed – coping with it. He and I had last been in a room together at this convention, in 2020, and he had been as jovial and as engaging as ever – a truly warm presence in the room. But the illness later seemed to take him over in a hurry and the news, when it came, knocked us all for six – a huge blow. He was just such a lovely man: naturally funny, brilliant company, and a really terrific storyteller.

I mentioned earlier the Beatles' film, *Magical Mystery Tour* – which the launch episode of *Do Not Adjust Your Set* had the daunting job of competing with at Christmas 1967. Well, John was offered a part in that movie. Apparently, at the audition, he'd told John Lennon that he was 'more of a Rolling Stones fan, really' – not necessarily the smartest tactic in the circumstances. Yet, a testament to his charm, he still got the job.

The problem was, John had a prior commitment to a BBC job that he couldn't get out of, so he had to let the chance go. Imagine that: it's the Swinging Sixties and you've got the opportunity to make a film with the Beatles, but the day job goes and gets in the way. Nobody would have found that easy to swallow – with the exception of my dad, of course. I think John was as sore about that twist of fate for a while as I was about being made to surrender a role in *Dad's Army*.*

---

* The role of Corporal Jones, which was mine for approximately three hours in 1968 – the time it took the BBC to discover that they could have

John was a genuinely talented actor. He'd had roles with the Royal Shakespeare Company and at the National The-atre. In 1995, when he'd become enormously famous for playing a honkingly superior second-hand car dealer from Lewisham, he chose to spend his summer onstage in Regent's Park doing Shakespeare – *Richard III* and *A Midsummer Night's Dream*. And he was equally happy during those years devoting his winters to hamming it up as various villainous figures in pantomimes. Captain Hook was a speciality. He'd seen *Peter Pan* at Christmas as a kid – his first time in a theatre – and been dumbfounded. As he once described it, he'd sat there thinking he was witnessing a chocolate box come to life.

Him too, then. Clearly there is no overestimating those Christmas shows and the impression they made on some of us young ones, staring up from the stalls. They put something in our minds which could never quite be dislodged.

There was something wonderfully unassuming about John. I remember being on a location shoot for *Only Fools* one time in Bournemouth. The show was in its heyday, and, once the

---

Clive Dunn instead. I wrote about this professional disappointment in my first volume of memoirs. It's quite possible that I mentioned it in my second, too. I may also have alluded to it in my third. And now here I am, briefly encountering the subject again in my fourth. Not that it left any kind of lasting impression on me, you understand. Anyway, what became of *Dad's Army*? The programme vanished without trace, didn't it? Some, sadly, wither on the vine.

word had got out that we were filming, people would gather on the street in quite large numbers to have a look at what we were up to. That meant a few security guys would be brought in to mind the perimeter of the set and make sure nothing unhelpful happened.

At one point, during a brief break in filming, John realised that he was running low on cigarettes and decided to pop to the shop. Of course, it wouldn't have occurred to John to send someone out to *get* him some fags, because that would have been too grand and lordly. But he did ask one of the guys on the perimeter if he would mind coming with him to the shop, get him off the set and guide him up the street and back without too much hindrance.

So off they went together and John bought his cigarettes and, mission accomplished, the pair of them returned. On the way back to the set, just by way of conversation, John asked the guy what time his shift ended.

'Oh, no – I'm not security,' said John's guide. 'I just came along to watch.'

John, by the way, was an excellent smoker, and very good at it – by which I mean he could smoke in a full range of styles: the secret smoker, furtively puffing away; the show-off smoker, letting the whole room know; the beginner, still getting the hang of it; the smoker who isn't really a smoker at all and who's only doing it because everyone else is . . . John could hold the room with a whole routine based on people's different ways with a cigarette.

240

But, of course, wherever he went, it was the laugh that people mostly wanted him to do – that terrible, high, mirthless bray that Boycie specialised in. That was John's personal gift to the show, modelled on the laugh of somebody in his local pub. John offered it up as a suggestion in rehearsal one day and everybody fell about. John Sullivan started writing it into the scripts: '*Boycie does one of his laughs.*'

Given what a solid part of the show he became, it's funny to reflect now how John just drifted in one afternoon to film what seemed to be a casual, come-and-go bit part. We were filming the second episode of the first series – 'Go West, Young Man'. In that story, Boycie has bought his girlfriend a classic E-Type Jaguar and pleads with Del to hide it in the Trotters' lock-up so that his wife doesn't find out. John was there for, literally, that one afternoon and, to be perfectly honest, the car is the thing I remember most vividly about making that episode.

Look, in my defence, it was a very special car, all right? Or it certainly was to me. Back when I was a naive twentysomething, dreaming of life as an international man of mystery from the front seat of an electrician's van, the E-Type Jaguar was, in my overawed opinion, the ultimate set of wheels. I was utterly convinced that the day I took delivery of an E-Type – preferably in red, preferably with white leather seats, and preferably with white-wall tyres – I would know for sure that I had made it, that my personal magnetism had peaked, and that life could show me no more.

I never did get that E-Type, as it turned out – yet now here I was, being handed the keys to one. And at work, of all places. OK, it was white, not red, but beggars can't be choosers. Nick Lyndhurst and I couldn't resist. We asked if we could take the car for a spin round the streets of London during our lunch hour – permission for which was very reluctantly granted.

'You won't be late back, will you?' was the slightly anxious question.

'Of course not!' we replied.

About a quarter of an hour of happy motoring pleasure through the streets of west London later, we realised that we were lost. I blamed Nick. Nick blamed me. Remember, if you can: these were the days before satnav – or 'satnaff' as I prefer to refer to it, having been sent up any number of blind alleys and dumped in any number of traffic jams by those oh-so-helpful electronic assistants. But we had nothing to help us that day apart from our senses of direction, and unfortunately they turned out to be worse than satnaff.

I still don't really know how we made it back that day. I can only think that a higher authority intervened and guided the steering wheel. Possibly a higher authority in the BBC budget department. However, make it back we did, albeit by the skin of our teeth and with filming just about to restart. 'We knew you'd be ready for us about now,' we blithely remarked, in true Del Boy style, as we clambered out. But the truth was we'd come close to holding up the production and embarrassing ourselves mightily. We swore each other to an oath of secrecy about it – which, oops, I seem to have broken. Sorry about that, Nick.

Anyway, that afternoon saw this actor called John Challis pitch up and film his sole appearance in that first series. John Sullivan only wrote Boycie into one episode in the second series, too – 'A Losing Streak', with the famous poker game; 'That wasn't the hand I dealt you,' and so forth. But, unsurprisingly, the character grew from there: Boycie was in two episodes of series three, and four episodes of series four, until it reached the point where those last Christmas specials would have been unthinkable without a part for him. And that was in no small measure because of John Challis showing John Sullivan what Boycie could be. It was the same with Sue Holderness's Marlene, with Patrick Murray's Mickey Pearce, with Roger Lloyd Pack's Trigger . . . The show evolved, far beyond its three-blokes-in-a-flat sitcom premise, and became an ensemble piece because of what those actors brought to their roles.

And that, incidentally, is another reason why programmes need time to develop – time which, I'm afraid, broadcasters are increasingly reluctant to give new shows and which has become a luxury in these more commercially intense times. It's not just about giving the audience time to find the show, although that's obviously important; it's about allowing time for the writer and the cast to find the show, too. Bear in mind that John Sullivan had written the whole of series one of *Only Fools* before the show had even been cast. He had imaginary faces and voices in mind for those characters, which Nick's, Lennard's and my actual faces and voices eventually supplanted. From the second series onwards John could have us in mind when he wrote and could craft the lines and situations to suit our deliveries.

If a show is given space, this feedback loop starts up in which the cast feeds back to the writer and the writer starts writing for the cast, and the programme, with any luck, advances and becomes deeper and richer for it. If the BBC had dumped *Only Fools* after series one – and given the less than spectacular viewing figures for that series on its first showing, they could easily have felt entitled to – none of this would have been able to happen and nobody would have been any the wiser. Fortunately, though, the commercial imperative didn't have to prevail, and the BBC kept faith with the show, and here we are.

When I think about John Challis, I remember in particular how good he was at handling his success in the show – dealing with the changes that inevitably happened in his life when he suddenly became very famous for playing *that character*. I certainly had my own struggles on that score. The success of the show was wonderful – and at the same time quite troubling, even alarming in some respects. Contradictions abounded. Del was the role of a lifetime – I knew that as well as I knew anything. He was an absolute gift, as far as I was concerned. You dream of being given a leading role in a show that really lands with people and embeds itself deeply in their affections, yet how often does that actually happen? I'd had more than a decade of false starts and dashed hopes on that particular quest, and watched a number of well-funded, nicely positioned shows leave the launch pad with a phut rather than a bang. In fact, it had happened to me so often that I'd started to think that my goose was cooked and that the big one would never arrive for me. And then, bingo, along came Derek Trotter.

And yet, at the same time, for all the wonderful things that I could attribute to him, that man was nothing less than a threat to my livelihood. How do you explain that to people? But it was true. Del Boy – lovable, energetic, roguish, playful, eternally optimistic Del Boy – sometimes seemed to be on nothing less than a mission to end my career as an actor.

The thing was, he became such a strong presence in the world, and my face, for obvious reasons, became so firmly associated with his, that he practically threatened to replace me. Wherever I went, Del would come barging through the door ahead of me. Which was all very well in some settings, but if the door in question led into an audition room where I was trying to be considered for another part, it could be less than helpful.

For example, in 1987 I went up for the role of Skullion, the Head Porter, in *Porterhouse Blue*, the Malcolm Bradbury adaptation of the Tom Sharpe novel, made by Channel 4. I had loved the novel and I loved the script and I desperately wanted to be a part of that production. Skullion was an ex-military man, a traditionalist determined to resist the tides of change, a behind-the-scenes wielder of dark power – a truly juicy role, and one that I was really confident I could bring something to.

I read for the part, in the usual way of these things, and it seemed to go OK. But then I had to audition again, this time in Skullion's costume – his dark suit and tightly buttoned waistcoat and his bowler hat. Auditioning in costume wasn't something that anyone had asked me to do before. I think I knew what was going on, though. The producers had to be absolutely convinced that I could come across as something other than an irrepressible, neck-flexing, cockney wheeler-dealer, which, at this point, was the first thing they thought of when they thought of me, and which they were absolutely convinced would be the first thing an audience thought of. And until I'd put on the clothes, and shown them good and proper that I could inhabit another character, one who wasn't going to shout 'Cushty!' at any moment, they couldn't convince themselves. In a strange way, then, I was fighting Del for that part. Successfully, as it turned out – but I had the feeling it was a close-run thing, and I also knew that there would have been other roles at this point in my career for which I wouldn't even have got into the audition room, let alone been invited to try on some clothes. Del would have seen to it.*

* I won a BAFTA for my performance as Skullion, which I mention here in the footnotes in order to seem like I'm being modest about it

Of course, Del's popularity brought its challenges beyond the professional realm, too. All of us who were in *Only Fools* saw our public profiles rise and reach a level that was entirely new to us. It worked like a switch. The outside world that you'd been moving around in without really thinking about it suddenly wasn't quite the same place. People were now noticing you, reacting to you, greeting you in the name of your character, quoting the scripts at you . . . None of us, I think, was quite prepared for how that would feel and the differences it would make, and we all responded to it in our different ways.

The morning after the first episode went out with Gwyneth Strong in it as Cassandra – 1989, the 'Yuppy Love' episode – Gwyneth remembers leaving her flat to go shopping, pushing the buggy containing her young son, and suddenly having this feeling that people were looking at her differently, more intently, as if trying to work out whether they knew her, and

---

but, in fact, trust me, in my entire career, it's the award that I'm most stonkingly proud of. And until the Oscar comes along – which must be any year soon, surely – it will remain so. And on the subject of Oscars and auditions, permit me here to recall a favourite story about the great American film star Shelley Winters, who, at an advanced stage in her career, was asked to audition for a role, and also to bring along a résumé and a headshot photograph. Apparently Winters duly attended with a large bag from which she withdrew one of her two Oscar statuettes and plonked it on the table in front of the producers. 'Here's my photo,' she said. Then she reached into the bag again and produced her second Oscar statuette. 'And here's my f***ing résumé.' Well, it's an approach. And one, I have to say, that I rather admire. Oh, and she got the part.

if . . . wait a minute . . . it's you, isn't it? Yes! It IS you! Look, everybody! It's her!

We all had moments like that, and it really was an eerie sensation. Again, this can be difficult to explain. It looks, I know, like such an odd thing to complain about. We spend so much time in our culture thinking about fame. Indeed, sometimes it seems to be the thing our culture prizes most: fame, stardom, recognition. For some people the idea of being recognised wherever you go is the dream – an ambition in itself, rather than the unlooked-for consequence of doing something else, which is how it comes to most of us who end up famous, and is certainly how it came to me.

But the truth is, these days when I sit at home and watch the reality shows and the talent contests where the first prize seems to be fame, above all, I can only shake my wise old head and say: be careful what you wish for, my children. Because, whatever it looks like, this may not be for everyone. Indeed, this thing you long for may end up bringing you only unease. Indeed, if there are aspects of your character which are in any way shy, withdrawn, self-conscious . . .

Let me put it this way: I'd never been a wearer of hats – with the solitary exception, I should perhaps declare, of the occasion of my mate Malcolm Taylor's wedding, somewhere in the seventies, where I gleefully discovered that the morning suit I was issued with, in my role as best man, came with a top hat. I was so delighted by this opportunity to look like Fred Astaire that I wore that top hat the whole day, including during the dinner at the reception, only removing it, extremely reluctantly, for the official photographs.*

After Del came into my life, though, hats became a part of my everyday wardrobe – not top hats, in this case, but certainly baseball caps, of which I suddenly amassed a small collection. I tugged their brims down over my face and pulled a scarf up over my chin and hoped to go unnoticed. Nick and Roger Lloyd Pack were very much of the same persuasion, wrapping themselves up tightly whenever they set foot outside the door. It didn't make us particularly comfortable, maybe, but the attention we would get otherwise made us even less comfortable.†

It was another reason I admired John Challis. He didn't let the fuss that came his way as a result of Only Fools trouble him or make him anxious, and if he found it tiresome, then he didn't let on. If people wanted him to 'do the laugh' (as almost invariably they did), he cheerfully obliged. I'm sure it must have irritated him sometimes – being asked to do the same thing, over and over, while seeming enthusiastic about it, is bound to – but I never saw him show it. Not once.

* And as a consequence of that heroic hat-wearing, my hair in those official wedding photos is utterly crushed flat and damp. I look as though someone has just dumped a bucket of water over me.
† Be aware that the hat-and-scarf wrap-up is a decent tactic for deflecting unwanted attention, except in warm weather when you end up drawing attention to yourself, which somewhat defeats the point. See also the wearing of sunglasses – especially indoors.

That attitude meant that he signed up wholeheartedly to the *Only Fools* conventions, where others among us, me included, were far more circumspect. John just thought, 'Why not?' When it emerged that *Only Fools* was an especially popular item in Serbia, several of us quietly made a note to cross that country off our list of potential destinations for a holiday. John, by contrast, flew straight out to Belgrade at the nearest opportunity and made a documentary about the show's success there. He greeted all the peculiar repercussions of his fame with wholesome curiosity, an arched eyebrow and a huge helping of good cheer. He was an example to us all, really.

That said, even John needed to be able to escape sometimes, and he and his wife Carol used to like slipping away to the Hotel des Arts in Paris. France, unlike Serbia, has never gone a total bomb on *Only Fools*, and John and Carol knew that, in the charming, quiet seclusion of the Hotel des Arts, John could be anonymous and enjoy his hotel breakfast at leisure, utterly undisturbed.

At least, they knew that until the morning when the journey of John's croissant from his plate to his lips was interrupted by the booming voice of a stranger.

'Bonjour, Boycie! What on earth are YOU doing here?'

Clearly nowhere, in fact, was safe.

But even that was fine by John. It became another story to tell – something else to go into the repertoire of amusing things that people would come out with in his presence and with which John would then merrily regale us all. 'I gather you're some kind of television personality,' a woman once said to him, rather crisply, and upon first introduction. 'Well, I'm here to tell you that I never watch television.' John tipped his head back and laughed loudly at that.

How could you not love a man whose death brought immediate tributes and messages of condolence from institutions as far-flung as Arsenal FC, the British Hedgehog Preservation Society and the American rap artist Ice-T? Well, John loved Arsenal, and he loved hedgehogs, and, as for Ice-T . . . Well, perhaps they were not the most obvious of buddies. Yet John and Ice-T had struck up a friendship on Twitter and every year, when Christmas came around, they would exchange a fond festive greeting – from the man behind Lewisham's most famous fictional car dealer to the man behind the O.G. *Original Gangster* album and back. When Ice-T was asked how the two of them knew each other, he replied, rather magnificently, 'Because I live on earth.'

I'm proud to be able to say that I knew John Challis not only because I live on earth, but also because I had the privilege of working with him and befriending him. I miss him badly. A T-shirt worn by one of the conventioneers in Bedford, and alluding to the florist's card on Del and Rodney's tribute at Grandad's funeral in series four, said it nicely, I thought.

RIP John Spurley Challis. Always in our foughts.

John would have tipped his head back and laughed loudly at that, too.

* * *

Ancient laws, set in stone by the founding fathers, dictate that there can be no fan convention without merchandise for sale. The *Only Fools* fortieth anniversary event certainly had no ambition to flout those laws. A souk to rival anything Marrakech can manage occupied the far end of the hotel's conference hall. But there was something about the fact that it was Trotters Independent Trading that had inspired this cheerful exploitation of a marketing opportunity that made it all the more appropriate, somehow.

I didn't linger too long among the groaning trestle tables for fear of getting purchased and bagged up myself and having to start a new life in, say, St Albans. (Nothing against St Albans. It's just that I'm happy where I am.) But I did observe, among the array of tempting items on offer, a Del Boy 'lounger blanket with sleeves' – a cosy one-piece outfit for at-home television-watching which I thought rather stylish, although my wife might not have agreed. There was also not just a 'Jolly Boys' Outing' beach towel, but a 'Jolly Boys' Outing' deckchair to go with it. There was no time to check the car park, but I wouldn't have been surprised to find a full-sized, limited-edition 'Jolly Boys' Outing' exploding coach out there, too.

There were Reliant Regal door panels and nose cones, with or without working indicators and available in your choice of clean or dirt-smudged finish. One of the oh-so-tasteful orangey-brown carpets used to dress the studio set appeared to have been divided into collectable carpet squares, each for sale, meaning that, just as sometimes football fans get given the chance to own their own small, potted patch of the hallowed Wembley Stadium turf, so *Only Fools* aficionados could take home a little plot of Trotter carpet and tread where the cast once trod.

There were wallets marked 'Loads of Bunce'. And there were bottles of Peckham Spring Water on sale at £3 a pop. Now that's what I call entrepreneurial – a fictional wheeze turned into an actual wheeze. Deeply impressive. I also saw a bloke head off with three rolls of 'Yuppy Flat Bamboo Wallpaper' under his arm. Maybe next time he'll bring photos of his newly decorated yuppy flat.

I lost count of the items from those mounds that I signed over the course of the weekend, and I lost track of the sheer range of those items, too. Plenty of Reliant Regal doors and panels, obviously, but more (as Del might have put it) *retroussé* objects, too: a framed elephant print, of the kind that could very easily have graced the wall of a certain Peckham flat; numerous china cats; at least one ceramic cheese dish (you knew it was a cheese dish because it helpfully came with the word 'CHEESE' printed on it to put the matter beyond doubt); and a sheepskin coat or three. The Monty Python team used to talk about getting cans of Spam thrust upon them to sign, as a result of the show's inadvertent and aforementioned association with that product – and maybe that still happens to them. But I wonder if any of them have ever been asked to put their name to a white leatherette-panelled free-standing cocktail bar, as I was in Bedford. I'd love to know where that ended up. Perhaps in the yuppy flat of the bloke with the bamboo wallpaper.

A small pile of second-hand Kylie Minogue albums now bear my signature, too. Is that OK? Will Kylie object? Too late to worry about it at this stage, I'm afraid. The top was back on my marker pen before I could really reflect on what I was doing. But the next time Kylie's in the house for one of my monthly Jason Towers karaoke nights, I'll try and find a moment to square it with her. If she can hear me above the music, of course. Those nights are always pretty raucous.

I also signed not one but two conventioneers' arms – having been asked to do so, let me make clear, rather than because I got carried away while signing other things, or went for one of the Kylie albums and missed. Both those conventioneers – one of whom apparently owns a barber-shop which is practically a shrine to *Only Fools* – told me that the idea was to create a template. They were intending to head off to the tattoo parlour to have my scribble inked over and rendered permanently.

I didn't know what to say, really – apart from maybe they should have tried it with a chequebook. Except, of course, nowhere accepts cheques any more.

Anyway, I complied to the best of my abilities – I don't know whether you've put your signature on anybody's arm recently, but it's not quite as easy as it looks. The surface moves under your pen in the way that, for instance, the side panel of a Reliant Regal doesn't. Yet, with my scrawl complete and more or less legible, the conventioneers went away content enough, one of them saying she was going straight to the parlour that very afternoon to complete the job.

The following day she returned for the second day of the event. My wife, Gill, spotted her and asked her how she had got on. She rolled up her sleeve and showed Gill her autographed arm – still inscribed in nothing more permanent than marker pen. Unfortunately, the tattoo parlour had been closed when she got there.

Again, correct me if I'm wrong, but the spirit of the Trotters seemed to hover lightly over that outcome, and I can only apologise to her if that was anything to do with me. I hope she found an open parlour before the template rubbed off.

Maybe Jay and Daryl could have pointed her the way of a good one. Jay and Daryl were the security guys appointed to keep guard over me at the conference. I'm sure they've had busier and more physically exacting jobs, because I've rarely felt safer than I did sitting among those *Only Fools* fans. But this was the arrangement, so there they were. They were twin brothers, which somehow made their smartly suited presence seem even more formidable. And, it probably goes without saying, they were both fit, strong blokes, dedicated, I have no doubt, to their duties and, if the situation arose, selflessly prepared to take, if not a bullet, then at least a thrown Kylie Minogue album for me.

They also had tattoos. Quite a collection of them. I know this because at one point, during a break, Jay and Daryl guided Gill and me out of the conference hall and upstairs towards a room on the first floor which had been set aside for me to rest up in and get a cup of tea when the opportunity arose. On the way up, we were talking about the limb that I had recently autographed and Gill asked Jay and Daryl if they had any permanently inked decorations themselves, none being visible, on account of the suits.

Indeed they did. Jay – or possibly Daryl – lifted the leg of his trousers to reveal an extensively illustrated calf. Then Daryl – or possibly Jay – unbuttoned his shirt and slipped it aside to display an equally lavishly decorated shoulder blade. Then Jay – or possibly Daryl – joined in by removing *his* shirt to show what was evidently the extensive diary of a tour of North America. An eagle, a bear and a trout figured, among many other mementoes, all exquisitely rendered. They stopped at their shirts, so who knows what other pictorial delights remained undisclosed to us in other areas, including, perhaps, the full instructions for replacing a filter on a Bosch dishwasher. What we did see, though, was beautifully done and one could only admire and applaud the detail and the craftwork.

Yet now I come to reflect on it, what a little tableau this scene must have presented to anybody who happened to be passing: me and my wife, in a hotel corridor, closely examining the tattoos of two stripped-to-the-waist security guards. I reflected later that it would only have taken one press photographer to have rounded the corner at that exact moment for me to have been left with an awful lot of explaining to do.

Anyway, break over and shirts back on, Jay and Daryl attentively guided me back to my headquarters for the weekend – a battered old armchair in a mock-up of the Trotters' lounge, where conventioneers could come and sit alongside me for a chat and a photograph. And, thus restored to my post, I continued to find myself on the receiving end of an absolute tidal wave of warmth and affection.

People had come from all over – from Leeds, Cornwall, Belfast, Scotland . . . Some just wanted to say thank you for all the laughter, the fun, the good times they associated with the show. Others struggled to speak at all, seemingly overcome by the moment. There were tears, young women going bright red, fanning their hands in front of their faces. 'You're going a bit red,' I would say, not making it any easier.

I would love to put that discombobulation and all those hot flushes down to the sheer awe that people routinely experience in the presence of a man of international jet-set

257

leisure – my pal TC knows all about this – and the phero-
mones no doubt coursing off me that weekend in Bedford-
shire. But I knew the truth: it wasn't me, it was that bloke
Del. And that series, *Only Fools*.

A hugely flattering experience, then – but at the same time
an enormously humbling one, and a frequently bewildering
one, too. What I have quickly learned in two appearances
at these kinds of convention is that I will be surrounded by
people who know those shows far better than I know them –
better than I ever knew them, actually. These are people who
can quote whole chunks of dialogue, verbatim, whereas I was
cramming those lines into my head as quickly as I could and
then moving on to the next script, never really to return.
These days, I don't tend to watch the shows, either. Not that
I wouldn't enjoy them and be proud of them. I catch clips
sometimes when they come up incidentally in other places,
and I always think they're funny; they still make me laugh
and I'm sure they always will. But it's never going to be my
idea of a good night in to sit down with the boxed set and
binge my way through a whole series.

Quite apart from anything else, those shows remind me
of a time when I had a full head of hair – a time, indeed,
when I firmly believed I would have that full head of hair
forever. So much for that. I've spoken about this before, but
the contrast between the person that appears on the screen
and the person that I then have to encounter in the mirror
these days is, I find, a little strong for me to take. All in all,

if it's OK with everyone else, I'd rather not subject myself to that particular contrast more frequently than I have to.

At the same time, I do entirely relate to the people who watch the show over and over and get it by heart. I completely understand that instinct, because I'm the same way about Laurel & Hardy. I watch Laurel & Hardy the way other people watch *Only Fools*: on repeat, with constantly renewed pleasure, as a fan. That look Oliver Hardy gives the camera when something has gone wrong or he's in the wrong, or he can't work out why Stan has done something – that little punctuation mark that only he does: I will never cease admiring the skill in that. Ditto the sequence in the hospital room, with Ollie's plastered leg in traction and the events that lead to him eventually getting flung out of the window: I will never cease taking pleasure from that, nor exhaust its brilliance. I could watch it on a loop.

Even so, it knocks you into quite a spin to learn so intimately, face-to-face, how much a comedy television series can sink itself into people's lives, and the effect it can have when it's there. I found myself deep in conversation with people for whom the show had clearly been a much-loved companion along the way – and in some cases far more than that. At one point, a guy in pink shorts sat down next to me and immediately started thanking me. The words were pouring from him in a torrent. He was telling me that I didn't realise what I'd done, that I'd saved his life, that he'd been through some really low times, hadn't known what to do or where to go, and had felt he was trapped in a tunnel – but right when he needed it, the show had made him laugh and given him a glimmer of hope, and it had helped him to turn around and start to come out of that darkness.

I felt like I didn't have any kind of adequate response to that. I think I ended up saying something about how if I'd made him laugh then I was very happy, because that was the job, but maybe we both ought to be thanking John Sullivan, because, after all, I was only doing what his scripts told me to do and delivering the lines that he wrote. As Nick Lyndhurst always said, when trying to deflect the praise that came his way: 'John made the bullets, we only fired them.'

Yet my friend in the pink shorts was by no means the only person that weekend who spoke in that way about the show. Sat there in that daft armchair, I heard a host of similar stories, each of them just as heartfelt and each of them just as trenchant – of lives rescued or reshaped or restored by the power of that programme. It made me think: what would it have been like if we had known at the time that the show would have these kinds of effects on people? We were enjoying ourselves – messing about, frankly. We all loved those characters and we loved going to work every day to portray them, and we all had a professional desire to do right by ourselves and do right by the scripts, and that was pretty much the extent of it, really. Beyond that, no pressure. But if we'd known all the ways in which the show would end up reaching out to people, I think we would have frozen solid and been unable to make it at all. It would have been too daunting.

So people came with their stories and some, in addition, came bearing gifts. No envelopes stuffed with cash, alas, which, obviously, I would not have encouraged.* But there were many other touching acts of generosity. Someone, by way of thanks, presented me with a DVD of Jacques Tati's *Monsieur Hulot's Holiday*, knowing (because I have written about it before) that going to see that movie as a child with my mother was a formative experience to rank alongside going to see Alastair Sim in *Scrooge*, and knowing also that I believe that film to be arguably the greatest sustained comedy performance ever recorded. I didn't have a copy, and I'm very grateful to own one. The project now is to try and organise a time when I can sit down and watch it with my wife and daughter – partly because I think they, in common with everybody else who likes funny things, need to see it, and partly because I want to find out if it lives up to my fondly admiring recollections of it, though I think I know the answer to that.

Of course, it's highly likely that I will turn into one of those annoying people who spends the film cajoling everyone else to pay attention and bossily pointing out the good

---

* I'm firmly of the belief that envelopes stuffed with cash should not be exchanged in the public arena of a fans convention. They should be exchanged afterwards, in the car park, or by prior arrangement at a motorway services.

bits just before they happen – not least that part where M. Hulot is changing a tyre on his car and the wheel rolls away into a pile of leaves in a cemetery, where he picks it up, gathering a bunch of leaves with it, so that he ends up appearing to hold, not a tyre, but a wreath, just as a funeral cortège comes past, all of whom solemnly shake his hand . . . I mean, the whole film is made up of these beautifully threaded-together moments, so I could become a very annoying presence indeed. But I hope not.

The only question is whether we can find a suitable slot between Richard Osman's *House of Games* and the American renovation show *Forever Homes*, both of which seem to be on heavy rotation in my house. When *House of Games* comes on, by the way, I tend to go and make the dogs' dinners. Nothing against Richard Osman, you understand, nor the show. But it's simply not fair to keep two hungry dogs waiting. Or that's my story, anyway.

And then, bearing a gift of another kind, came the person who told me about watching *Only Fools* on television in India, and realising that the all-important term 'plonker' had no natural Hindi equivalent. This I was delighted to discover. In the Hindi dubbed version, apparently, it is rendered simply and consistently as 'plonker'. Don't ask me how the translators got on with 'dipstick', but it seems they found a way. No such luck with plonker, though. As my friend at the convention explained, for her, as a non-Hindi speaker watching the Indian broadcasts, the dialogue would be a long stream of incomprehensible sounds from which, just occasionally, the solitary word 'plonker' would brightly leap out, like the linguistic equivalent of a sore thumb.

Ah, the things that Britain has given the world – in this case, it seems, an untranslatable insult. Or perhaps more likely, looking at it the other way, an insult in no need of translation, whose meaning globally transcends the barriers of language and culture alike, with the consequence that you can say 'plonker' in India and in literally dozens of other countries around the world and be sure that you will be understood. For my own small part in bringing the people of the globe together like this, I couldn't be more proud, I'm sure.*

A hectic weekend, then – one which I spent most of sitting at an odd angle, twisting towards people to hear their

---

* According to the *Oxford English Dictionary*, the actual derivation of 'plonker' is a nineteenth-century word meaning something unusually large that you might have to *plonk down* – a 'whopper', you might also say. The *OED* cites an illustration from 1903: 'That turnip's a plonker.' This notion of something outsized, or bulking embarrassingly large, seems then to have loaned itself to slang usages, particularly in the military, for, ahem, the male member, and also for 'a foolish, inept or contemptible person'. Here the *OED* cites usages dating back to 1955, and also quotes a certain John Sullivan, writing in 1981, specifically for episode three of the first series of *Only Fools*: 'Rodney! I didn't mean drive off! What a plonker!' That, clearly, was Del's first public use of the term, though there were to be many, many more, carrying the word very firmly into popular currency. Again, to be at the heart of linguistic history in this way . . . well, my heart can only swell and tears of pride rise to my misty eyes.

stories, and never stopping talking and engaging. It took me three days at home for my back to recover and my neck to untwist so that I was facing the right way again.

But what a privilege: that was all I kept thinking. What a privilege and a fantastic stroke of luck to end up in a programme that inspired that kind of loyalty, and over such a long period of time. And what a privilege, at this point in my life, to be able to bask in the warmth of it every now and again. What's so striking is that the love for the show holds firm. I wasn't the only member of the cast who watched *Only Fools* become successful and then waited for the backlash. That's the fate of most comedy shows, after all. Comedy, like everything else, with the exception, obviously, of Cliff Richard, ages. If nothing else, I thought, our programme would end up getting found out by changing fashions and new ideas about what's funny and the simple passing of time. In due course, *Only Fools* would be obliged to head off into fusty oblivion and we'd all console ourselves that, well, at least we had a decent run.

But somehow it never happened. The backlash never came.

Why should that be? What was the show's precious secret? People much cleverer than me will be able to come up with some properly smart answers to that question, I'm sure. But when I try to explain it, the thing I keep coming back to is the show's innocence. Which might seem an odd thing to say about a programme whose central character was a dedicated rule-bender and determined tax avoider. (I always used to think that if Derek Trotter had spent half the energy he expended doing things dishonestly on trying to do them honestly, he could have been a millionaire in no time at all. But, bless him, he was too busy trying to get there by the bent route and getting nowhere the long way round.)

What I mean by innocence, though, is that *Only Fools* didn't depend on extremes. There was no bad language in it. It never deliberately sought confrontation in the aim of getting a reaction. In that sense, it was a powerful testament to the power of good, clean entertainment. It remains a beacon for what you can achieve if you try and go down that road, as opposed to going in the direction of comedy that is deliberately divisive, comedy that's straight away spoiling for a fight, comedy in which crudeness replaces wit – comedy that seeks to separate us rather than bring us together on some kind of common ground that we recognise. And I do often find myself wondering whether comedy on television these days has lost its faith in trying to take that route. Maybe the times are just too fragmented to make it possible, but I like to think they're not, and I like to think the abiding popularity of *Only Fools* indicates that I might be right – possibly even reveals a gap that nobody is trying to fill any more.

Then there was the nature of the show's characters and the warmth they generated. Yes, it was a sitcom and its ultimate ambition was to go looking for laughs wherever laughs could be found. Yet it was also obviously built on real people with real dreams, who had the kinds of hopes and aspirations for their lives that ordinary people have. And in the pursuit of those hopes and aspirations, they faced real adversity and real disappointment, things that make up ordinary people's lives and that ordinary people can directly relate to – birth, death and everything in between. It was quietly and gently inclusive, too, without feeling that it had to hammer that point home. It reflected life in London as John knew it, where people from all kinds of backgrounds simply rubbed along together without thinking very much of it.

Most of all, though, the show was, in the most literal sense, family entertainment: it was entertainment about a family – about the relationships between brothers, the relationships between husbands and wives, girlfriends and boyfriends, the relationships with grandfathers, with great-uncles, with absent parents . . . And that would explain, I think, why it worked so well at Christmas, and why Christmas became such a particular niche for it and so strongly bound up with the fate of the show. Because Christmas, too, for better or worse, is about family. And in *Only Fools*, people could see family life, with all its wrinkles and its ruptures, its pleasures and its frustrations, its golden times and its dark spells, played back to them, at a moment in the year when those things were most firmly in their minds. It was inherently a family show for a family time of year.

And on the subject of family, did my 21-year-old daughter gleefully depart the fortieth anniversary convention with, under her arm, the plush mannequin she had purchased of her father looking an absolute idiot? And did my wife quietly descend one evening to take part in the karaoke session, giving the room her renditions of those stone-cold *Only Fools and Horses* classics, 'Everybody's Talkin'' and 'Holding Back the Years'?

Reader, I prefer to make no comment either way on these rumoured developments. I only know that each of us, in our own ways, enjoyed our experience in that hotel conference centre near Bedford that weekend.

Twice in two years, though . . . This might be turning into a habit.

ON THE TWELFTH DEL OF CHRISTMAS

Regals and royals

'To look back is not necessarily to be nostalgic,' said the Queen in her Christmas message to the nation in 1996, before going on to stress the importance of using the lessons of the past in order to look forward 'with courage and optimism'.

Or as Derek Trotter put it, in *his* message to the nation that year, a few hours later on the same channel, at the end of 'Heroes and Villains': 'Not a bad old world, is it, bruv?'

It is – and I think at this stage in the book, we can agree on this – what has ultimately linked the reigning monarch and *Only Fools and Horses* through the years: a quiet determination to use the twin powers of Christmas and television to bestow upon the country a message of comfort and hope to take forward into the new year. Albeit that we tended to get a bigger slot in the schedule for our message and have a slightly greater quotient of punchlines.

That said, for all that obvious sense of a shared mission, I

268

wasn't expecting the Trotters to pitch up during the Queen's Platinum Jubilee celebrations in 2022. Or rather, the 'Platinum Jubbly', as one Chinese manufacturer of china-ware apparently labelled it by accident on about £30,000 worth of commemorative mugs and plates which then had to be scrapped when the error was pointed out. Oops. There were, no doubt, all sorts of ways of sending your very best wishes to Her Majesty on the seventi-eth anniversary of her ascent to the throne, but 'Have a luvvly Platinum Jubbly, ma'am' probably wasn't a line that even Derek Trotter would have been gauche enough to try.

That said, thinking about it, I wouldn't mind owning one of those plates if you know of any that survived the cull. Collector's item, and all that.

Anyhow, the point at which the Trotters definitively took their place at the centre of the formal ceremonies marking that historic moment in the national life came at Bucking-ham Palace on 5 June. Maybe you watched the special parade that concluded that holiday weekend: the huge carnival-style procession up the Mall designed to reflect the Queen's seventy-year reign and the years of change over which she has ruled. And if you did see it, maybe you observed in the ceremony a moment of cultural contrast that still makes me laugh to think about now.

One moment the crowds lining the route were being invited to feast their eyes on the four-ton gold state coach, commissioned by King George III in seventeen-hundred-and-frozen-to-death, and now seen rumbling along the avenue with great dignity behind its eight plumed horses, while a mounted military guard in full regalia rode in attendance; the next (give or take a few moments, and a few bits of marching, and one or two buses with people waving from them) they were watching a yellow Reliant Supervan III puttering in the same direction, with 'Trotters Independent Trading' painted on its side and a camel-coated elbow hanging out of its side window.

New York, Paris . . . Buck House?

I've got to say, I found the sight of that stupid van, in those regal surroundings, both hilarious and moving. Of course, the wonderful incongruity of that vehicle in any kind of grand or formal setting was something that the show itself made merry with on many occasions, perhaps most memorably in 'A Royal Flush', the Christmas special from 1986, mentioned earlier, when Del and Rodney pull into the country estate of the Duke of Maylebury, ready for a weekend of romance (Rodney) and clay pigeon shooting with a borrowed shotgun (Del).

You only had to bring that van into shot in a context like that – show it nosing onto the gravel drive of a sumptuous country house or bumping across a field among the gentlefolk's Range Rovers and BMWs – to be sure of hearing a knowing laugh in the audience when those scenes were screened at the eventual studio recording. There was nothing that Nick Lyndhurst and I needed to do to embellish things, either. In fact, the less we reacted to the van and the more we appeared to think that it was the perfectly natural mode of transport for our characters to be going about in – simply part of the air that we breathed – the funnier it became. And, frankly, because there were very few settings in which that soppy vehicle *wasn't* to some degree incongruous, the van was its own punchline practically every time it appeared.

But for a properly riotous and genuinely deafening clash of tones, this Jubilee pageant set-up, with the Reliant making its way along that famous, broad red-paved avenue in central London and then ceremoniously rounding the Victoria Memorial in front of Buckingham Palace . . . well, that took it, I thought, to another level.

Watching the Trotters' innocent little van perform that magnificent journey, I was reminded of a little royal adventure that once happened to a friend of mine. When I had my London flat in Newman Street, I lived opposite a couple called Micky and Angie McCaul, and we became firm friends. Indeed, let the history books show that it was the McCauls who were frequently appointed to tend to my later worldrenowned grapefruit plant, watering it in its infancy when I was off on tour. And let the history books equally show that sometimes they even remembered to do so.

Micky worked as a lettings agent and a lot of his job was driving around London to meet clients and show them properties; and one day – this would have been in the late 1970s – heading home after an appointment in Victoria, he found himself taking his car past the garden wall of Buckingham Palace and then up the Mall in the direction of Whitehall. There was a line of quite slow-moving traffic ahead of Micky, but he simply followed along behind it, having no real alternative. He hadn't gone very far when a policeman stepped out in front of his car and gestured at him to turn left, which the cars ahead of him were also doing.

Micky, naturally, did as he was told, assuming the road ahead was closed or there was some kind of problem necessitating a detour. Very soon after making his turn, however, he was aware of passing through a broad gateway, after which the line of vehicles ahead of him came to a halt. Micky stopped, too, and noticed in his rear-view mirror that the gate was now closing behind him.

At this point, another policeman appeared, this time in Micky's side window. This one was bending down and he had a searching and possibly rather anxious expression on his face. Micky wound down the window.

'What do you think *you're* doing?' asked the policeman.

'Well, I was told to turn in,' said Micky, understandably a touch confused.

The policeman stood up and did some shouting and some gesturing in the direction behind Micky's car. Micky saw the gate that had closed behind him now reopen.

'Back out,' said the policeman, in a tone which brooked no argument.

So, with no further ceremony, Micky reversed off the drive of Clarence House, which was at that time the residence of Queen Elizabeth the Queen Mother, watched the gates again close after him, and somewhat sheepishly resumed his journey along the Mall. Apparently this is what could happen if you accidentally stuck yourself on the end of a member of the royal family's official motorcade – or rather if a policeman accidentally stuck you there. Micky had ended up going home with the Queen Mum.

It had been but the briefest of visits, of course. If the kettle had been on, no one had mentioned it to Micky, who left without so much as a 'thank you for stopping by'. Still, he was able to dine out on the story forever afterwards.*

---

* Just to repeat, this was the 1970s when security was a little less, shall we say, attentive than it tends to be these days. In 1962, during an outbreak of smog in London that reduced visibility to fifteen feet in places, someone was stopped by a police officer driving their car innocently and very gingerly across the parade ground in front of Buckingham Palace. I think it's safe to say that wouldn't happen nowadays, and not just because we don't get smogs like that any more. And on that subject, I was twelve when the properly legendary Great Smog of 1952 descended on London and the winter air was so thick then that a gentleman passing the end of Lodge Lane in a rather superior car asked me and my mate Tony Brighton to guide him to Woodside Avenue – which we did, one of us walking ahead of the car, the other guiding the driver along the kerb. It was about three miles and it seemed to take forever, travelling at a crawl, but we each got five bob for our trouble so it was more than worth it. File under

The Trotters' van, however, did not owe its place in the procession on the Mall in June 2022 to misdirection, by a policeman or anybody else. It really was meant to be there. And I guess that was what was even more moving, from my point of view, about the sight of it in that exceptionally grand context: the fact that this daft vehicle had been selected for the parade in the first place – lobbed in, on this giant public occasion, with all these other wheel-borne icons of British life: the Minis, the Morris Minors, the Land Rovers, the Jags and the double-decker buses.

And once again I could only scratch my head in bewilderment at the niche that this simple sitcom has somehow ended up carving itself in the national consciousness. This, the parade seemed to be saying, is historic Britain: a place defined by hallowed, regal pomp and ceremony dating back centuries, and by iconic feats of engineering that speak for the country nationally and internationally, but also, while we're mentioning it, by a dodgy three-wheeler belonging to a couple of fictional chancers from Peckham.

You can say this much about that battered old Reliant, though: at least it lasted the course under its own steam during that parade, which is more than can be said for the vintage Jaguar bearing the great chef Prue Leith that

---

'wouldn't happen now', although maybe climate change might have its own ideas about that.

afternoon. That car conked out and had to be pushed along the Mall by a small team of stewards in hi-vis jackets.

You want to get yourself inside a reliable motor next time, Prue.

Just to be clear about it, I was not at the wheel of the Trotters' Reliant Supervan III that day – and that was not my camel-coated elbow protruding from its window. Nor did I get to be borne along in the class-leading luxury of its passenger seat. And was I disappointed about that outcome? Well, on balance, not exactly.

Don't get me wrong: I associate that vehicle with extremely cheerful memories – some of the most cheerful memories of my working life, actually. Indeed, the first thing that comes to mind when I think of that yellow van is sitting next to Nick Lyndhurst and trying – and frequently failing – to get takes done without one or both of us cracking up. Throughout the filming of *Only Fools* Nick and I were constantly on the verge of setting each other off. 'Giddy' might be the word I need here. Often that was just the irresistible consequence of the scripts, many of which seemed to have the rare attribute of becoming funnier the more often you said and heard them. Containing ourselves in the face of that kind of writing was a constant challenge, not just for Nick and me but for all the cast.

On top of that, though, Nick and I had both worked in the theatre, and we knew from rich experience that, irrespective of how good, bad or indifferent the script was, getting one of your colleagues to crack up and break character – or, as we say, to 'corpse' – was one of our chosen profession's most satisfying pleasures and, indeed, one of its most noble callings. Nick and I duly considered it a point of honour, and practically a duty, to get each other to corpse whenever the opportunity arose.*

It was all about not taking things too seriously, I guess – and certainly about not letting your colleagues take *themselves* too seriously. And, yes, in some of the more, shall we say, trying theatrical productions which it had been the lot of both Nick and myself to endure on our thespian journeys, I guess it was also about finding a way simply to get through it all with your spirits intact. When the mission was spirit-preservation, theatre actors could be pretty ingenious. Nick told me he was once in a production where members of the

---

* To corpse: ancient theatrical expression denoting the unsuccessful suppression of extraneous and inappropriate laughter by an actor, mid-performance. Said to originate from an incident of yore in which an actor, lying on the stage playing dead, got the giggles after somebody fluffed their lines, thereby treating the audience to the sight of a body oddly heaving with badly contained laughter. Word spread, and the concept of 'corpsing' was born. This is distinct, of course, from what it could easily seem to describe: an actor forgetting their lines and freezing. The term for that is 'drying'. At moments of drying an actor has essentially two options: to call for assistance from the prompt in the wings or to seek help from a fellow cast member. A stuck Jenny Seagrove once famously took the second, more ambitious option. 'Darling, what do *you* think?' she asked Tom Conti, who was playing her lover. 'I don't know,' said Conti. 'I haven't been listening.'

276

cast organised a nightly game of 'pass the golf ball'. According to the rules of this improvised sport, it was your duty to find a moment during the performance when you could slip one of your participating colleagues a golf ball which they, in turn, had to fob off on someone else – all entirely unbeknown to the audience, and certainly unbeknown to the director of the play, who would almost certainly have taken a dim view. The loser was the actor in possession of the golf ball when the curtain came down – or, of course, anyone who gave the game away by corpsing in the meantime.

I think I can honestly say that I never played 'pass the golf ball' during my career as a theatre actor, but I did get involved in any number of pitched corpsing battles – and, indeed, in some of the lesser plays I was in, and during some of the more gruelling tours and summer seasons, I relied upon those battles to keep life interesting and morale high. And I frequently found willing adversaries. That's why I am able to disclose to you here that there was nothing that the great Bob Monkhouse wasn't prepared to reveal to you from a position in the wings if he thought it would cause you to lose your concentration and come out of character for a moment. Absolutely nothing.

Anyway, something about the confines of that Reliant, and being necessarily shut in there for long spells while cameras and lights were being positioned and lines were being run through, only encouraged the emergence from Nick and me of our inner schoolboys, which were always

277

pretty close to the surface in any case. I don't know whether other owners had the same experience but, for us two, extraneous giggling seemed to come that much more automatically when we were in the seats of a Reliant Supervan III.

So, yes, happy memories. At the same time, all these glad associations aside, if you added up all the hours I must have spent in one of those cars down the years, all things considered, it would amount to . . . well, probably whole weeks of my life that I will never have again. And, with all respect to the manufacturer, since the show ended I have rarely found myself bursting to clamber back into one of those tiny cockpits, settle myself into the thinly upholstered seat, fire up its buzzy little engine and take the thing out on a road trip, just for old times' sake. These days, given the choice between driving a Reliant Regal Supervan and watching it go past, I'd generally choose the latter, is basically what I'm trying to say.

And that, as it happened, was the position I found myself in at the Platinum Jubilee parade that Sunday in June: watching it all go past – and from an exclusive front-row seat in the grandstand, I might add. And for this I had to thank my official royal appointment to the status of 'national treasure'.

Seriously. It was there in black and white on the invitation that arrived, summoning me to Her Majesty the Queen's Platinum Jubilee Pageant – and specifically the Marlborough House Reception for 'national treasures'. The accompanying letter informed me that not only would I be enjoying the opportunity to get an extremely privileged view of the parade, from a position 'in the heart of the celebrations', I would also be able to participate in 'the iconic national anthem moment' – taking my place on the stage outside Buckingham Palace at the climax of the proceedings, and, with Her Majesty surveying the scene from the balcony, joining a choir of my fellow 'national treasures' in a rousing rendition of 'God Save the Queen'.

Had these people ever heard me sing? Clearly not. But no matter. Given a fair wind and a decent amount of cover from my fellow national treasures, even I could probably get through the national anthem without the police needing to be called.

And cover it seemed there would be. 'You will be among many other national treasures during this moment,' the accompanying literature informed me. Which I suppose was a comforting thought. At the same time, what *is* a national treasure? I wondered about this for quite some time. Is it something that's recently been dug up? Something that could be cashed in if the economy takes a serious dive? A museum piece? And could one ever be classified as a buried national treasure?

That last question didn't bear too much thinking about.

All I can tell you on this matter is that, around my house, I have never been referred to as a national treasure. Indeed, at home the preferred term for me is 'legend' – pronounced 'leg end', ever since my daughter saw me being referred to as a 'legend' and, honking with laughter, adopted the alternative pronunciation as standard. My wife then gleefully joined her in this act of mockery. I don't see 'national treasure' replacing 'leg end' among the people closest to me any time soon, whatever the organisers of Her Majesty the Queen's Platinum Jubilee Pageant might have to say about it.

Anyway, I was keen to know what a national treasure might be expected to wear at an elite event such as this, and was quite relieved to discover that it was merely 'smart summer attire and comfortable footwear', suitable for an event which would apparently require us to 'be seated in an open-air stand for a number of hours'. I was equally relieved to discover that 'hats, fascinators and morning suits are by no means obligatory'. I always tire of my fascinator – find it less and less fascinating, if you will – and especially on those days when I'm spending a number of hours in an open-air stand.

I also learned that I would be required to produce 'one form of photographic identification' in order to be admitted: none of that 'Don't you know who I am?' stuff was going to wash in the vicinity of Marlborough House that day, clearly. And I also read up on the strictly prohibited items that should not be about my person on the day: 'umbrellas, alcohol, large flags, buggies, poles, knives . . .'

Quite right, too. The last thing you would want, on a royal occasion such as this, would be packs of armed national treasures, drunk on their own alcohol, roaming about the place in buggies, with knives and poles. It's a recipe for disaster.

'It is reasonable to expect large crowds after the show is finished,' the literature further warned me – knowledge which, I must admit, didn't make my heart sing. One huge plus, though: no mention of any kind of red carpet activity prior to the event. I know I made the claim earlier in this book that the three most depressing words in the English language are 'replacement bus service', but I've got to say, from my point of view, 'red carpet activity' runs them close. I'm very aware that this will sound baffling to the kind of people who love that sort of thing, and will only earn me limited amounts of sympathy among everyone else. After all, in the global league table of human suffering, having to walk a red carpet while a few flashbulbs go off is never going to feature very high – not as long as war, famine, plague and pestilence are in the pecking order, not to mention panto-mimes, and none of those show any sign of packing up and leaving us all alone any time soon.

But I can only speak for myself and be honest about it: and the truth is, nothing makes me feel more awkward and self-conscious than having to dawdle in front of the photographers like that. I would almost rather swim to the venue through shark-infested waters than walk the red carpet, and Gill feels exactly the same way.

Anyway, whatever the challenges, physical and mental, of

the Marlborough House reception for national treasures and my part in the 'iconic national anthem moment', I could at least assure myself that I had been putting some training in. Indeed, some of us began warming up for the Queen's Platinum Jubilee well before the long weekend in June – even before we had been officially designated as national treasures. In my case the limbering-up for the big anniversary commenced one day in March, with a spot of light cherry tree-planting in Aylesbury.

And by the way, I take back that stuff I said earlier in this book about my position as Britain's leading cultivator of grapefruits having been cruelly overlooked by the wider horticultural community. At any rate, someone, clearly, in a position of authority had noticed that I could be trusted with a bag of fertiliser and a shovel, and that's why I was called in to Aylesbury that day to do my bit for the Queen's Green Canopy initiative.

This was a brilliant, Jubilee-inspired idea that I was all in favour of: a project to get at least three million new trees in the ground all over the UK by the end of 2022. Prince Charles had launched this mission in May 2021 by planting an oak sapling in the grounds of Windsor Castle. That was also the occasion, as I recall, when the Prince tried to get a line in about thinking of the Jubilee as a 'Treebilee' – a catchphrase which never quite stuck and which was probably never really going to.

Ah, well: all of us who work in comedy have been there.

You've got a line you think is a real zinger and you absolutely can't wait to get to that point in the script where you can land it on the audience – and then it dies on the air in front of your lips and goes for sweet nothing. If it's any consolation to Prince Charles, it even happened with John Sullivan scripts once or twice. Peril of the job.

Anyway, going to Aylesbury for a spot of planting that morning was a job that I was very happy to do. May that cherry tree flourish, along with all the other 2,999,999 trees that got planted all over the country as a consequence of that initiative.

One morning, very shortly after that, there came another Jubilee-related call. Once again my writerly labours were interrupted by the arrival in the study of Gill, bearing a sheet of paper: I had been summoned to Windsor Castle.

'Given that my horticultural expertise is now a matter of public knowledge, they'll probably be wanting me to have a look at Prince Charles's Treebilee sapling,' I said, 'and offer some tips on upkeep, watering, etc. And maybe I can do something about fixing that "Treebilee" catchphrase at the same time.'

'I don't think so,' said Gill, still examining the piece of paper.

Apparently ITV were organising a television spectacular which would take place in the presence of the Queen and form that broadcaster's main tribute to her in this Platinum year. The idea seemed to be to stage a pageant telling the

history of our islands, with more than a thousand performers and hundreds of horses, and with the great Dame Helen
Mirren, no less, playing the role of Elizabeth I. This was all
set to go off in May, a few weeks before the Jubilee weekend
itself. ITV were wanting to know if I was available.

Well, of course, it stood to reason that, at such a moment
in history, a national broadcaster would want to gather the
nation's beknighted and be-damed thespians and instruct
them to lead the country in its celebrating and reflecting.
Setting down my quill, I rose slowly and crossed the room to
the study's mullioned window. There I stood for a moment
and looked out thoughtfully across the rolling lawns of Jason
Towers, where members of the estate's gardening staff were
busy feeding the peacocks and pruning the azaleas. Or were
they feeding the azaleas and pruning the peacocks? From
that distance, it was quite hard to tell. And anyway, my mind
was on other things. I was wondering which great figure from
British history ITV were considering asking me to portray.

So many sprang instantly to mind. Winston Churchill,
maybe? The role of our nation's greatest ever wartime leader
would be a fairly natural fit for someone with my actorly
gravitas and instinctive level-headedness in an emergency,
not to mention my way with a cigar and a V-sign.

Or perhaps Sir Walter Raleigh? As I hope I've made clear
by now, you don't spend years in repertory theatre in Bromley without becoming a dab hand with a cloak. And maybe
it would be good to be back in tights after all these years . . .

Or wait, what about Isambard Kingdom Brunel, the greatest engineering visionary Great Britain has ever known? Wasn't that the role that went to Sir Kenneth Branagh in the opening ceremony of the London 2012 Olympics? Overdue a revival, then. And who better than me to pick up Sir Ken's distinguished mantle, don a stovepipe hat and a frock coat and bring Brunel back to life in a way that the nation might well feel compelled to talk about for years, and even decades afterwards?

But wait again. If this was a history of the British Isles, they were going to have to cover the Gunpowder Plot at some point, weren't they? Maybe I could pitch up in the middle of that as Guy Fawkes, confound people's expectations, play the bad guy, show the more villainous side of my BAFTA-winning range . . . And the more bonfire-lighting side, bonfire-lighting being another of my largely unheralded but indisputable skills.

At that point, however, a thought suddenly entered my mind that caused my excited musings to freeze and a chill to pass like a cold hand around my kidneys.

Great figures from British history . . . Oh no . . . Surely not . . .

I turned to Gill, my tone suddenly full of foreboding.

'They don't want me to turn up as Derek Trotter, do they?'

Suddenly it seemed all too plausible: Dame Helen Mirren as Elizabeth I and Sir David Jason as Del Boy – all in the presence of the Queen. 'Oi! Oi! Have a luvvly Jubbly, Your Majesty!'

In fact, they didn't. Indeed, as Gill explained, they didn't want me to turn up as anybody, actually. Nobody, at least, apart from myself. The idea was that I would say a few words in tribute to the Queen and her long reign. Oh, and this wouldn't be during the show at Windsor, either. It would be filmed beforehand and dropped into the broadcast.

So, my Churchill, my Raleigh, my Brunel, my Fawkes, even my Trotter – all shelved until the next great pageantry-based occasion in the nation's history.

Still, I refer you at this point to one of the business's most important sayings: there are no small parts, there are only small actors. And for me, at five foot six, this phrase has always held a particularly profound resonance. As has wisely been remarked: for the true actor, every role is an opportunity – even, I'm here to tell you, a role as a police-man in *Aladdin*. And perhaps *especially* a role as a policeman in *Aladdin*. If a brief cameo as myself was where ITV saw me on this occasion, rather than appearing opposite Dame Helen as, for example, a young William Shakespeare, then so be it: I would swallow my disappointment and I would rise to that opportunity and give it my very best.

Plus I suppose you could say, being myself was a role which I was extremely well placed to perform. Better placed than anybody, potentially. Indeed, you could go even further and say that myself was the role I was born to play.

Except that, strangely enough, that's not really the way I see it at all. Tracing it back, one of the fundamental reasons I became an actor, I think, was because being myself was something I didn't seem to be particularly drawn to or excited by, or even especially good at, and because it seemed to me there were all sorts of other roles that I might be better at, or certainly have more fun filling, which acting – uniquely among all the available professions, or definitely the non-criminal ones – magically opened the door to.

And then, as a consequence of performing in some of those roles, people start asking you to come along to things and be yourself again – the person you were doing your best to escape from all along. Ironic that, isn't it? I'm not sure I'll ever quite get my mind around it.

Anyway, once again, the suggestion seemed to be hovering that I might shoot this little personal message for ITV's Jubilee tribute show myself, at home. I guess that would have been the simplest option – Gill and I rigging something up as we had done for Jay Blades on that *Strictly Come Dancing* Christmas special. However, call me old-fashioned – and no disrespect intended to Jay here – but the idea of phoning in a tribute to the Queen seemed borderline treasonous to me. Why, surely, that was the kind of disrespectful behaviour for which you would have got yourself banged up in the Tower back in the day – or, at least, if they'd had television in the seventeenth century. Certainly, being asked to pay tribute to the reigning monarch on the seventieth anniversary of her crowning, and delivering a murky, hand-held iPhone recording shot against a conveniently blank patch of wall in the sitting room would feel to me a bit like turning up at the Palace for dinner in your gardening clothes: not quite the done thing.

So I told ITV that I'd be more than happy to oblige, but we'd need to film it properly, with a camera and some lights, operated by professionals, and maybe also some make-up, also operated by a professional – the way these things were traditionally done before the pandemic rewrote all the rules.

Believe me, I wasn't being a diva here, nor trying to imply that the exquisite nuances of my performance would be tragically lost if brought to the nation via the medium of my wife's phone (although the fact is, frankly, they would); I just thought that, in this special case, if the job was worth doing, it really was worth doing properly. I mean, how often does a queen get to celebrate seventy years on the throne? Fortunately ITV agreed and the message was filmed, using the conventional apparatus, in the distinguished surroundings of Hartwell House, a hotel just outside Aylesbury.

I, of course, can remember watching Queen Elizabeth's Coronation. Not having this new technological marvel called television in our home at that point – very few houses around our way did – come 2 June 1953, with a national holiday declared, we Whites all piled round to where my mate Ronnie Prior lived, a couple of terraces away from Lodge Lane, in William Street. There we were joined by the rest of the population of Finchley and several other neighbouring London boroughs, or so it seemed. The Priors had never been so popular, nor their tiny front room so in demand. We all wedged in as best we could and I – then at the tender age of twelve – remember sitting on the patterned carpet in a huddle of other junior members of the party, and gazing in wonder at the thick, curved glass of the Priors' goggle-box – which was, I'm almost certain, not the Priors' goggle-box at all, if we're going to be precise about it, but more likely a goggle-box belonging to Radio Rentals, from whom they would have had it on loan.

We watched and listened solemnly, as the occasion seemed to demand. Every now and again, not entirely in keeping with that solemnity, the picture would start to roll – literally sliding up the screen and coming round again like the reel in a fruit machine. At which point, it would be time for Ronnie Prior's dad to make an important adjustment to the internal aerial, whose job of decoding the signal on its journey from Westminster Abbey, via the antenna at Alexandra Palace, to the Priors' front room, can't have been made any easier by the presence of half of London taking up all the air in the final couple of yards.*

---

* I may be wrong, but the method of attempting to cure faulty picture reception by slapping or thumping the top of the box came in a few years later, when people started having fixed, external aerials which did not lend themselves to adjustment, short of going outside and nipping up a ladder – broadly considered too much of an interruption to one's viewing. In more recent times, the advent of the flat screen, entirely dispensing with the idea of the television as a solid piece of furniture, has altogether

Yet, the occasional technical hitch aside, I can't even begin to explain to you how magical those pictures coming from the Abbey that day seemed, just by existing at all. Round about this time, I would have been regularly staring in a state of astonishment at Dick Tracy's two-way radio wristwatch, the miracle of technology via which, in the comic strips, our intrepid detective could communicate with the rest of his crime-busting force. Utterly incredible that seemed to me – and, in a way that is hard to recapture now, the concept of moving images on a television, in those early days, felt equally far-flung. Yet here it was, the stuff of science fiction come to life. And in Ronnie Prior's front room, of all places.

Those images made a huge impression on me, and on all of us who watched them at the time, and I think the nature of them explains a lot about how people of my generation continue to feel about the Queen – this woman whom we first saw, by the miracle of television, at the centre of this massive ceremonial event. The pomp and the majesty of the Coronation seemed so grand to us, so imposing and other-worldly. Yet at the centre of it all was this young, slight-seeming woman. I tried to speak about some of this in the message that I recorded for that Windsor pageant. I talked about the mettle the Queen had shown, taking over from her father at the age of twenty-five, and how she came to

---

signalled the end for improvised hands-on technical adjustments to the broadcast image – which is probably for the best, all things considered.

embody dedication – the idea of putting something first. Did I manage to convey what I meant? I don't know. I certainly hope so. But I do think it wouldn't have been the same, somehow, if I had tried to say all this into a hand-held iPhone.

Having done my bit earlier, I didn't go to Windsor Castle for ITV's big show, but I did notice that my colleague in the friendly skies, Tom Cruise, was on hand for that one – covering for me, as ever. We've got each other's backs, you know. I believe the topic of what was then Tom's latest movie, *Top Gun: Maverick*, came up during his appearance that night and consequently a few people raised their eyebrows afterwards about him seeming to use this august, royal occasion as a handy platform for a spot of cross-promotion.

Now, I don't really know what went on, and I certainly don't know what the terms of Tom's appearance on the show were. But what I can say is that, in fairness to Tom, he is, without question, a raging Anglophile. As one of his closest friends – or certainly one of his newest friends – I can vouch for that. He absolutely loves and respects this place and does as much of his work here as he possibly can. So nobody ought to doubt the sincerity of his desire to be part of it all that night.

But you'd expect me to defend him, the pair of us being so close.

Of course, I'm not sure *he* knows that.

* * *

Sunday 5 June, though – that was the big one. Leaving nothing to chance, Gill and I were dropped outside the Ritz, bright and breezy, by my wise and accomplished driver, Les 'there are drivers, and there are drivers' Davis. And then we set off on the walk down St James's Street.

Smart summer attire? Check. Comfortable footwear? Check again. One form of photographic identification? Naturally. It dawned on me, bantering with members of the security staff as we made our way through the various security checks, that, courtesy of *Only Fools*, I must be one of a very small number of people who can call a policeman a plonker and be entirely sure he'll get away with it. My newly confirmed 'national treasure' status was already yielding dividends.

So now I was inside the grounds of Clarence House, just as my friend Micky McCaul had been when he followed that mistaken policeman's signal all those years ago, although I was planning on staying for longer than Micky did and definitely intended to have something to eat and drink.

It was all very luscious, as you might expect. Waiting staff circulated with trays of drinks and canapés. (I declined the alcohol. Not during the daytime, thank you, and with a national anthem to sing.) Marquees fluttered in the breeze. Flowers nodded in their borders. There was soft seating to sink into, and, of course, there were Portaloos. You shall know the poshness of an outdoor event, I always say, by the grandness of its Portaloos, and in this case I would score Her

Majesty the Queen's Platinum Jubilee Pageant (Marlborough House Reception Division) a resounding overall nine out of ten, with strong performances in the key categories of roominess, decor, fragrancing and generally not looking like the kind of thing you see on a building site. Indeed, I would say the Marlborough House Portaloos were outscored only by the Portaloos in the VIP enclosure at the annual Fairford Air Show in Gloucestershire, which, in this user's humble opinion, continue to set the standard for demountable, mass-use khazi facilities.

I'm glad to be able to share with you the fruits of my hard-won observational expertise in this important area. Remember: I went so that you don't have to. It's a service I'm happy to provide.

It was, of course, both thrilling and strange to be in an isolated enclosure so thickly peopled with faces you recognised – a national treasure island, as it were. As we sat together and took in the scene, Gill and I kept nudging each other, surreptitiously pointing and saying, 'Ooh, look – it's him/her off the telly.' I know that if you yourself are a him or a her off the telly, then people imagine that you don't really do this. But I'm here to tell you that you do – or that I do, at any rate. How could I help myself? It's not every Sunday that I get introduced to Deborah Meaden from *Dragons' Den*, watch the newscaster Michael Buerk make his way across the grass with a glass in his hand, and then, with Sir Chris Hoy the Olympic cyclist hovering in the background, fall into a conversation with Patrick Mower about Leeds, where I filmed *A Touch of Frost* and where he films *Emmerdale*.

Eventually, after this period of gentle mixing and mingling, a nice person with a clipboard came up and told us it was time for those of us who were national treasures and our partners to take our seats for the parade. So Gill and I gathered up our stuff and prepared to join the migration to the grandstand.

Actually, gathering up our stuff took a little doing, now I come to mention it. Because this was the British summer, and because the day was clearly going to be a long one, and because we are British, Gill and I had come equipped for every possible eventuality, bringing two bags between us containing rain ponchos, scarves, sweaters, gilets and other oddments of warm clothing, along with emergency provisions in the form of biscuits and bottled water. None of which, in fact, we ended up needing but, of course, it always pays to be prepared.

Note, however, that at an event at which champagne was served along with food supplied by Fortnum & Mason, I was going about the place with a packet of biscuits that I had brought from home. Old habits die hard, clearly.

Heading, as instructed, across the gardens through the throng in the direction, allegedly, of the grandstand, I concentrated on following a tall and prominent figure in a broad-brimmed hat, a riding overcoat, trousers with leather gaiters and buckles and straps on them, and a pair of magnificent brown boots. It was reassuring to think that, from here on in, if I got lost, I would at least know that Jeremy Irons was also lost.

And that was good news for Jeremy Irons, too, I suppose, because if we got really profoundly lost and hours went by and hunger set in, then I had biscuits, which I would possibly be prepared to share with him.

Although maybe he too had biscuits, stowed in that riding overcoat, or under that hat. I somehow doubted it, though.

Keeping our eyes firmly on Jeremy Irons's hat up ahead, we left Marlborough House and followed the circuitous route to the back of the grandstand – not the one in which the royal party and the political guests of honour were ensconced at various times during the weekend, but the block of seating directly next door to it. Gill and I were escorted to seats in the front row, next to Dame Jessica Ennis-Hill, the Olympic heptathlete, who was there with her mum, Alison – both lovely people. It was sobering to reflect that Jessica has been known to clear 1.91 metres in the high jump, which is nearly 30cm more than I clear when I stand up. Still, I took the opportunity to assure her, athlete to athlete, that if she ever wanted tips on landing a fall through the gap where a bar flap used to be, she should have no hesitation about getting in touch.

Incidentally, on the subject of my height, I was mildly disappointed to realise that, although our seats afforded a splendid and relaxed view of the giant screen mounted opposite the grandstand, the two horizontal metal poles forming the guard rail directly in front of us neatly obstructed my view of the parade itself. However, if I leaned forward and twisted my head slightly to one side I could get a perfect view between the poles. This didn't look especially dignified, and risked giving a bad public impression of my posture. 'Sit back,' Gill kept saying. 'Yes, OK,' was my reply, 'but all I'll be able to see is some tops of heads and some feet with a steel pole in between.'

In due course, the parade began – that famous gold coach trundling along, pulled by white horses and flanked by black ones. You've got to love the way Britain does these things, haven't you? No missiles and tanks, no overt displays of military might or proudly flaunted weapons of mass destruction, but fairy-tale horse-drawn coaches, soldiers in historic uniforms and, shortly after that, a flatbed truck full of people break-dancing. Well, it made me proud, anyway.

There was also a series of double-decker buses, representing the decades, with various celebrities waving from the top of them. Almost the first person whose wave I recognised was Nigel Havers. Perhaps he was thinking the same as I was: that it's a lot further from Bromley Rep to the Mall than it looks.

At another moment a float went past containing a gaggle of characters from children's television across the years – the Wombles, the Tellytubbies, Peppa Pig and his various relations. And there, in among them, was Danger Mouse. Now, that really did stir something in me. Whisper it, but I think I'm as proud of having given a voice to that little character as I am of anything I've done in my career, and the fact that not only is he still fondly remembered but is deemed significant enough to rub padded shoulders on a bus with such timeless small-screen icons as the Wombles, touches me profoundly.*

And then, eventually, there it was – that only-too-familiar Reliant Regal Supervan III, a mere yellow dot on the Mall at first, but slowly getting bigger and bigger until it was unmistakable in all its tatty glory. I'd had no idea it was going to feature and I couldn't have been more delighted at what its presence said about John Sullivan and the show we all created. And I thought about how hard John would have laughed to see it there that day.

As the van rounded the Victoria Memorial, directly below us, people around me were urging me to stand up and take the salute – just as, earlier in the parade, in the front row of

---

* Unlike 26 Lodge Lane or the site of the New Theatre at Bromley, Danger Mouse's former home does have a blue plaque. Just as 'Sherlock Holmes, Consulting Detective', is properly commemorated as a former resident at 221b Baker Street, so does the nearest postbox, a bit further up the road, have a blue disc stuck to its base marking it as the erstwhile home of 'Danger Mouse, the greatest secret agent in the world'. So at least one of us got our dues. In truth, though, I think a fan of the show may have stuck that tribute there, rather than the official heritage authorities, and I'm not entirely sure how permanent it may be, so see it while you can. It's an excellent little gag, though. Danger Mouse and his sidekick Penfold really did operate out of a postbox in Baker Street, so the tribute is entirely fitting.

the directly adjacent grandstand, Prince Charles had taken the salute from the passing military. For a moment there, I was sorely tempted. But I thought it might have looked as though I was trying to draw attention to myself, and I was also worried that it might have come across as disrespectful. Silly, really. I wish I had done it now. It would have been a good gag.

As the parade drew towards its end, another clipboard-wielding member of staff appeared beside me and asked me to follow him out in readiness for the 'iconic national anthem moment'. Several others stood up and joined me, and we were led out of the back of the grandstand, along a series of paths, through a set of wrought-iron gates at the side of the Palace and into a completely canopy-covered area just to the side of the stage, where we all stood and waited. It was exactly like being backstage in a theatre, with crew, in black and wearing headsets, rushing about, while we, the national treasures, waited for our cue.

I took a moment to look about me. There were people there – no names, no pack drill – about whom my immediate thought was, 'Blimey, they've got older.' Which, of course, is a ridiculous thing to find yourself thinking. Of course they'd got older. That's what happens, if fate smiles on you and you are fortunate enough to stick around for a while. And that's the way to be thinking about it, surely: getting older is what *fortunate* people do. It's the biggest stroke of luck you'll get.

But then my next thought was equally obvious: 'If I'm

looking at them and thinking, "Blimey, they've got older," then they're looking at me and thinking the same.'

There were some mixed feelings there, let me tell you.

Because age and fame are locked in a particularly troublesome tango, aren't they? It's often said that people freeze at the age they were when they became famous – that, to some extent, the age you are when you get well known is the age you will be for the rest of your life. I'm not sure I recognise that phenomenon in myself. But then I became famous relatively late on – in my late thirties and early forties – when I'd already had a decent chance to find out the kind of person I was and the kind of work I was interested in doing, so maybe it works slightly differently in that case.

But what I do think is true is that we freeze other people at the age they became famous *to us*. We freeze them in our minds. How we see them from then on is always with reference to how they were at that original point when they most fully entered our lives. So, even as time forges on in the opposite direction, visiting its inevitable ravages, we're always referring back to that first image that we had of someone. Which is not especially useful and incredibly unfair, of course, but I can hardly complain about it when it happens to me, because I do it myself.

That said, standing just in front of me as we gathered for choral duty that Sunday afternoon was Sir Cliff Richard, to whom none of the normal rules on ageing seem to apply and who appears to be successfully taking all his cues in this

matter from Peter Pan. Sir Cliff was wearing an extremely
bright jacket made from a Union Jack. He'd been up all
night with the sewing machine, by the look of it, and he was
moving as spryly as if he had just hopped off a double-decker
bus in 1963, rather than, as was the case, off a double-decker
bus in 2022. Clearly the day that someone says Sir Cliff isn't
what he used to be will be the day we can all give up. That
blinding jacket, by the way, even outdid the flowery shirt
Sir Cliff was wearing in the pictures I mentioned of the
burned-out New Theatre in Bromley, a shared episode in
our life stories about which I would have loved to shoot the
breeze with him, while also seeking his advice on how not
to age in any of the traditional physical senses, but sadly a
moment of togetherness for us never arose.

Finally the crew in black with the earpieces began to wave
us forward. It took a little while to get us all onto the stage, but
once we had sorted ourselves into something like an order, I
found myself at one end of the group, quite far back. Again I
was struck by the thought of how different this was from the
ways in which I might normally pass a Sunday afternoon.
In my immediate vicinity at this point were the legendary
former newscaster Angela Rippon, the chef Rick Stein, the
television presenters Rylan Clark and Holly Willoughby,
and the entertainer Timmy Mallett, who had thoughtfully
brought a large sponge hammer with him. I racked my brain
to recall whether giant foam tools were listed with umbrellas and knives among the items that we were not allowed to

carry with us on the day, but self-evidently they weren't, or not in Timmy Mallett's case. He may have applied for and been granted an exemption, of course.

Not that Timmy's mallet formed any kind of obstruction to my view of what was going on. That job was done by a large piece of hanging scenery, dressing the rear of the stage and, just by chance, given the position I had taken up, completely removing the Buckingham Palace balcony from my eyeline.

Nothing I could do about that now, though. Ahead of us, with the parade complete, the barriers had been opened up and thousands upon thousands of people were streaming out onto the Mall and up to the Victoria Monument, massing in front of the stage and the Palace. Whereupon Ed Sheeran, looking almost as young as Cliff Richard, promptly serenaded them, and us, from an open area off to our right. Sheeran completed his performance, set down his guitar and walked off, brushing directly past me on his way through. I toyed with stopping him and running by him an idea that was rapidly forming in my head for an album of duets together, me and him, but, whether he read that intention in my eyes or not, he seemed to be in a blazing hurry to get away and was gone before I could grab his elbow. Maybe he had been booked to do a couple of numbers privately for the Queen. Or perhaps he needed to get to a gig somewhere else for which he was actually getting paid. I wouldn't blame him.

Then, finally, it was our big moment – our 'iconic national anthem moment', indeed. Our cue was supposed to be the arrival of the Queen on the balcony, followed by the usual trumpet fanfare, issued from the forecourt of the Palace. But would she even come out? The Queen had been carefully rationing her public appearances all weekend, had not thus far appeared during the parade, and nobody seemed to know for certain, even at that late point, whether she would now emerge. During those moments, in her continuing absence, a certain amount of confusion rippled through those of us waiting on the stage.

No need to worry, though. After a brief delay, the balcony doors finally opened and a deafening roar peeled off the crowd as the Queen appeared, followed out into the open by Prince Charles and Camilla, Prince William and Kate and Prince George. Or so I was told, anyway. I, of course, was still standing at the back of the choir, with that piece of scenery in the way. I couldn't see a thing. It could have been Alan Titchmarsh up there for all I knew about it. Except that it couldn't, in fact, because he was down here, with us.

Somewhere behind us, though, the trumpets blared and the drums rolled and, waved in by the arms of a producer, the national treasures on the stage launched into the national anthem, joined by the crowd who took over and, with the greater numbers on their side, rather drowned us out which, in my case, may have been just as well. And then the anthem ended, and those in our choir whose view was not obstructed by a piece of low-hanging scenery looked across to the balcony to drink in the celebration's climactic moment: the

Queen receiving the acclaim of her subjects on the occasion of her Platinum Jubilee.

There I was, then, uniquely placed to witness history – and yet, on account of that rogue piece of scenery, not witnessing it, or certainly not witnessing the person at the heart of it. At this point, I had a terrifically good view of Jimmy Tarbuck and, of course, of Sir Cliff Richard's jacket, and I didn't take either of those privileges for granted, but I had not so much as a glimmer of the royal party.

Suddenly I was back in the stalls before the pantomime at Golders Green, in that moment which I wrote about right at the beginning of this book, experiencing an eerily similar sense of imminent deflation. Imagine going to *Jack and the Beanstalk* and not seeing the giant. And now imagine going to the Queen's Jubilee parade and not seeing the Queen.

But what happened next was rather touching. Somehow sensing my predicament, my fellow treasures began to organise a concerted effort to shuffle this particular, shorter treasure across to a position on the stage where he might have a chance of seeing the scene on the balcony. It was very generous of everyone. I felt like a small child, getting passed through a football crowd to a place where he could get a view of the match.

It would be impossible to recount the full list of national treasures with whom I found myself literally rubbing shoulders or thereabouts during these improvised manoeuvres, but suffice it to say that, stepping into a gap created by Anita

Harris and Harry Redknapp, climbing around an obliging Sir Steve Redgrave, and taking care not to step on the toes of a sweetly encouraging Bonnie Langford, I eventually, after a long and circuitous journey through seventy years of British celebrity, made it to a spot where, by craning my neck and twisting my upper body, I could lean out and bring the balcony of Buckingham Palace into view.

Just in time to catch a glimpse of a woman's retreating back, the briefest flash of emerald green, returning through the glass doors into the Palace and out of sight.

Damn it. Missed her. And despite the best united efforts of the country's national treasures, too.

Ah, well. With our duties done, and the doors behind the Palace balcony now firmly closed, the choir began slowly to shuffle away to the side of the stage to rejoin our partners, waiting in the adjacent tented village, and head for home. As we departed, some among our number – and, again, discretion being so much the better part of valour, I won't be putting any names to any faces here – were delaying our progress by taking a moment to stop and turn to the crowd and raise their arms, before basking in the cheers and applause that came their way as a result. And I found myself thinking, rather sniffily, 'Oh, come on – you've only been part of a hundred-strong choir that's sung the national anthem. Are you really taking a curtain call here? And also, you're holding some of us up.'

But then I listened to the extraordinary noise washing up

from that crowd and looked out at the sea of faces, extending seemingly forever down the Mall. And I thought to myself, 'Well, actually, how many times is *this* opportunity likely to present itself?'

So I, too, stopped and I turned and looked out at all those people, the biggest gathering by a literal country mile that I had ever found myself standing on a stage in front of, and I raised my hand and gave a wave.

'Acknowledging the crowd,' I think they call it in the world of sport. And from those close enough to the stage to see me do it, a huge cheer went up and a host of hands waved back.

And what can I tell you? Those self-indulgent national treasures ahead of me in the queue to get off the stage had had exactly the right idea. It felt absolutely amazing.

EPILOGUE

. . . and a partridge up your pear tree

Only *Fools and Horses* came back, of course. We'd wrapped up the story with 'Time on our Hands' in 1996. The Trotters were millionaires. The arc was complete. We had reached the perfect end point.

But people wanted more. Five years later, we started making what would become a further set of three Christmas specials, the first of which, 'If They Could See Us Now', went out on Christmas Day in 2001. It was watched by 21.35 million people, suggesting the show had, indeed, been missed.

That was a mixed Christmas for me, though. On Boxing Day, twenty-four hours after the triumphant return of *Only Fools*, ITV launched *Micawber*. Boy, did we think we were onto a winner with that one – my and John Sullivan's second venture together. The press lines wrote themselves really. 'From the team that brought you *Only Fools . . .*'

John was a huge Charles Dickens fan, and had tried to

interest the BBC in an adaptation of *David Copperfield*. They turned it down, though, so he went away and came up with this instead – a kind of prequel to that novel, in the form of a comedy drama series, centred on the roguish but ultimately good-hearted character of Wilkins Micawber.

I have a letter John wrote me, typically long, in the excited build-up to the project, addressing me as 'Wilkins' and using John's own adopted Victorian persona, Adolphus Snuggs-Sullivan. It's on the headed notepaper of 'The Acton Theatrical Touring Ensemble – founded 1803, proprietor: Adolphus Snuggs-Sullivan', a reference to the BBC's Acton rehearsal rooms, the 'Acton Hilton', mentioned before.

'We should meet soon to further discuss our forthcoming theatrical venture,' John/Adolphus wrote, 'with which we shall enthral the denizens of the kingdom with intrigue, veracity, humorous alliterations and fierce battle scenes (apologies, sir, wrong play! By the by, many thanks for that flask of your famous punch).'

He closed with a PS: 'What a joyous day it will be when some clever git invents the telephone.'

ITV apportioned the show a budget of around £1 million per hour, which was serious money, and let us shoot an initial run of four episodes. Each of those episodes got an average of nearly six million viewers, for which terrestrial television would happily bite off your hand at the wrist these days, but which didn't really come anywhere near to cutting the mustard back then – or not when something was costing £1 million per hour. After those initial four episodes, the show was quietly shelved.

And our hopes had been so high. Rogues with golden hearts, people who are nearly always jovial and whose generosity exceeds their means . . . that was Del, and that was Pa Larkin in *The Darling Buds of May*, and that was Micawber, surely. This was a winning formula.

But it wasn't to be. There are no winning formulas, it turns out. There are shows that work and shows that don't work and this was a show that didn't work. I was dashed.

But you get up and move on. A producer called Rod Brown got in touch. He was involved in making a film for Sky of *Hogfather*, Terry Pratchett's Christmas-on-Discworld fantasy story. He wanted to know if I fancied playing Albert, the pork-pie-loving manservant of Death, who is Discworld's rather kindly and philosophical version of the Grim Reaper.

This was 2006, and I'd been playing Detective Inspector Jack Frost in *A Touch of Frost* for fourteen years, so I was rather attracted to the idea of acting the fool again. I was a big reader of Terry Pratchett's novels, but the character of his that I had always dreamed of playing was Rincewind, the hapless wizard from *The Colour of Magic*. So I told Rod I'd sign up for *Hogfather*, but he had to promise me that if they ever made *The Colour of Magic*, they'd give me the role of Rincewind.

We filmed *Hogfather* at Pinewood Studios, out to the west of London. Going through its border-patrol-style gates on the first day, I was transported effortlessly back to a warm Sunday afternoon in the fifties, when I and my pals, Micky Weedon and Brian Barneycoat, taking our motorbikes out joyriding, as we used to on those wonderfully traffic-free weekends, had come upon Pinewood entirely by accident. The sight of it, coming out of nowhere, had a powerful effect on all three of us – the centre of British film entertainment suddenly in front of us. We parked up and just stood and looked at it for a while, as if thinking: 'Beyond this gate lies the world of magic.' And now I was inside it, and part of it. What a journey I had come on.

Not long after that, I got stuck up in its roof. Typical. I was riding the Hogfather's hog-drawn flying sleigh at the time, in the company of Death – as you do. Death's voice in that film was supplied by Ian Richardson, with whom I'd worked on *Porterhouse Blue*. This was to be Ian's last role, sadly.

But Death's body was being provided by a six-foot-seven Dutch actor called Marnix Van Den Broeke, who would later become the requisite cloaked skeleton courtesy of some CGI trickery, post-production. So there we were, the pair of us, a contrast in lengths, you could say, borne aloft in one of Pinewood's cavernous studio spaces by a sophisticated system of hydraulics, and merrily flying our sleigh against a green screen, when – whump. The power went out, along with the lights, and our sleigh froze.

Somewhere below us, an enormous downpour of rain had abruptly flooded the studio. The crew duly evacuated the building, as instructed. But Marnix and I were in no position to do any evacuating. We were left high and dry in the dark for what felt like hours, and would no doubt have got many games of noughts and crosses played, had we only had a pen, and had there only been enough light.

Left hanging about, yet again: it really does seem to have been an unusually strong theme in my career.

Still, the electricity went back on eventually, and the film got made and it seemed to go over well – and still goes over well each year, in fact. In a celebratory mood, I took home, courtesy of the props department, Death's giant hour-glass 'life-timer'. It stands to this day on the stairs in my house and prompts me to reflect every time I pass and notice it, not on Death and our ever-elapsing time on earth, as it happens, but on what a laugh it was making *Hogfather*. Tremendous fun.

Rod Brown was as good as his word, and two years later I got to play Rincewind in *The Colour of Magic*. This time I took home what Pratchett fans know well as the Luggage. Well, nobody else seemed to want it, and I thought it would make a nice ornament for the house – a conversation piece, if you will. After all, how many homes do you know that have large, polished trunks with multiple human feet pro-truding from the bottom of them?*

Don't get me wrong, by the way: I don't always walk away from shoots with the furniture. There are actors who are a little notorious for backing their cars round on the final day of production. No names, no pack drill. But I am not one of them. My total haul from all those years on *Only Fools* was a pair of bottles of Peckham Spring Mineral Water, with authentic labels (if not authentic mineral water), and, as already declared, a few prize items from Del's exclusive ward-robe, including one sheepskin coat, which my wife is very keen that I shouldn't wear. And though I have fought her on this, I must reluctantly admit, with the passing of time, that she's got a point. Age has slightly withered that coat now, and in some areas slightly expanded it, and it makes me look less like Del these days and more like a moulting camel.

It possibly makes me smell a little like a moulting camel, too. But let's not go there.

However, the Luggage did accompany me home, in all its fibre-glass glory. And when Gill suggested that the kinds of conversation this intended conversation piece would inspire weren't necessarily the kinds of conversation anybody

---

* The Luggage is a highly useful invention: a capacious storage unit which nobody ever needs to lift or carry because it gets itself around on its own many feet. Just to be clear, the feet on my prop version were fibre glass, not human, and didn't actually work.

sensible would be keen to have, I placed it on the little island in the middle of our pond where it could serve magnificently as a feed storer for the pair of swans who descended to live on that island one breeding season. (We seem to be pretty busy with the birds round my way. Swans, geese, owls – you name it. If it's got feathers on, the chances are it will stop by for a free meal.)

And then one evening I got to thinking: props from popular TV shows and films are worth a bit of money. The Luggage probably deserved a more dignified fate than to sit out there in the elements, in the middle of somebody's garden, storing bird feed. Maybe I could auction it off for charity and raise a few hundred quid for some deserving cause. Wouldn't that be a good thing to do?

I resolved to go out there the very next day, bring in the Luggage, clean it up a bit and start to look into ways that I might sell it.

The following morning I set out across the garden. It had been a stormy night – indeed, a dark and stormy night, just like in the very best stories. The grass was scattered with bits of debris torn off the trees by the wind. It looked like the Luggage's last night in the open had been a real tester.

A tester indeed. When I reached the pond, I saw that a tree had blown down and fallen directly on my piece of precious film memorabilia, splitting it neatly in half.

Anybody want to buy half the Luggage? With a bag of related splinters? One previous slightly careless owner?

I didn't think so.

Only one possible conclusion can be formed about this strangely timed intervention. It was a cautionary message from the spirit of Sir Terry Pratchett himself – a warning to yours truly not even to entertain the idea of converting purloined elements of the late novelist's franchise into filthy lucre.

* * *

God bless Derek Trotter. I've had some causes to curse him down the years, but I know what I owe him. Basically he launched me into the nation's Christmas tree and I never came down. It amazes me, the things I now get asked to do simply because I once appeared on the television at Christmas, running through the mist in a daft Batman outfit.

For instance, in the summer of 2021, I was asked to record a message of support for Gareth Southgate and the England football team on the eve of their European Championship final against Italy. Now, what I know about football could be written on the back of a stamp and leave room over for illustrations. At Popes Garage, the car repair shop where I got my first job after leaving school, there would often be a bit of a kick-about during lunch hour in the yard, and I would take part in a desultory and frequently satirical manner and in the hope of being regarded as one of the boys. It rarely went well. It was also probably the last time I kicked a ball.

If you had told those guys, during one of those lunchtimes, that one day I'd be giving the England team a pep talk ahead of a major final, they would have laughed themselves so rigid they would have had to go home for the afternoon.

Lo, though, once again that which was unlikely came to pass. Always willing to play our part, Gill and I got the phone out. I said hello to Gareth – asked him if he was still over at Southgate, which isn't that far down the road from where I grew up . . . I made a lot of silly jokes, basically, and then told the boys to give it their all, make us proud, win it for England.

After I'd sent it off, I thought about the players, watching this piece of nonsense. Those guys are mostly in their twenties; many of them weren't born when *Only Fools* was regularly on telly. And yet the show would still mean something to many of them. It gets passed down, and I can never quite get my head around that – around having been part of a television programme, not just that families would watch together back then, but that families might watch together now: that generational legacy, each new generation passing the show on to the next and all of them still able to enjoy it. That was the unifying force which John Sullivan dreamed of creating when he was writing *Only Fools and Horses*, and I can only think it would delight and amaze him to see it in action all these years later.

Anyway, I did my bit for Gareth and for England, and then I sat back and watched the game on the night, quietly confident that my intervention would produce the desired result.

And what happened? They lost on penalties.

I felt a bit guilty, really. Could I have done more? Surely not. I gave it 100 per cent – honest, Gareth.

But even this pales beside the invitation that came my way via email in the summer of 2022. A statue was going to be unveiled at RAF Hawkinge in Kent, the former RAF station from which planes flew for the Battle of Britain and many other aerial missions during the Second World War. The statue was of a group of airmen at rest on the grass between missions, and relatives of those airmen would be present. Prince Charles had been going to attend the unveiling, but something had come up. Would I consider stepping into the breach and doing the honours?

Now, I would have responded warmly to this invitation in any circumstances. It's in my roots as a war baby who survived the Blitz to welcome any chance to pay tribute to the sacrifices made by airmen, and so many others, in that awful conflict. And I loved the fact that relatives were going to be there – a really important reminder of something we should never lose sight of about those who served and gave their lives: they were people with families and loved ones.

But I did, I admit, have a little chortle at the thought of the organisers going down their list of possible unveilers.

'OK, so sadly the heir to the throne is out. Let's try David Jason.'

Do I glimpse a hint of a possible future for me here – some kind of job-share arrangement with Prince Charles, helping out when the royal schedule gets a bit tight, and picking up the slack? Well, OK. I do have one or two projects of my own on the go, and, of course, I'm still waiting for Tom Cruise to get back to me on the body-double thing. But we could probably work something out, if that's the direction this is going. Maybe we should put a lunch in the diary and see where we all stand.

But let's get Christmas out of the way first, shall we? By the time you read this, likely as not, the nights will have drawn right in and a tangible sense of anticipation for the 'big day' will be brewing. At Jason Towers, the paper chains will be going up, a warm fire will be crackling in the grate, the cooks will be energetically basting meats in the kitchens, and the peacock pruner will once again be looking forward eagerly to his annual morning off.

I've been given to a little grumbling about the festive season and its various trials and tribulations down the years, I don't deny. But looking back in order to put this book together, I realise that, give or take a couple of pantomime experiences and one or two tight moments in harnesses, Christmas has been quite good to me, really. Overwhelmingly good, in fact.

And yes, there's the forced jollity and the shopping and the possibility of that tricky annual drinks party, and the thousand tiny stresses and irritations the season is prey to.

But maybe, if we're ever tempted to feel vexed about it all, we should cleave to the words of Scrooge's nephew, Fred, in *A Christmas Carol* – words on this matter that nobody, surely, will ever better.

For it is Fred who describes Christmas as 'a good time; a kind, forgiving, charitable, pleasant time; the only time I know of, in the long calendar of the year, when men and women seem by one consent to open their shut-up hearts freely, and to think of people below them as if they really were fellow-passengers to the grave, and not another race of creatures bound on other journeys'.

Well, amen to that, Fred. Amen to that.

Now, if you'll excuse me, I have a pressing appointment with a Victorian gazunda.

Those amaryllis bulbs don't plant themselves, you know.

And this year, surely this year . . .

APPENDIX

Covid and carpet burns

I didn't get to unveil that monument at Hawkinge. Instead of standing in for Prince Charles that day, I was sealed up in my bedroom staring miserably at the ceiling. After two and a half years of dodging it, I had tested positive for Covid-19.

I was bitterly disappointed. I'd been so looking forward to meeting everyone there and doing my bit. (Go, dear reader, if you get the chance, to the Kent Battle of Britain Museum at Hawkinge airfield. Tell them I sent you.)

My symptoms: severe cough, sore throat, loss of appetite, and carpet burns. The last of those was my fault for getting up to go to the loo. Well, when you've got to go . . .

Boom: my legs turned to jelly and I went down like a ton of bricks. Thankfully, the radiator cushioned my fall. I tried to stand, but my limbs had all the strength of overcooked spaghetti. With my pasta arms, I couldn't reach the mobile phone that Gill had left with me, and my throat was so sore that I could only manage a hoarse croak, rather than an audible cry for help.

So I had no choice but to improvise. I set off for the bedroom door, face-down, via the carpet.

In the whole of my acting career, I believe this was the only time I have ever been called upon to portray a caterpillar. With my legs and arms failing me, I resorted to using my head to propel me forward for good measure. It was a long struggle. Doomy thoughts began to overcome me. Was this how it would end? Face-down in the shagpile in my underpants? I began to regret not pinning my knighthood to those underpants – some shred of dignity at the last.

I may have been getting a little delirious.

But then, at the moment of maximum despair, the door flew open and a figure burst in wearing a *Better Call Saul* onesie with its hood up, two face-masks and a pair of disposable gloves. It was Gill in her improvised PPE (*Better Call Saul* is our favourite Netflix series; we've seen it and bought the onesie). At the sight of me face-down on the carpet in my underpants, my wife let out a scream of horror, assuming I had collapsed and banged my head. Her fears were by no means alleviated when she saw two big marks on my bonce.

'Carpet burns,' I explained, wheezily. 'It's a long story . . .'

Gill helped me back to bed and issued me with strict instructions not to venture forth again unaccompanied. She also added a walkie talkie to my communication system and put up a camp bed for herself right outside the bedroom door in case of any more hoarse croaks in the night.

After four days in bed, my limbs resumed the strength of uncooked rigatoni and I was on my way back. I was lucky. I got Covid-19 late, and with four doses of the vaccine inside me. I wonder, though: how many people can add 'carpet burns to the forehead' to their list of Covid symptoms?

INDEX